Experiencing Reading and Writing

Sandra G. Brown

Ocean County College

Kendall Hunt
publishing company

Kendall Hunt
publishing company

www.kendallhunt.com
Send all inquiries to:
4050 Westmark Drive
Dubuque, IA 52004-1840

ISBN 978-1-4652-3726-2

Printed in the United States of America
10 9 8 7 6 5 4 3 2 1

To My Husband Dick

Contents

CHAPTER 2

Descriptive Voices: The First Message of Intent—What's Happening?   39

CHAPTER 3

CHAPTER 4

Expository Voices: The Third Message of Intent— What Usually Happens?   97

CHAPTER 5

Persuasive and Argumentative Voices: The Fourth Message of Intent—What Should Happen?   125

Preface

Experiencing Reading and Writing is presented to both the college instructor and, more importantly, the college student as a road map to navigate the twenty-first century's information highway. While society throws up its hands in dismay at the declining literacy level, this practical guide intends to move the developmental reader and writer forward, beyond the dry, didactic materials commonly in place for their introductory remedial courses. Even though past failures may place these students at high risk, no one deserves to be directed away from the intellectual world. *Experiencing Reading and Writing* respects the student who tried, did not at first succeed, and now tries again.

Belief in these scholars who never were, but now *want* to be, coupled with an adult lifetime of teaching experience, resolutely drives this text. However, the author does not drive alone. My colleague, William J. McGreevy, professor of English at Ocean County College for nearly three decades, collaborated with me on several editions of a reading text used for fifteen years in our developmental reading courses. As a Rutgers graduate student, I set course early, compelled to follow the teachings of the ultimate pragmatist John Dewey. James Moffett's humanistic view of the universe of discourse helped to refine and focus my romance with experiential learning through his definition of reading and writing acts he called "happenings." My personal mentors, Janet Emig and Louise Rosenblatt, imparted to me an entirely fresh perspective of language and cognition; to them I owe the greatest debt. Their landmark studies in the writing process and transactional reading form the basis for the present conceptual framework—what Emig might call my "governing gaze." Remarkable parallels between *extensive* and *reflexive* writing modes and *efferent* and *aesthetic* reading stances mandate recognition and deserve the widest possible audience.

Happily, Emig's pioneering work on the writing process is today an accepted part of the language arts curriculum in almost every college in our country. Many instructors translate as well transactional reading theory into classroom practice; but no college text, as far as I can see, overtly combines the two. *Experiencing Reading and Writing* does so. It not only makes this important connection, but further brings it directly to the students who most need to see it: developmental college freshmen.

Experiencing Reading and Writing transforms theory into practice in myriad ways. Each chapter furnishes to the student and the instructor:

- clearly written information about written language
- "do-able" strategies for mastery of each mode of discourse
- readily accessible multicultural readings
- open-ended questions for writing and discussion to encourage critical thinking, based on each selection
- measures for evaluation of comprehension
- opportunities for vocabulary building
- ideas for dynamic individual language projects
- suggestions for collaborative learning events

- recommendations for related films and internet research
- questions that focus on each reader's transaction with the text

A concise "Writer's Handbook" clarifies standard writing protocol at the conclusion of the discrete chapters. Some instructors will prefer to omit certain applications or features, while others may prefer to enhance each chapter and the Handbook with ancillary materials. The format is eminently flexible.

Using both cognitive and affective learning strategies to facilitate the move from concrete to divergent thinking, *Experiencing Reading and Writing* builds on successively intricate voices of discourse, linking each rhetorical register with its most appropriate writing mode and reading stance. This textual configuration encourages students to deconstruct and construct meaning, empowering them first to examine the literal content and design of the selection; then, to infer its meaning; and last, to question, decide upon, and critique its significance, applying the reading's thesis, issue, or them to themselves and the world around them.

This text's focus is the seemingly uncomplicated student—more complex than many would believe—intending to regenerate in and restore to each young man and woman not only language skill proficiency, but also recognition of the importance of writing and reading to the highway of life as it is traveled, lived, and imagined.

Sandra G. Brown
January 2014

To the Student

The Triple-Entry Journal: Catalyst for Experiencing Reading and Writing

Reading and Writing Improvement

Everyone wants to be a better reader and writer. But how can we do it? Carmen Collins, author of essays, children's literature, and college textbooks, said that not only can a good deal of reading improve our writing, but also that a good deal of writing can improve our reading![1]

If we want to write a wonderful story or a powerful essay, good sense tells us to read as many stories and essays as we can. But how many people know that the reverse is just as true? That same good sense ought to tell us that writing can help us read more effectively. The truth is, the more we write when we read, the better we'll read. And, chances are, we'll enjoy it more, too.

Journals as a Way of Learning

In the last decade, journals have become very popular as a way of learning. They serve not only as a record of your coursework for review purposes, but also as a means of exploring your topic as you move through it. What is more, our classes as well as your texts can be easier to comprehend if you take a few minutes to write about your feelings each day, before work actually begins.

The following plan defines three separate writing acts: before, during, and after reading.

Each has its own function which can improve your reading behavior dramatically. It can also serve as the source of ideas for the many suggested essay topics in this book and others your professor will assign to you throughout the semester. The triple-entry journal can serve as a catalyst for deep comprehension, efficient note-taking, and rich, personal enjoyment. Importantly, it is a way to remember and review each class in preparation for quizzes and tests.

How to Keep a Triple-Entry Journal

Each journal-keeping day consists of three journal entries: one written before class actually begins, one during class, and one sometime after class is over.

Freewriting

The first entry consists of freewriting for five minutes. You can consider in writing what you may learn in the class session, how you feel about learning, how you feel about the assignment done the night before, or any other personal idea regarding the experiences of reading, writing, and learning. To expedite the writing of this section, your instructor may choose to write a question or topic on the chalkboard.

---

1. Carmen Collins. "The Effect of Writing Experiences in the Expressive Mode Upon the Reading, Self-esteem, Attitudes, and Academic Achievement of Freshmen in a College Reading Course." Dissertation, Rutgers University, 1979.

Note-taking and Homework

The second entry each class day will consist of the taking of class notes. Everything of importance spoken or written on the board should be recorded. If you work in a peer group, the jottings of your project should be included in this section of your journal. If you are given a homework assignment that does not require a written response in the textbook itself, you may also use the second section for this home assignment. A space between the class notes and the homework done later can clarify each for later study.

Reflection

The third entry of the day will consist of your personal response to the ongoing work—your problems with it as well as your breakthroughs. This section can become a place to ask questions you do not care to ask out loud in class. Consider this section of your journal as the "reflection section"—a place to think back about your class that day. Write this section sometime after class is over, perhaps in the evening. You might think about how well you enjoyed the class that particular day, or how you learned something completely new (or something old that you had not thought about for a long time). Of course, you may reflect your feelings of dissatisfaction with the day's work. Perhaps you may feel that the reading is too difficult or easy for you. Perhaps the writing assignments are too hard to complete, or that you cannot meet the instructor's demands for excellence. This is the place to say so! Use this section as well to make important connections between lectures and readings, internet or library research, the instructor's questions to you or her answers to yours. Write questions about your difficulties with essay-writing, or comments about your consults with a writing tutor. Importantly, try to connect each day's work with something you already know.

Journal Do's and Don'ts

Save events that are of a personal nature to you for another kind of diary. A triple-entry journal is not a personal diary.

Fullness is the single most important feature of a successful journal. Therefore, continue to explain what you think, what you see, what you hear, and what you read and write in a free, unedited manner.

Journals should always be spontaneously written. Don't retype or recopy!

Journals may be read, on occasion, by other students or your instructor. Most of the time, however, they will be a private affair. If you would like to share a dialogue with a reader, leave a three- or four-inch margin on each page for comments. Reading another student's journal can be a wonderfully social event. Dialoguing is a way of extending and enriching your classroom experiences. See for yourself!

Collaborative Projects: Working Well with Others

Did you ever start a conversation and have your listener interrupt by finishing your sentence? That can be annoying! Do you feel like saying "don't put words in my mouth"? Are you guilty of doing this to someone else? Speaking to others successfully—that is, cheerfully, and getting your point across at the same time—is one of the goals of working collaboratively. Collaboration in the classroom can be one way to learn a great deal about a subject, but it also can be a way to learn about yourself. Moreover, it can help you to be successful in the workplace, in social gatherings, in professional meetings, in legal discussions; anywhere that public dialogue can take you.

By definition, collaboration is working together, co-laboring, with another to create a jointly accredited work. It is a balancing act; a state of being where all partners contribute equally to a finished project that reflects every member's voice. The goal of collaboration in the classroom is to create knowledge together—new knowledge that is a synthesis of ideas.

To work on a collaborative project, whether it is dissecting a frog, sewing a quilt, or writing a report, requires respect of others; listening attentively with a positive attitude, and, when it is your turn to contribute, being clear about what you think, and keeping it short so others can understand what you mean.

Collaborative projects connect people and ideas. They connect not only students with students but also students with teachers and even students with sources, both primary and secondary. All form a mix of learning and learning styles, creating a dynamism like no other, because the result is original, fresh, and personal.

A "Collaboration Sensation"—a group project—concludes each chapter of this book. These are suggested as ways to join together a variety of viewpoints on a topic related to the issues in each chapter. The focus is on you, the learner. You have control over your work; your voice counts. Writing the group process from start to finish (including difficulties!) in your journal as you move through it can allow you to see how the process works/worked/could work better in the future. Try it!

CHAPTER 1

FROM WRITING MODE
TO READING STANCE

Responding to the Writer's Message of Intent

THE READER-WRITER RELATIONSHIP

The "Scientific" Approach

In the "good old days," a cigar was a nickel and the corner drugstore had the only phone in the neighborhood. Back then, Ernest Hemingway's novel *A Farewell to Arms* was thought to be shocking, while the work of famous writers like D. H. Lawrence and James Joyce actually was banned.

Turn-of-the-century English teachers (some called them "preacher teachers"), influenced by Charles Darwin's theory of evolution (published in 1859), sought to apply certain laws of nature to writers and their writing. The so-called "scientific" approach of teaching reading and writing included learning information about literary history and authors' biographies. Each author's politics, social status, and choice of language was studied closely, as if those features could reveal what made him (women authors were nearly non-existent) famous. Young children as well as college students commonly were required to stand and recite memorized textbook material; they were immediately reprimanded or even physically punished in various ways for not knowing their "lessons." Repeating taught information was thought to be the hallmark of a "good student."

Students wrote reports only about the facts taught to them, not their interpretation of the work studied. Spelling, grammar, punctuation, and neat handwriting were the most important parts of every writing assignment.

The New Criticism

But as the years passed, those methods went out of style. From the 1920s until the 1950s, the spotlight shifted from the author to the book itself. The historical perspective, previously prized in scholarship, was largely ignored; this new type of scholarship cared nothing for the author's intent, much less the reader's or writer's response. Professional critics were born who based their judgment purely upon features of the text itself. These men (for women were still largely absent from the literary world) analyzed images, metaphors, and other symbolic language forms, judging the worth of the text-as-art object by criteria they authorized themselves. Students dared not explain what they personally thought of a poem, novel, or short story; indeed, they were taught to listen to the critics and cite them carefully in their essays. The critics were always right. This movement was called the "New Criticism."

During these early phases of English education, very little attention was given to the ordinary reader of books. The fairly common Latin dedication, *Lectori Benevolo,* meaning "to the kind and gentle reader," was all but ignored in the classroom. The man or woman turning the pages was in the shadows.

The Emergence of the Reader

Today, we know that reading is not a one-way relationship. Every living reader responds actively to the text. We interact with each book we pick up. While it reflects its author's historical, political, social, and psychological orientation as well as his or her intention for writing it, we must bring to it something of ourselves. We now know that reading is not passive reception, but active participation. There is truth in the saying "a book is dead until it's read."

Today, students in every discipline have the right and the responsibility to think for themselves, to move through the writing process, responding to each text in unique ways. As a writer responding to reading, you have a voice; you are in control. Certainly, you will need to read critical opinions (and the more you read, the better), but you must judge for yourself whether or not you agree with the published articles. Your essays must be clearly and honestly written, demonstrating your personal knowledge.[1] Every writer's voice counts.

This book takes the reader and writer out of the shadows. Its focus is less concerned with authors and their texts than the art and science of bringing ourselves to them. This book is concerned with you and me, as readers and writers.

You, Me, It

Before you read and write about all the selections in this book, consider these three little words: You, Me, and It. In following the story, "A Woman on the Street," YOU are the reader. ME refers to the writer, Jeannette Walls: "It was months since I laid eyes on Mom, and when she looked up, I was overcome with panic that she'd see *me* . . ." And what is the story? Why, IT, of course. IT is intended for YOU, the reading audience. Every encoded message relies upon these three components. When you write, you become the ME, and your audience becomes the YOU. The IT always stays the same, doesn't it? But the relationship of the writer to the reader and the reader to the writer always changes ITS meaning.

Six Types of Questions

We can approach a discussion of any reading experience by asking six different types of questions, although sometimes these "types" overlap. Some address your first, personal response to the reading. Some address your relationship to the writer. Others address the actual form of the

---

1. See Michael Polanyi's ground-breaking work *Personal Knowledge.*

reading itself. Others address your solid knowledge of the writer's background (and whether you need to know it). Still others address the kinds of questions many teachers will ask, those that will check your close attention to the reading. Last, there are the kinds of questions that look at your own reading process. This last type, especially, are *metacognitive* questions. These intend to make you aware of what you do when you read, so that you can begin to think about your own style of learning. These are questions particularly about YOU.

Read "A Woman on the Street" from the memoir *The Glass Castle* by Jeannette Walls. The six types of questions that follow will not check your knowledge as much as your relationship to the piece. Don't worry about knowing "answers!"

"A WOMAN ON THE STREET" FROM *THE GLASS CASTLE*

Jeannette Walls

I was sitting in a taxi, wondering if I had overdressed for the evening, when I looked out the window and saw Mom rooting through a Dumpster. It was just after dark. A blustery March wind whipped the steam coming out of the manholes, and people hurried along the sidewalks with their collars turned up. I was stuck in traffic two blocks from the party where I was heading.

Mom stood fifteen feet away. She had tied rags around her shoulders to keep out the spring chill and was picking through the trash while her dog, a black-and-white terrier mix, played at her feet. Mom's gestures were all familiar—the way she tilted her head and thrust out her lower lip when studying items of potential value that she'd hoisted out of the Dumpster, the way her eyes widened with childish glee when she found something she liked. Her long hair was streaked with gray, tangled and matted, and her eyes had sunk deep into their sockets, but still she reminded me of the mom she'd been when I was a kid, swan-diving off cliffs and painting in the desert and reading Shakespeare aloud. Her cheekbones were still high and strong, but the skin was parched and ruddy from all those winters and summers exposed to the elements. To the people walking by, she probably looked like any of the thousands of homeless people in New York City.

It had been months since I laid eyes on Mom, and when she looked up, I was overcome with panic that she'd see me and call out my name, and that someone on the way to the same party would spot us together and Mom would introduce herself and my secret would be out.

I slid down in the seat and asked the driver to turn around and take me home to Park Avenue.

The taxi pulled up in front of my building, the doorman held the door for me, and the elevator man took me up to my floor. My husband was working late, as he did most nights, and the apartment was silent except for the click of my heels on the polished wood floor. I was still rattled from seeing Mom, the unexpectedness of coming across her, the sight of her rooting happily through the Dumpster. I put some Vivaldi on, hoping the music would settle me down.*

---

* To hear what Jeannette listened to, watch and listen to YouTube videos: *Vivaldi Four Seasons (Winter) & Four Seasons I Musici 1988.*

I looked around the room. There were the turn-of-the-century bronze-and-silver vases and the old books with worn leather spines that I'd collected at flea markets. There were the Georgian maps I'd had framed, the Persian rugs, and the overstuffed leather armchair I liked to sink into at the end of the day. I'd tried to make a home for myself here, tried to turn the apartment into the sort of place where the person I wanted to be would live. But I could never enjoy the room without worrying about Mom and Dad huddled on a sidewalk grate somewhere. I fretted about them, but I was embarrassed by them, too, and ashamed of myself for wearing pearls and living on Park Avenue while my parents were busy keeping warm and finding something to eat.

What could I do? I'd tried to help them countless times, but Dad would insist they didn't need anything, and Mom would ask for something silly, like a perfume atomizer or a membership in a health club. They said that they were living the way they wanted to.

After ducking down in the taxi so Mom wouldn't see me, I hated myself—hated my antiques, my clothes, and my apartment. I had to do something, so I called a friend of Mom's and left a message. It was our system of staying in touch. It always took Mom a few days to get back to me, but when I heard from her, she sounded, as always, cheerful and casual, as though we'd had lunch the day before. I told her I wanted to see her and suggested she drop by the apartment, but she wanted to go to a restaurant. She loved eating out, so we agreed to meet for lunch at her favorite Chinese restaurant.

Mom was sitting at a booth, studying the menu, when I arrived. She'd made an effort to fix herself up. She wore a bulky gray sweater with only a few light stains, and black leather men's shoes. She'd washed her face, but her neck and temples were still dark with grime.

She waved enthusiastically when she saw me. "It's my baby girl!" she called out. I kissed her cheek. Mom had dumped all the plastic packets of soy sauce and duck sauce and hot-and-spicy mustard from the table into her purse. Now she emptied a wooden bowl of dried noodles into it as well. "A little snack for later on," she explained.

We ordered. Mom chose the Seafood Delight. "You know how I love my seafood," she said.

She started talking about Picasso.* She'd seen a retrospective of his work and decided he was hugely overrated. All the cubist stuff was gimmicky, as far as she was concerned. He hadn't really done anything worthwhile after his Rose Period.**

"I'm worried about you," I said. "Tell me what I can do to help."

Her smile faded. "What makes you think I need your help?"

"I'm not rich," I said. "But I have some money. Tell me what it is you need."

She thought for a moment. "I could use an electrolysis treatment."

"Be serious."

"I am serious. If a woman looks good, she feels good."

"Come on, Mom." I felt my shoulders tightening up, the way they invariably did during these conversations. "I'm talking about something that could help you change your life, make it better."

"You want to help me change my life?" Mom asked. "I'm fine. You're the one who needs help. Your values are all confused."

"Mom, I saw you picking through the trash in the East Village a few days ago."

"Well, people in this country are too wasteful. It's my way of recycling." She took a bite of her Seafood Delight. "Why didn't you say hello?"

---

* Pablo Picasso (1881–1973). One of the most influential artists of the 20th C. Co-founder of Cubism.
** 1904–1906, a period influenced by Picasso's love affair with Fernande Olivier, when he used many pink and reddish tones in his painting.

"I was too ashamed, Mom, I hid."

Mom pointed her chopsticks at me. "You see?" she said. "Right there. That's exactly what I'm saying. You're way too easily embarrassed. Your father and I are who we are. Accept it."

"And what am I supposed to tell people about my parents?"

"Just tell the truth," Mom said. "That's simple enough."

The following questions ask YOU about the way you responded to "A Woman on the Street." If you share your answers with other students in this class, you will notice that everyone's answers may be a little bit different. Each of the forty reading selections in this book will be followed by some questions, but not every one of the following will be asked. Questions of your own can be written in your journal throughout the semester. Ask some of them in class, and see how different students answer them!

The Reading Experience: Questions for Study and Discussion with Six Types of Questions

You and the Story

1. How does the story make you feel?
2. Do you want to discuss it with others? Why or why not?
3. Does it remind you of any similar experience in your own life?
4. Does it remind you of anything else you have read?
5. To whom is it addressed?
6. Is "A Woman on the Street" believable?
7. Do you think everyone will read this story the same way you did?

You and the Writer

1. Why do you think Jeannette Walls is is writing this episode in her life?
2. In your opinion, how many years have elapsed between this episode on the street and its telling?
3. How did the experience of seeing her mother rummaging in the dumpster affect Jeannette?
4. At the time Jeannette Walls is writing her memoir, do you think she feels the same way about her mother as she did then? What reasons can you give for your answer?

You and the Form of the Story

1. Do you think this is an effective opening for a book? What is the effect of the first sentence? Would you have started the story differently?
2. Do you think this is written in clear language? What words don't you understand?
3. Should the author have explained any section of her opening chapter more specifically? Should she have added more information?

4. How do the references to cultural features (e.g., Vivaldi, Georgian maps, Park Avenue) add to the story? Do you think every reader can identify with these references? What would you do, if anything, about those you aren't familiar with?

5. Do you feel comfortable with the length of this story as an opening chapter in a longer work?

You and the History/Background of the Writer

1. Do you have to study any history to understand the story?

2. Do you have to know the author's background (e.g., biography, previous publications) to understand the story?

You and the Limits, or Facts of the Story

1. What is the story about? Does it have a plot? Can you follow its time sequence?

2. Who are its characters? Are these people described well, so the reader can envision them?

3. What is the setting? What details bring the setting to life for you? Is it contemporary, or a historical piece? Will it ever become dated, or is it timeless? Why or why not?

4. Is it open ended, or does it lead to a "finale"? How may it continue?

5. Who is the narrator? When does this take place in the narrator's life?

You and the Reading Process

1. Did you read this slowly or quickly?

2. Did you re-read any lines as you were reading, or after you were finished?

3. Did you think you misunderstood any part of the story as you were reading it?

4. Is this the first time you are reading this story? If not, do you remember it? Do you read it differently now?

5. Did you ever read a story like this one? What was it about? How was it similar? Which one do you prefer? Why?

6. Would you like to continue reading more about Jeannette Walls and her mother? Explain.

The Writing Experience: Tips for Writing

- Always begin a writing assignment by freewriting all your thoughts, without stopping. Jot down in short phrases or sentences whatever comes to mind as soon as you read the assignment.

- When you have run out of ideas, recheck the reading selection and underline or circle any sentences or words you would like to use in your paper.

- If you need to quote directly, make sure you use quotation marks and give the author credit in your paper.

- Next, organize your paper so that it flows, following these suggestions:

  (a) If you write your own memoir, keep the sequence in order so your reader can follow it easily.

  (b) If you write a letter, have a broad, cheerful opening paragraph before you begin to get into the details. Make sure you close with a friendly message.

(c) If you write an essay on the homeless involving research, make sure that you open with a clear statement of your purpose before getting into specific details in your internal paragraphs. Write a clear conclusion stating what you have found out, and how it makes you feel. Cite your sources carefully. Refer to any videos you may watch, websites you may visit, or, of course, books or magazines that you read!

(d) If you write about values, begin in the same way, stating your purpose. Divide your internal paragraphs so that each person is discussed in a single paragraph, before reaching your own conclusion in the last paragraph.

- If you choose (c) or (d) for this reading selection, make sure you use the author's full name and the title "A Woman on the Street" when you begin.

Suggestions for Writing

1. "A Woman on the Street" is the first chapter is Jeannette Walls' memoir. A memoir is a true story, taken from the life of its writer. It's more than a "history" — its intention is to reveal to the reader the writer's point of view about people and events that shaped her life. Not every day or every person is recorded — just events and people that made a difference. Choose one such person or event in your life for a short one- or two-page paper. Use clear, vivid images that will let your reader see what you saw and feel what you felt. Include some dialogue, if you think it is important and will move your tale along.

2. Write a letter as if you were Jeannette to a friend who lives out west, perhaps in a rural area. For one reason or another you have lost touch with this person, but you would like to reconnect. Explain to her — or him — what your life is like now. Include a description of your beautiful apartment, your professional and social life, and what has happened to your mom. Explain your dilemma.

3. Write an essay about the homeless in New York City. Use the internet to find out about the 50,000 people who sleep in shelters every night. Provide reasons for homelessness and solutions to this enormous problem. You may want to compare and contrast homelessness in New York City with one other large American city, a smaller suburb, or even a city in a foreign country.

4. In an informal essay, respond fully and thoughtfully to these issues raised in "A Woman on the Street": how values affect behavior, and how behavior can affect one's values. Discuss both Jeannette's and her mother's values. How might they have been formed? How does their clothing, their lifestyle, and their conversation reflect their values? Allow the essay to conclude with a discussion of your own feelings about the experiences in this reading.

Recommended Films and eConnections

Jeannette Walls Lets Go of her Shame — Oprah's Lifeclass. 14 Oct.2011. YouTube video.

Record NYC Homeless Population Rises to 50,000 in Shelters Each Night. Huffingtonpost. 5 Mar. 2013. YouTube Video.

The Glass Castle. Dir. n.d. Perf. Jennifer Lawrence. Lionsgate. Date forthcoming. Film.

Inocente. Dir. Sean Fine and Andrea Nix Fine. Perf. John Leguizamo. Shine Global, Salty Features, Fine Films and Unison Films. 2012. Film.

Quiz

_____ 1. "A Woman on the Street" is: (a) a true story; (b) amemoir; (c) an autobiography; (d) all of the above.

_____ 2. The story opens with the author on her way to: (a) a party; (b) a business meeting; (c) the opera; (d) an unspecified event.

_____ 3. Mom's conversation reveals: (a) a woman who has always lived on the street for years; (b) a woman who was born and raised in New York; (c) a woman who was culturally knowledgeable; (d) a woman who, along with her husband, was only very recently made homeless.

_____ 4. The story reveals that Jeannette feels: (a) ashamed of her parents; (b) a need to help her parents; (c) disgusted with her parents; (d) both (a) and (b) are correct.

_____ 5. "Just tell the truth" is a sentence that indicates that: (a) Mom is angry at Jeannette; (b) Mom is mentally more well balanced than Jeannette realizes; (c) Mom is mentally unstable; (d) Mom would like Jeannette to help her.

EFFERENT AND AESTHETIC READING

Have you ever wondered why some people get so much out of reading and others don't? Many people dive into a book while others put one toe in first. If it's too cold, they won't go in, or if they do, they do so very slowly without much enjoyment.

Those who enjoy reading and do so briskly are like accomplished swimmers, out for a day of fun. Those who don't enjoy reading are often like people afraid of water, perhaps because of bad past experiences. The former concentrate on the swim; the latter on the water.

Interestingly, the people who don't get much out of their reading, like the reluctant swimmer, do need to concentrate on the medium (text/water)—at first. Often certain texts are easier and more enjoyable to read than others, but problems with the hard ones trigger the hasty, general response, "I'm not a good reader." Actually everyone has a preference—even excellent readers. But good readers can vary their _approaches_ to different texts; the reading _stance_ can be quite different for different types of texts.

Putting YOU in the Reading and Putting the Reading in YOU

Basically, there are two ways to read: _putting YOU in the reading_ and _putting the reading in YOU._ "Putting YOU in the reading" simply means to live through the reading; to feel your way through it; to sense its meaning; to predict what will come next; to let yourself respond naturally. This kind of reading has been called _aesthetic_ reading.[2] On the other hand, "putting the reading in YOU" entails extracting information from the reading material to use at a later time; to take note of the most important facts given. This kind of reading has been called _efferent_ reading.[5]

Some people read to enjoy a good cry, have a good laugh, or solve a deep mystery. Others prefer reading scores on the sports page, editorials, or the weather, and have no problems at all with how-to manuals, recipes, or maps. Ideally, all readers should be able to approach and to understand all kinds of material. That is a goal of this book.

---

2. Louise Rosenblatt. _The Reader, the Text, the Poem: The Transactional Theory of the Literary Work._ (Carbondale and Edwardsville, Ill.: Southern Illinois University Press, 1978), pp. 24–5.

The first step toward becoming a brisk, accomplished reader is to become aware of your reading preference. Is it easier to put yourself into the reading, or to put the reading in you?

Living through the Text and Extracting the Text: Two Reading Selections

Read the following selections. If you can, comment quickly in the margins as you read. Use question marks if anything isn't clear and a check, asterisk, or star if you like something (even if it's only one word). If it's too much of a bother to do this, very briefly jot your thoughts afterward in Part II of your Journal. Before you look at the questions and writing assignments that follow, consider this: Which piece did you enjoy more? Which was easier to follow? Write that in the margin!

Guns

WD Ehrhart

Comments

Again we pass that field
green artillery piece squatting
by the Legion Post on Chelten Avenue,
its ugly little pointed snout
ranged against my daughter's school.

"Did you ever use a gun
like that?" my daughter asks.
and I say, "No, but others did.
I used a smaller gun. A rifle."
She knows I've been to war.

"That's dumb," she says,
and I say, "Yes," and nod
because it was, and nod again
because she doesn't know.
How do you tell a four-year-old

what steel can do to flesh?
How vivid do you dare to get?
How explain a world where men
kill other men deliberately
and call it love of country?

Just eighteen, I killed
a ten-year old. I didn't know.
he spins across the marketplace
all shattered chest, all eyes and arms.
Do I tell her that? Not yet,

"Guns" is reprinted from *Greatest Hits 1970–2000* by W. D. Ehrhart, Puddinghouse Press 2001, by permission of the author.

though one day I will have
no choice except to tell her
or to send her into the world
wide-eyed and ignorant.
The boy spins across the years

till he lands in a heap
in another war in another place
where yet another generation
is rudely about to discover
what their fathers never told them.

The Reading Experience: Questions for Study and Discussion

1. How does the poem "Guns" make you feel? Do you want to discuss it with others? Why or why not? Are Ehrhart's feelings revealed in the poem? Explain the points of view of both the poet and his daughter.

2. The poem consists of seven *stanzas* (poetic paragraphs) written in *blank verse* (lines that do not rhyme) and uses dialogue (speech). Would it be more or less effective if it had a traditional rhyme? Would it be more or less effective if it were written as a short story, with traditional paragraphs? Would it be more or less effective without the dialogue? Explain.

3. Think about the first stanza. What is the effect of opening with the description of the "artillery piece" with its "ugly little . . . . snout" "pointed" at the poet's daughter's school? How does it set up the conversation to follow?

4. Why does the poet avoid telling his daughter that day about guns? Ehrhart, who served as a U.S. Marine for three years, spent thirteen months in Vietnam and earned the Purple Heart. When will he explain to her what he has been through?

5. How does the poem end? What does he think will happen if "another generation" is never told the truth about war and guns? Do you share the poet's point of view?

The Writing Experience: Suggestions for Short Papers

1. Experiment with blank verse. Using no rhyme whatever, create approximately eight to twelve lines that tell about one of the following:
   - the death of an animal
   - a winning lottery ticket
   - a job interview
   - first love

2. Experiment with dialogue and point of view, either in verse or short story form. You may want to begin with a description, as Ehrhart does, or not. Then create a conversation between two people, of different ages, genders, or professions. Some suggestions are:
   - student and professor discussing a grade
   - celebrity and fan at a concert
   - boy and girl's first meeting at a party, wedding, or school cafeteria
   - parent and son or daughter discussing money

3. Write a short essay, using any of the questions for discussion above. Begin with a clear introduction and statement of thesis. Build your internal paragraphs with solid examples. End with a strong conclusion about your topic, especially for the arguments set up in #2 and #5.

Recommended Films and eConnections

Points of View in Literature – (Somebody's Watchin' You). Chris Warner. 12 Jan. 2012. YouTube video.

He Said, She Said. Pauline Jones. <cozyread.com> 12 Feb. 2010. YouTube video.

The Deer Hunter. Dir. Michael Cimino. Perf. Robert De Niro, Meryl Streep, Christopher Walken. EMI-Warner, 1978. Film.

Platoon. Dir. Oliver Stone. Perf. Tom Berenger, Willem Dafoe, Charlie Sheen. Orion, 1986. Film.

POLITICS, RELIGION, AND WAR

John P. McKay, Bennett D. Hill and John Buckler

In 1559 France and Spain signed the Treaty of Cateau-Cambrésis, which ended the long conflict known as the Habsburg-Valois Wars. This event marked a watershed in early modern European history. Spain was the victor. France, exhausted by the struggle, had to acknowledge Spanish dominance in Italy, where much of the war had been fought. Spanish governors ruled in Sicily, Naples, and Milan, and Spanish influence was strong in the Papal States and Tuscany.

Emperor Charles V had divided his attention between the Holy Roman Empire and Spain. Under his son Philip II (r. 1556–1598), however, the center of the Habsburg Empire and the political center of gravity for all of Europe shifted westward to Spain. Before 1559 Spain and France had fought bitterly for control of Italy; after 1559 the two Catholic powers aimed their guns at Protestantism. The Treaty of Cateau-Cambrésis ended an era of strictly dynastic wars and initiated a period of conflicts in which politics and religion played the dominant roles.

Because a variety of issues were stewing, it is not easy to generalize about the wars of the late sixteenth century. Some were continuations of struggles between the centralizing goals of monarchies and the feudal reactions of nobilities. Some were crusading battles between Catholics and Protestants. Some were struggles for national independence or for international expansion.

Source: "Politics, Religion, and War" by McKay et al. A History of Western Society, 5e, 1995, p. 489.

The Reading Experience: Questions for Study and Discussion

1. How did you read the excerpt "Politics, Religion, and War," quickly or slowly? Did it make you feel sympathetic to any of the military men from Spain, France, or Italy? As a reader, do you want to discuss this article with others? Why or why not?

2. The authors talk about "two Catholic powers" who in 1559 "aimed their guns at Protestantism." Do they explain why? What do authors tell the reader about the Treaty of Cateau-Cambrésis? How is it connected to Philip II? What is the central issue, or main point of this article?

3. Do the writers reveal any particular point of view? Is the writing of this excerpt clear and effective? Are there any words that you do not understand? Are there any concepts that you do not understand? Can you envision any other way to present this material, or can you suggest what may be lacking, if anything? What more would you like to know about?

4. List three important facts that you learned from reading this article. Compare this to three facts from WD Ehrhart's poem "Guns." Can you see a difference? Which reading selection gives you more information? Which one teaches you more? Explain.

5. Are people or countries the focus in "Politics, Religion, and War"? Have the three authors respected historians' intent upon providing the reader with a full understanding of the sixteenth century shift in the reasons for going to war, successfully portrayed the situation?

The Writing Experience: Suggestions for Short Papers

1. Write a 500-word essay about the weapons used in the late sixteenth- to early seventeenth-century wars in central Europe. Include an explanation of the discovery of gunpowder and the use of cannons and their effect on public opinion toward war at that time. You may want to use some of the verse of the Italian poet Ludovico Ariosto to illustrate the sentiments of civilian population.

2. Write a letter from the outgoing Spanish Emperor Charles V to his studious son, Philip II, giving advice on how to govern; write a response from Philip, explaining how he intended to strengthen Spain and make its civilization flourish.

3. The great Miguel de Cervantes, author of *Don Quixote* (later made into the long-running Broadway play *Man of La Mancha*), was twelve when France and Spain signed the Treaty of Cateau-Cambrésis.

   At twenty-two, he served for seven years in the Spanish Navy under Emperor Philip II. In his famous work, the main character, Don Quixote, symbolizes the impractical dreams of seventeenth-century Spain. Write a diary entry in your own handwriting as it may have appeared in Cervantes' daily journal, written after a day's combat on the high seas.

4. Using question #4 above, explain how the content of WD Ehrhart's poem "Guns" differs from that of McKay's, Hill's, and Buckler's excerpt "Politics, Religion, and War" from their textbook *A History of Western Society*.

Recommended Films and eConnections

Several student YouTube films are made about Charles V and his son, Philip II. These posts are generally temporary in nature.

Don Quixote, Part 1: Chapters I–X. Professor González Echevarría. Yale Courses (Span 300). 1 Mar. 2011. YouTube video.

Man of La Mancha. Dir. Arthur Hiller. Perf. Peter O'Toole, Sophia Loren, James Coco. Produzioni Europee Associati, 1972. Film.

Quiz

_____ 1. Aesthetic reading: (a) puts YOU in the reading, recreating in a personal way the writer's presentation; (b) puts the reading in YOU, absorbing facts to obtain knowledge about the world; (c) means to underline the main idea and list important specific examples of that idea as you read; (d) none of the above.

_____ 2. Efferent reading: (a) puts YOU in the reading, recreating in a personal way the writer's presentation; (b) puts the reading in YOU, absorbing facts to obtain knowledge about the world; (c) means to put yourself in the writer's place, openly experiencing what is written; (d) none of the above.

_____ 3. Aesthetic reading: (a) is the most appropriate, "readerly" way to read "Guns"; (b) is the most appropriate, "readerly" way to read "Politics, Religion, and War"; (c) is a methodical, analytic type of reading; (d) requires that you study, or deliberately store information in your memory for later retrieval.

_____ 4. Efferent reading: (a) is the most appropriate, "readerly" way to read "Politics, Religion, and War"; (b) requires you to live through the writer's experience; (c) requires that you study, or deliberately store information in your memory for later retrieval; (d) both (a) and (c) are correct.

_____ 5. Both "Guns" and "Politics, Religion, and War": (a) treat the subject of combat; (b) treat the subject of loss; (c) present conflict; (d) all of the above.

WISHING CAN MAKE IT SO: FROM THE REFLEXIVE WRITER TO THE AESTHETIC READER

Best wishes!

Make a wish!

We wish you a Merry Christmas!

Wishes come in many forms. Did you ever wish you were taller, older, or smarter? Have you ever wished for anything special? Of course, we all make wishes—and send them; birthday wishes, wedding wishes, holiday wishes. This sensitive, often fantastic, and always private side of peoples' natures accounts for our desires and our goals—and often, what we become.

Reflexive Writing

Some people wish to write. No one asks them to do it. They record their personal thoughts about others and the world not only outside but also inside themselves. They have a strong desire to recreate in written form their experiences, feelings, reflections, and dreams. In a sense, they're fulfilling a wish.

This type of writer usually uses a personal tone, whether shaping a story, crafting poetry, or jotting thoughts in a diary. You saw this in the poem "Guns," in the previous section. There is a sense of closeness, sometimes even intimacy, about the writing. The words "I" and "me" appear often in a perfectly natural way, and the writer comfortably uses the word "you," as well. This personal, self-sponsored act has been called _reflexive_ writing.[3]

---

3. Janet Emig. _The Composing Processes of Twelfth Graders._ (Urbana, Ill.: National Council of Teachers of English, 1971), p. 37.

When a man or woman muses thoughtfully, allowing ideas to flow freely and warmly, the writer either wishes to satisfy himself or to move the kind of reader (YOU) who will flow with him. The writer often wishes to bare heart and soul, and envisions someone who will not judge, but understand; someone who can openly experience what is written.

Reading Reflexive Writing

Such a message may affect you, the reader, in various ways. You may laugh, cry, feel afraid, or be moved passionately. If you put yourself into the work (IT), you will respond like an artist would, recreating in a personal way the writer's presentation. The words will then become alive, real, and new. They will grow and change as you read them. As you can see, the *reflexive* writer needs an *aesthetic* reader.

Read the following poem, "Rednecks," by Martín Espada, and let your imagination float freely.

REDNECKS

Gaithersburg, Maryland

Martín Espada

At Scot Gas, Darnestown Road,
the high school boys
pumping gas
would snicker at the rednecks.
Every Saturday night there was Earl,
puckering his liquor-smashed face
to announce that he was driving
across the bridge, a bridge spanning
only the whiskey river
that bubbled in his stomach.
Earl's car, one side crumpled like his nose,
would circle slowly around the pumps,
turn signal winking relentlessly.

Another pickup truck morning,
and rednecks. Loitering
in our red uniforms, we watched
as a pickup rumbled through.
We expected: "Fill it with no-lead, boy,
and gimme a cash ticket."
We expected the farmer with sideburns
and a pompadour.
We, with new diplomas framed
at home, never expected the woman.

Her face was a purple rubber mask
melting off her head, scars rippling down
where the fire seared her freak face,
leaving her a carnival where high school boys
paid a quarter to look, and look away.

No one took the pump. The farmer saw us standing
in our red uniforms, a regiment of illiterate conscripts.
Still watching us, he leaned across the seat of the truck
and kissed her. He kissed her
all over her happy ruined face, kissed her
as I pumped the gas and scraped the windshield
and measured the oil, he kept kissing her.

The Reading Experience: Questions for Reading and Discussion

1. How does the poem make you feel? Do you want to discuss it with others? Does it remind you of any similar experience in your own life? Do you think everyone will read it the same way you did?

2. Is "Rednecks" believable? Why do you think the poet is writing it? In your opinion, how did the experience affect the high school boy who pumped the gas? Do you think he is the poet himself? Why?

3. Do you think the three stanzas are arranged/divided effectively? Would the poem be less or more effective if it had a strong rhyme? Would the feeling of the poem change? Is the language of the poem difficult to understand?

4. Do you have to study any history, or know the author's background to understand the poem, or is it timeless? Do you think you understood it, or was it somehow confusing? Did you reread any lines as you were reading, or after you were finished?

5. Who are the "rednecks"? Who is "the woman" and what is her relationship to "the farmer with sideburns and a pompadour"? What is the poem about? How does the poem end? Why does the farmer keep "kissing her"?

The Writing Experience: Suggestions for Short Papers

1. Gaithersburg, Maryland, remained a rural farming community until the 1970s, which is approximately the era in which the action of the poem "Rednecks" takes place. Compose a short 2–3 page essay discussing this largely blue collar culture. Include such information as the average income, the job market, housing, forms of entertainment, local places of worship, geographical landmarks, etc. You may want to illustrate your essay with a photocopied map of the area, showing its proximity to larger cities, like Baltimore.

2. Stereotyping—categorizing people by age, race, religion, gender, physical appearance—or any other common feature—is irrational, and always negative. How does it start? What does it say about the person who is doing the stereotyping? Compose a short essay explaining this issue.

3. Consider the relationship of the farmer and the woman in the poem "Rednecks." Using your imagination, write a short narrative telling how they may have met, whether or not they married, and what happened to her. Explain how they feel about each other at the gas station.

4. Write a letter to a friend or cousin in another town, as if you were the high school graduate who pumped the gas, explaining what happened that day. Include as well what you may have realized about yourself, for the first time.

Recommended Films and eConnections

Alabanza. Connections Literary Series: College of Southern Maryland. 8 Jan. 2009. YouTube video.

Martín Espada discusses poetry and activism. HoCoPoLitSo. 20 Mar. 2012. YouTube video.

In the Heat of the Night. Dir. Norman Jewison. Perf. Rod Steiger, Sidney Poitier. United Artists, 1967. Film.

A League of Their Own. Dir. Penny Marshall. Perf. Geena Davis, Lori Petty, Tom Hanks, Madonna, Rosie O'Donnell. Columbia Pictures, 1992. Film.

GO FOR THE GOLD: FROM THE EXTENSIVE WRITER TO THE EFFERENT READER

Olympic athletes must train long and hard to enter the competition. The champions' final moments of glory represent the culmination of many years of preparation and dedication. Although the dream of winning begins as a wish, without the daily workouts and the right instruction by trainers and coaches, the gold medals would remain only a dream.

College students go through similar experiences. Your diploma, your medal of glory, will signify years of hard work and dedication. Your professors will require that you read a great many texts and write as many papers before you can realize your dream and claim your degree with honor.

To accomplish our goals, we often have to do more than wish upon a star; we often have to go through experiences and tackle tasks we would not otherwise choose. Recognizing the divisions between wish and task, as well as self-motivation and other-directed behavior, can be of help in understanding responses to written language.

Extensive Writing

Most of your essays will be assigned by your instructors to help you understand their subject. These writings may require research and adherence to a traditional format. The model for your papers often will be the textbooks and essays that you are required to read. As you compose your material, you will keep purpose, detail, clarity, and grammatical correctness uppermost in your mind. The writing, like that in your texts, will be formal, with little or no trace of "me" or "you." This other-directed, intellectual inquiry has been called *extensive* writing.[4]

Extensive writing may not be as much fun to write as *reflexive* writing. Its more formal structure, its "distance" also may make it less fun to read. In order to read it most effectively, just accept its purpose: to provide you with facts, to help you understand the world in a more knowledgeable way. You will need to "put the writing into YOU." Going for the gold requires tenacity and knowing the rules. An extensive writer needs a tenacious, efferent reader who knows all the rules of extracting and retaining information from the text.

Read the next article, "Where Does the Term Redneck Come From?" and see how much factual information you can absorb. This is your chance to learn what Martín Espada was writing about, if you still aren't sure, and to learn where that odd term comes from!

---

4. Janet Emig. *The Composing Processes of Twelfth Graders.* (Urbana, Ill.: National Council of Teachers of English, 1971), p. 37.

WHERE DOES THE TERM REDNECK COME FROM?

N. L. West

To us, a redneck is someone who is from the South. They love being in the South and to them they are the only great people in the country. They do all that they can to show people their love of huntin', fishin', and of course, their tractors!

It is true that we associate rednecks with this definition in this modern age—but in truth, the name was given another way. There are many different backgrounds that people believe the term redneck was derived from

1. Many believe that the term was given to people who had a red neck from the sun that was caused by the fact that they constantly worked outside their whole life. When the sun is beating on someone for years, the effect can cause the skin that is exposed to redden what was once fair skin and cause it to be tough and leathery. By middle aged these workers were often very wrinkled.

2. Others believe that people would use red bandanas and tie them around their necks to show others their loyalty to the union affiliations during the violent fight between owners and the United Mine Workers.

3. There are some historians that believe the term originated in Scotland. The National Covenant and The Solemn League and Covenant signed special documents that stated that Scotland wanted to become a Presbyterian Church Government and would reject the Church of England from being their official church.

Many of the Covenanters signed these documents by using their own blood. They also began to wear red pieces of cloth around their necks to show where they stood in the public eye. Soon people began to call them rednecks. Because many of the early inhabitants lived in the southern parts of the U.S. and came of Scottish descent they were given this term.

It is obvious that the reason has evolved into what we know it today. Many from the South will gladly be called rednecks and feel a sense of pride from it. But as proud as they might be we aren't sure if they can still endure the many redneck jokes that have been created on their behalf. I guess we'll have to try a few on them and see what happens.

From "Where Does the Term Redneck Come From?" by N. L. West, http://www.articlesbase.com/culture-articles/where-does-the-term-redneck-come-from-649511.html. Copyright © 2008 by www.wemfo.com. Reprinted by permission.

The Reading Experience: Questions for Reading and Discussion

1. Does the explanation above feel satisfactory? Or do you want to research this question further? Do you think every reader will have the same interest in this subject as you have? Did you know any of this information before reading it here?

2. Is the language difficult to understand? Are there any terms that you need to research further, like "bandanas"? Do you need to know more about the proper names used in this article, like the "United Mine Workers" or "The Solemn League and Covenant"?

3. What is English? There are approximately 500,000 words in the English language (the unabridged Oxford English Dictionary currently catalogues about 600,000). Our standard hardcover abridged college dictionaries include about half that number, and

paperbacks much less—only about 40,000. But is the English language only content-discrete words, or is it something more? Is it form as well? Is it not also the way we use these words and their forms? Or is it a combination of all three—content, form, and use? "Redneck" is a compound word, made up of *red* and *neck*. But as we can see, the way it is used today, it is not an innocent description of sunburn. It's a loaded word—and its meaning is perjorative (look that up in your dictionary).

4. As you read this article, did you think of taking notes? Can this information be studied in preparation for an objective quiz? Did you think of taking notes when reading Martín Espada's poem, "Rednecks"?

   Can the message in his poem be studied for an objective quiz? Would it be appropriate to do so?

5. Which selection about *rednecks* is written reflexively? Which is written extensively?

The Writing Experience: Suggestions for Short Papers

1. Write a short essay that explains the meaning, and the origin of three to five currently used compound words. Explain how these may have come into use by doing some library or internet research, but if no information exists, hypothesize about their origin. In an essay of this nature, wit can be very effective!

2. English is an extremely flexible language that is constantly changing. Every change reflects some feature of our culture, whether it is scientific, technological, professional, or social. Some of the ways new words replace old are through the use of acronyms (CBS, ttyl), clipped forms (math), trade words (band aid), and of course, slang (waddup), which changes almost daily. Compose a short essay that explains each of these categories, using plentiful examples. Consider how the words you have chosen reflect our contemporary culture.

3. Using the question "What is English?" as a starting point for a short essay, write your own explanation. Some of the questions you may want to consider are: Why is it a required school subject? How does it differ from any other language? Does the term "the English Department" indicate just the study of language, or grammar? What else does it include?

4. If you speak another language, write a short, personal essay that explains your experiences in learning English.

Recommended Films and eConnections

The Adventure of English, Episode 8: Many Tongues Called English, One World Language. RainbowEyes1000. 7 Oct. 2012. YouTube video.

Etymology. Sound change, roots and derivation. NativLang. 7 July 2011. YouTube video.

The Immigrant Experience: The Long Long Journey. Dir. Joan Micklin Silver. Perf. John Kowalczyck, Thomas Kubiak, Joan Kendall. Learning Corporation of America, 1972. Film.

Quiz

_____ 1. Reflexive writing indicates: (a) the writer is self-motivated; she *must* write; (b) the writer is motivated by someone else to perform a task; (c) the writer first does a significant amount of research befor beginning her project; (d) the writer prepares an outline for the writing experience before beginning the task.

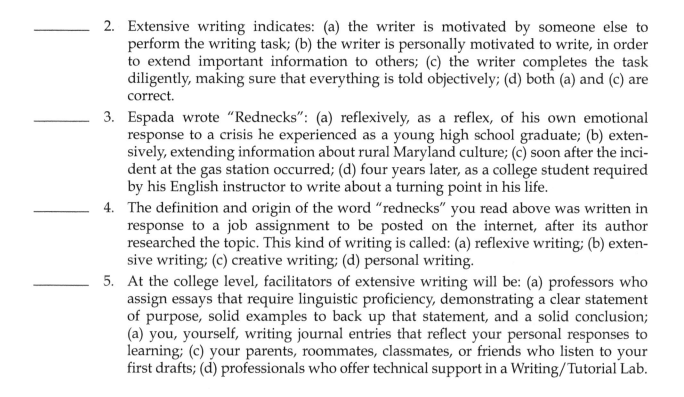

2. Extensive writing indicates: (a) the writer is motivated by someone else to perform the writing task; (b) the writer is personally motivated to write, in order to extend important information to others; (c) the writer completes the task diligently, making sure that everything is told objectively; (d) both (a) and (c) are correct.

3. Espada wrote "Rednecks": (a) reflexively, as a reflex, of his own emotional response to a crisis he experienced as a young high school graduate; (b) extensively, extending information about rural Maryland culture; (c) soon after the incident at the gas station occurred; (d) four years later, as a college student required by his English instructor to write about a turning point in his life.

4. The definition and origin of the word "rednecks" you read above was written in response to a job assignment to be posted on the internet, after its author researched the topic. This kind of writing is called: (a) reflexive writing; (b) extensive writing; (c) creative writing; (d) personal writing.

5. At the college level, facilitators of extensive writing will be: (a) professors who assign essays that require linguistic proficiency, demonstrating a clear statement of purpose, solid examples to back up that statement, and a solid conclusion; (a) you, yourself, writing journal entries that reflect your personal responses to learning; (c) your parents, roommates, classmates, or friends who listen to your first drafts; (d) professionals who offer technical support in a Writing/Tutorial Lab.

MESSAGES OF INTENT

Why do writers write? We've heard students say that they do it "for the money." Although dollars and cents certainly motivated F. Scott Fitzgerald, that's rarely so. Sometimes authors write because it's actually fun! But the answer closest to the truth has several components.

The Intent to Portray: Spatial Description

Like all of us, writers have complex needs. These needs translate into messages of intent. Writers appear to be more keenly aware of sights and sounds than the rest of us. They seem to need to describe everything they sense. Perhaps the act of writing helps them to see better themselves. They are intent on portraying, much like a portrait painter is intent on capturing someone's likeness on canvas. We think that sensory description may be the primary reason why writers write.

The Intent to Sense a Flow: Chronological Description

Writers also need to organize their world, to put things in order. Here their intent is to be able to sense a direction, a flow, or a trend. To do this, they make lists, charts, tables, outlines, and other sequential devices which they use to more fully describe processes that explain the progress of our existence on earth. These depictions are the closest thing to graphic art.

The Intent to Interest and Entertain: Narration

Further, writers need to relate things that they experienced, real or imaginary. Their intent is to interest others in what they have seen or projected, to entertain them or to otherwise engage them in conversation. To make this happen, writers strive for excitement. They use heightened, rich phrases that may rhyme or ring, sometimes even long afterward. Entertaining the audience does not necessarily mean to relate things are pleasant or funny. The classic masks of comedy and tragedy remind us that the early Greeks staged a festival of plays that entertained their audiences on many levels. Novels, short stories, plays, and films that remind us of the frailty of the human condition outnumber comedies by a wide margin. In any event, plainly, writers of narration want attention and they want their tales to be remembered. This social aspect of language is most likely the oldest form that appears in writing in every culture.

The Intent to Teach: Exposition

In addition, many writers want to teach what they know, to explain phenomena they have studied. This phenomena can be either the ordinary stuff of life that we take for granted or a startling discovery that can change the way all of humankind thinks. Sometimes, the information is so clearly told that it is used in textbooks. Therefore, the need to inform translates into the intent to teach.

The Intent to Convince: Persuasion and Argument

Finally, many writers clearly love to argue! They want to convince others to believe as they do. Sometimes, the need can be named as the need for power; other times, the need for money. Although these reasons sound selfish at first, upon closer inspection one can recognize how forceful writing can be used in myriad ways to achieve all sorts of benefits — mental, physical, and spiritual — for individuals and society at large. The message of intent is to change people's ideas and their behavior.

But above all, the primary need of all writers is to have an audience. Writers need readers.

Reflect upon the intentions of each writer you have just read. Listen to the writers' messages of intent that follow. Carefully consider each one's intention. Why did they write the article? Why did they write it the way they did? For whom were they writing? Ask yourself, which may be written reflexively and which extensively? That may have a great deal to do with their intent.

READERLY RESPONSES

Hearing and Listening

What's the difference between hearing and listening? To help yourself answer, consider these sentences:

"Can you hear me?"
"Are you listening"

If you said that the first sentence asks about volume while the second deals with attention, you're right. Current slang or even military jargon, however, can confuse their meanings in sentences like "I hear you, dude!" or "Now hear this!" — where the meaning of the word *hear* refers to attention, as well. The two meanings, therefore, can be confusing. It is important to clarify each, for interpretation often affects behavior. Too many people think they're paying attention if they merely hear words or if they pronounce them silently to themselves as they read.

The daughters of the poet John Milton wrote down what their father dictated to them, but they did not pay attention to what he said. In other words, they took motes, but then, did not take note! They heard, but they did not listen.

Readers are writers, listeners. As a college student, your first task is to become a listener — not only to lectures, but also to textbooks. This listening entails both taking notes as well as heeding, or taking note of what is said and written. In order to become a good listener and heedful note-taker, you will need to know what to listen *for*.

HOW TO LISTEN TO MESSAGES OF INTENT

Readerly Response #1: To Envision

Cartographers transcribe the overview of geographical formations as maps. Statisticians describe the dimensions of ethnographic groups with charts. Advertisers create layouts to pictorally and verbally represent their products. Similarly, poets, novelists, biographers, journalists, playwrights and screenwriters portray persons and scenes, using words that rely upon the senses. All hope to evoke the same readerly response, which is *to envision* what is shown. As a reader, your task is to call upon your senses of sight, smell, hearing, taste, and touch to evoke the description. Of course, the writer's words will limit that projection, but your past experiences will dictate precisely what you will picture. For example, the word *red* for you may bring to mind a ripe tomato, while someone else may think of a drop of blood. However, that word will never suggest the pallor of snow.

Objective, extensively written descriptions, such as the dimensions of a wooden birdhouse or a recipe for mince pie require "putting the reading in you" — the efferent stance. On the other hand, subjective, reflexively written description, such as Gustave Flaubert's portrait of Madame Bovary, require "putting you in the reading" — the aesthetic reading stance. Above all, don't just hear the description — listen to it.

Readerly Response #2: To Live Through the Experience and Predict What's Coming

Not all movies or novels are "cliffhangers," but when writers intend to interest an audience in what they have seen or fantasized, they hope wholeheartedly that readers will follow the action with emotion, living through the experience as if they were actually there. Poets tell in intense, often symbolic language of the significance or poignancy of events; novelists recreate the panorama of life as it is lived through the eyes of their fictional characters; biographers and journalists relate what they have seen and heard in the world around them, aiming not only for accuracy, but also the thrill of the moment; those who craft scripts strive for the rapt attention of their audience with special effects that condense time and magnify reality. The readerly response called for is your participation. Open your mind, give full rein to your imagination, and guess what will happen every step of the way. Feel free to tremble, to laugh, to weep. Subjective, reflexively written narratives require the aesthetic stance — "putting you in the reading" — fully. Although the writing will relate the circumstances, remember that each of us will interpret them in our own personal ways

Readerly Response #3: To Learn

What do textbook authors, your professors, scientists and doctors who write articles have in common? That should be an easy question — they all want to inform you about the world. For their messages to create an impact, you must do so much more than merely hear them! Your listening must become extremely sharp and focused. You have to *study* what they say — both as they say it and afterward.

This may sound difficult at first, but there's an easy way to do it. Most informative writers begin by stating the main idea of the message, and end by repeating it. If you know this readerly response, you will be adequately prepared to listen efferently to any extensive message, and to learn from it. You will begin to extract and "put the reading in you," perhaps even forever.

Readerly Response #4: To Judge

"Friends, Romans, countrymen, lend me your ears." When Shakespeare's Antony speaks these words, does he want his audience to *hear* him, or to *listen* to him? Remember that Antony understands how to "work a crowd". His message of intent is to turn them against Brutus, Cassius, and the others who have murdered Caesar. To do this, he surely wants them to listen closely—to "lend him their ears" .

Modern politicians, advertising executives, and lawyers, too, want you to listen. All intend to convince you to change your mind and your behavior. Their arguments can be very persuasive. They turn the heat up, and emotions run high. It takes a cool, efferent reader who can extract the main idea and analyze its development to deal with this powerful language.

Such a reader will know how to *judge* evidence by separating valid arguments from fallacious thinking. Voters, shoppers, and jurors who hear speeches and slogans, but don't really listen to them, may very well end up with something they won't like.

Of course, persuasive language also can be effectively used to convince people to help themselves. Clergy and health professionals, for example, know how such *effective* language can be *affective* as well.

When you "lend your ears" to an argument, hold your emotions in check. Listen efferently. Judge all information. Decide whether you want to accept the premise.

Which readerly responses are most appropriate for the following pieces of writing? Should each piece be read efferently or aesthetically?

TARZAN OF THE APES

Edgar Rice Burroughs

On this day, then, he went directly to the door and spent hours examining it and fussing with the hinges, the knob and the latch. Finally he stumbled upon the right combination, and the door swung creakingly open before his astonished eyes.

For some minutes he did not dare venture within, but finally as his eyes became accustomed to the dim light of the interior he slowly and cautiously entered.

In the middle of the floor lay a skeleton, every vestige of flesh gone from the bones to which still clung the mildewed and moldered remnants of what had once been clothing. Upon the bed lay a similar gruesome thing, but smaller, while near-by was a third, a wee mite of a skeleton.

To none of these evidences of a fearful tragedy of a long dead day did little Tarzan give but passing heed. His wild jungle life had inured him to the sight of dead and dying animals, and had he known that he was looking upon the remains of his own father and mother he would have been no more greatly moved.

The furnishings and other contents of the room it was which riveted his attention. He examined many things minutely—tools and weapons, books, paper, clothing—what little had withstood the ravages of time in the humid atmosphere of the jungle coast. He opened chests and cupboards, such as did not baffle his small experience and in these he found the contents much better preserved.

Source: Tarzan of the Apes by Edgar Rice Burroughs, 1913.

Among other things he found a sharp hunting knife, on the keen blade of which he immediately proceeded to cut his finger. Undaunted he continued his experiments, finding that he could hack and hew splinters of wood from the table and chairs with this new toy.

For a long time this amused him, but finally tiring he continued his explorations. In a cupboard filled with books he came across one with brightly colored pictures—it was a child's illustrated alphabet—

A is for Archer
  Who shots with a bow.
  B is for Boy,
  His first name is Joe.
The pictures interested him greatly.

There were many apes with faces similar to his own, and further over in the book he found, under "M," some little monkeys such as he saw daily fitting through the trees of his primeval forest. But nowhere was pictured any of his own people; in all the book was none that resembled Kerchak, or Tublat, or Kala.

At first he tried to pick the little figures from the leaves but soon saw that they were not real, though he knew not what they might be, nor had he any words to describe them.

The boats, and trains, and cows and horses were quite meaningless to him but not quite so baffling as the odd little figures which appeared beneath and between the colored picture—some strange kind of bug he thought they might be, for many of them had legs though nowhere could he find one with eyes and a mouth. It was his first introduction to the letters of the alphabet, and he was over ten years old.

Of course he had never before seen print, or even had spoken with any living thing which had the remotest idea that such a thing as a written language existed, not ever had he seen anyone reading.

So what wonder that the little boy was quite at a loss to guess the meaning of these strange figures. Near the middle of the book he found his old enemy, Sabor, the lioness, and further on, coiled Histah, the snake.

Oh, it was most engrossing! Never before in all his ten years had he enjoyed anything so much. So absorbed was he that he did not note the approaching dusk, until it was quite upon him and the figures were blurred.

He put the book back in the cupboard and closed the door, for he did not wish anyone else to find and destroy his treasure, and as he went out into the gathering darkness he closed the great door of the cabin behind him as it had been before he discovered the secret of its lock, but before he left he had noticed the hunting knife lying where he had thrown it upon the floor, and this he picked up and took with him to show his fellows.

The Reading Experience: Questions for Reading and Discussion

1. How does Burroughs describe the three skeletons so that the reader knows more than Tarzan does?

2. Provide three descriptive details of the room. To which of our senses do they appeal?

3. Why could Tarzan not find any words to describe some of the pictures in the illustrated alphabet book?

4. If you did not know what printed letters symbolized, how could you describe them? Compare your description to Tarzan's.

5. What is the writer's intent in describing the skeletons, room, and the printed letters? Do you think Burroughs was writing reflexively or extensively? For whom is he writing?

Which readerly response is most appropriate? Should "Tarzan" be read efferently or aesthetically?

The Writing Experience: Suggestions for Short Papers

1. After asking the parents' permission, read a storybook to a three-year-old child. Ask the child what the pictures are, and what the letters look like. Record his or her answers. Write a short paper describing in your own words the pictures shown, comparing your description to the child's. Analyze to the best of your ability the toddler's description of the letters. Use this information to compare with Burroughs' chapter in *Tarzan*.

2. Describe your feelings on the first day of college. How did you respond to your new surroundings? Describe your first class, the instructor, and the students you met. Omit actual names!

3. Compare Burroughs' description to another medium in which Tarzan is portrayed: either in TV cartoons, the Broadway play, the Disney full-length feature, or any of the Hollywood films made of this character.

4. In 1800 a feral child about twelve years old was found outside the woods in Sernin-sur-Rance, in France. He was wearing no clothes, and could not speak. Raised by a young medical student, Jean Itard, "Victor," as the wild child was called, eventually did learn some of the habits of civilization, but only learned to write two words: *lait*, meaning "milk," and *Oh Dieu*, meaning "Oh God." Using library resources or the internet, describe Victor as he appeared, and compare him to the fictional Tarzan.

Recommended Films and eConnections

Tarzan (1932–1940): Johnny Weissmuller sound track. (107 videos). The People's Museum. 1 May 2008. YouTube video.

Trailer: The Wild Boy. The CineLady. 25 Aug. 2012. YouTube video.

The Wild Child. Dir. Francois Truffaut. Perf. Jean-Pierre Cargol, Francois Truffaut. Les films du Carrosse, 1970. Film.

Tarzan. Dir. Chris Buck and Kevin Lima. Perf. Tony Goldwyn, Minnie Driver, Glenn Close, Rosie O'Donnell. Walt Disney Animated Classics, 1999. Film.

Quiz

_____ 1. As a writer, Burroughs' primary intent in writing this chapter of his full-length novel *Tarzan* is: (a) to portray the cabin and Tarzan's response to it; (b) to relate the rising action of the plot; (c) to compare and contrast articles from nature with man-made objects; (d) to persuade the reader that lack of a formal education can lead to adult illiteracy.

_____ 2. As a reader, you should: (a) envision the cabin through Tarzan's eyes; (b) underline and then list all unknown vocabulary items; (c) skim the selection to find the thesis statement and the conclusion; (d) judge whether or not you ought to believe this writer.

_____ 3. The five senses are used to convey Tarzan's experience as he enters and finds his way around the cabin. Which one of the following phrases specifically uses the sense of touch? (a) the door swung creakingly open; (b) the dim light of the interior; (c) mildewed and moldered remnants of what had once been clothing; (d) on the keen blade . . . he immediately proceeded to cut his finger.

4. Which of the following phrases specifically uses the sense of hearing? (a) the door swung creakingly open; (b) the dim light of the interior; (c) mildewed and moldered remnants of what had once been clothing; (d) on the keen blade . . . he immediately proceeded to cut his finger.

5. An example of the "strange kind of bug" Tarzan sees is: (a) "A is for Archer"; (b) Histah, the snake; (c) little figures in the leaves; (d) cows and horses.

Image Courtesy of Library of Congress.

EASTER SUNDAY

Marian Anderson

The excitement over the denial of Constitution Hall to me did not die down. It seemed to increase and to follow me wherever I went. I felt about the affair as about an election campaign; whatever the outcome, there is bound to be unpleasantness and embarrassment. I could not escape it, of course. My friends wanted to discuss it, and even strangers went out of their way to express their strong feelings of sympathy and support.

What were my own feelings? I was saddened and ashamed. I was sorry for the people who had precipitated the affair. I felt that their behavior stemmed from a lack of understanding. They were not persecuting me personally or as a representative of my people so much as they were doing something that was neither sensible nor good. Could I have erased the bitterness, I would have done so gladly. I do not mean that I would have been prepared to say that I was not entitled to appear in Constitution Hall as might any other performer. But the unpleasantness disturbed me, and if it had been up to me alone I would have sought a way to wipe it out. I cannot say that such a way out suggested itself to me at the time, or that I thought of one after the event. But I have been in this world long enough to know that there are all kinds of people, all suited by their own natures for different tasks. It would be fooling myself to think that I was meant to be a fearless fighter; I was not, just as I was not meant to be a soprano instead of a contralto.

Then the time came when it was decided that I would sing in Washington on Easter Sunday. The invitation to appear in the open, singing from the Lincoln Memorial before as many people as would care to come, without charge, was made formally by Harold L. Ickes, Secretary of the Interior. It was duly reported, and the weight of the Washington affair bore in on me . . . I studied my conscience. In principle the idea was sound, but it could not be comfortable to me as an individual. As I thought further, I could see that my significance as an individual was small in this affair. I had become, whether I liked it or not, a symbol, representing my people. I had to appear.

I discussed the problem with Mother, of course. Her comment was characteristic: "It is an important decision to make. You are in this work. You intend to stay in it. You know what your aspirations are. I think you should make your own decision."

Mother knew what the decision would be. In my heart I also knew. I could not run away from this situation. If I had anything to offer, I would have to do so now. It would be mis-leading, however, to say that once the decision was made I was without doubts.

We reached Washington early that Easter morning and went to the home of Gifford Pinchot, who had been Governor of Pennsylvania. The Pinchots had been kind enough to offer their hospitality, and it was needed because the hotels would not take us. Then we drove over to the Lincoln Memorial. Kosti was well enough to play, and we tried out the piano and examined the public-address system, which had six microphones, meant not only for the people who were present but also for a radio audience.

When we returned that afternoon I had sensations unlike any I had experienced before. The only comparable emotion I could recall was the feeling I had had when Maestro Toscanini had appeared in the artist's room in Salzburg. My heart leaped wildly, and I could not talk. I even wondered whether I would be able to sing.

The murmur of the vast assemblage quickened my pulse beat. There were policemen waiting at the car, and they led us through a passageway that other officers kept open in the throng. We entered the monument and were taken to a small room. We were introduced to Mr. Ickes, whom we had not met before. He outlined the program. Then came the signal to go out before the public.

If I did not consult contemporary reports I could not recall who was there. My head and heart were in such turmoil that I looked and hardly saw, I listened and hardly heard. I was led to the platform by Representative Caroline O'Day of New York, who had been born in Georgia, and Oscar Chapman, Assistant Secretary of the Interior, who was a Virginian. On the platform behind me sat Secretary Ickes, Secretary of the Treasury Morgenthau, Supreme Court Justice Black, Senators Wagner, Mead, Barkley, Clark, Guffey, and Capper, and many Representatives, including Representative Arthur W. Mitchell of Illinois, a Negro. Mother was there, as were people from Howard University and from churches in Washington and other cities. So was Walter White, then secretary of the National Association for the Advancement of Colored People. It was Mr. White who at one point stepped to the microphone and appealed to the crowd, probably averting serious accidents when my own people tried to reach me.

I report these things now because I have looked them up. All I knew then as I stepped forward was the overwhelming impact of that vast multitude. There seemed to be people as far as the eye could see. The crowd stretched in a great semicircle from the Lincoln Memorial around the reflecting pool on to the shaft of the Washington Monument. I had a feeling that a great wave of good will poured out from these people, almost engulfing me. And when I stood up to sing our National Anthem I felt for a moment as though I were choking. For a desperate second I thought that the words, well as I know them, would not come.

I sang, I don't know how. There must have been the help of professionalism I had accumulated over the years. Without it I could not have gone through the program. I sang—and again I know because I consulted a newspaper clipping—"America," the aria "O mio Fernando," Schubert's "Ave Maria," and three spirituals—"Gospel Train," "Trampin'," and "My Soul Is Anchored in the Lord."

I regret that a fixed rule was broken, another thing about which I found out later. Photographs were taken from within the Memorial, where the great statue of Lincoln stands, although there was a tradition that no pictures could be taken from within the sanctum.

It seems also that at the end, when the tumult of the crowd's shouting would not die down, I spoke a few words. I read the clipping now and cannot believe that I could have uttered another sound after I had finished singing. "I am overwhelmed," I said. "I just can't talk. I can't tell you what you have done for me today. I thank you from the bottom of my heart again and again."

It was the simple truth. But did I really say it?

There were many in the gathering who were stirred by their own emotions. Perhaps I did not grasp all that was happening, but at the end great numbers of people bore down on me. They were friendly; all they wished to do was to offer their congratulations and good wishes. The police felt that such a concentration of people was a danger, and they escorted me back into the Memorial. Finally we returned to the Pinchot home.

The Reading Experience: Questions for Reading and Discussion

1. How does Marian Anderson's story make you feel? Do you want to discuss it with others?

2. How crucial is the advice Marian Anderson's mother gave her? Do you think it is good advice?

3. How do you respond to the cultural references made in this episode in Anderson's life, in particular, Constitution Hall and the Lincoln Memorial? Is it important to understand the significance of the following references: Gifford Pinchot, Caroline O'Day, and Oscar Chapman? Why does Anderson point out their home states?

4. Why does Anderson feel as if she were "choking" when she got up to sing the National Anthem?

5. In 1955, Marian Anderson became the first African American to sing at the Metropolitan Opera; in the 1960s, she served as ambassador to the UN travelling the globe. Is her story of Easter Sunday as meaningful today as it was in 1939, or is it more meaningful?

The Writing Experience: Suggestions for Short Papers

1. Read on the internet the *LIFE Magazine* article: "Marian Anderson and the Concert that Sparked the Civil Rights Movement" (April 2013) or the *New Yorker* article "Voice of the Century: Celebrating Marian Anderson" (April 13, 2009). Explain how her decisions changed First Lady Eleanor Roosevelt's mind about the DAR, inspired the Rev. Martin Luther King, and resonates today as a lesson to this generation of Americans.

2. Use Marian Anderson's story as the basis for a personal response to a contemporary issue involving racial or religious tolerance. If you use any TV or news articles, be sure to cite your source.

3. How does visual media affect a reader's perception of a story? After you watch the newsreel taken on the steps of the Lincoln Memorial on Easter Sunday, 1939, comment on how reading the excerpt "Easter Sunday" above and then watching it unfold changed your perception of that event.

4. How would this story be different if told from another person's point of view? In your opinion, are autobiography, biography, and journalism equally effective as narratives?

Recommended Films and eConnections

Marian Anderson Sings at the Lincoln Memorial Newsreel Story. UCLA 15 September 2010. YouTube video.

Marian Anderson, 1950. Newsreelvideo 13 April 2009. YouTubevideo.

Marian Anderson: A Portrait in Music. VAI 4278. 2004. DVD.

Marian Anderson On Stage and At Home. Dir. Allan Altman. Perf. Marian Anderson, Franz Rupp. 1950. Film.

Quiz

_____ 1. In her biography, *Oh My Lord, What a Morning,* Marian Anderson relates how she sang to a crowd of 75,000 on Easter Sunday, 1939: (a) at the Lincoln Memorial; (b) at the White House; (c) at Carnegie Hall; (d) in Constitution Hall.

_____ 2. When Anderson was informed that she could not enter the public building, she sought advice from: (a) her minister; (b) her agent; (c) Eleanor Roosevelt; (d) her mother.

_____ 3. Marian Anderson wrote about that Easter Sunday because: (a) she was personally motivated to do so; (b) her agent advised her to do so; (c) her mother told her it would be important to do so; (d) the press was insistent that she reveal the events of that day.

_____ 4. As a reader, the most appropriate way to read this selection is: (a) to try to envision the scene; (b) to try to live through Anderson's experience, understanding her situation, and trying to predict what will happen; (c) to take notes and underline important ideas as you read; (d) to judge whether you believe that her account is truthful.

_____ 5. The reason Anderson writes "I report these things now because I have looked them up" indicates: (a) that she has a poor memory; (b) that she was too overwhelmed with emotion to remember the titles of the selections she sang—her "head and heart were in such turmoil"; (c) the order of the program was changed many times; (d) photographers' flashbulbs were popping every moment as she was performing, blurring her vision.

FLIGHT OF THE BUMBLEBEE

Mary Jones

There's an old joke about bumblebees: According to aerodynamic theory, it's impossible for them to fly. No way could those short wings of theirs provide enough power to lift their comparatively stout bodies off the ground.

Scientists, who have naturally been curious about how bumblebees *do* manage to fly despite the presumed hindrance of rotund bodies, are now finding that these creatures fly in the face of another theory too. Contrary to expectations—and quite unlike airplanes—they they do not have an optimum cruising speed.

For the first time for any free-flying insect, Rutgers professor Timothy M. Casey, who heads the entomology department at Cook College, and a British colleague at the University of Cambridge, Charles Ellington, have directly measured the oxygen consumption of bumblebees. In effect, in what the British scientific journal *Nature* calls "a remarkable achievement," they have found out how much energy it takes for a bumblebee to hover and to fly at various speeds in a wind tunnel.

These measurements are hard to make for insects because of the extremely tiny amounts of oxygen that such small creatures use. The only previous measurements of energy expenditure concern a few tethered insects, not free-flying ones. But Casey and Ellington devised a specially sealed wind tunnel and a highly sensitive oxygen analyzer that enabled them to make the tests.

The researchers discovered that the bumblebees, which flap their wings an astonishing 160 times a second, used just about the same amount of oxygen hovering as when they flew forward at various speeds (up to a nearly top pace of 13 feet per second). Previously, it had long been assumed that an optimum flight speed, where power demands are at a minimum, must exist for insects and birds in the same way that such an efficient speed exists for aircraft.

"Hovering, which is flying at zero speed, is very expensive," Casey says. "It takes a lot of power to generate lift in still air. But this lift component of aerodynamic power requirements declines as forward speed increases." With faster and faster flight, however, the other aerodynamic components—the power needed to overcome the drag of the wings and the body—increase. For airplanes, these varying power components are known to result in a total energy cost that form a U-shaped curve; that is, the overall cost gradually decreases from a high start-up cost until an optimum cruising speed is reached and then rises again. It had generally been accepted that the same thing applied to the flight of living creatures.

Casey's new results on the flight of the bumblebee, which contradict previous aerodynamic theory, are similar to those from some studies of bats and birds, especially hummingbirds, which also show little change in energy costs except at very high speeds, he says. The explanation, Casey believes, is that current theory is "too simple" to accurately describe the flapping flight of birds and insects since it doesn't take into account the large vortices produced at the end of each wing stroke.

The energy any animal or insect expends—from muscle performance to site limitations—is Casey's specialty as an environmental physiologist. "Energy is the way you keep score in evolutionary biology," he explains. "It's the currency of fitness to survive."

The Reading Experience: Questions for Reading and Discussion

1. Does the explanation above feel satisfactory? Or do you want to research this question further? Do you think every reader will have the same interest in this subject as you have? Did you know any of this information before reading it here?

2. Is Jones' language difficult to understand? Are there any terms that you need to research further, like "aerodynamic"? Do you feel you need to know more about Charles Ellington or the journal *Nature?*

3. Are you aware of the classical musical piece, *The Flight of the Bumblebee* by Rimsky-Korsakov? It is frequently a solo performance piece used to demonstrate the skill of the musician, due to its intensely frantic pace. Try listening to a performance on either clarinet or flute. How does this frenzy of music compare to the content of the article? How does knowing the semantic connection (word meaning) alter your understanding of Jones' article?

4. What is the main idea of the article? Can you underline its thesis statement? What is Jones' purpose in writing this article?

5. Is this article written extensively, to offer the reader information, or reflexively, because the writer needed to express herself?

The Writing Experience: Suggestions for Short Papers

1. Write an introductory paragraph for a hypothetical essay which sets out your intention to explain at least one of the following situations. In your thesis statement, include your reason for choosing this subject.

    (a) How nature/heredity or nurture (the environment; how we are raised) is more important in determining personality

    (b) How electrical storms/hurricanes/tornadoes originate or why they seem to be getting more frequent and more violent

    (c) Under what circumstances and how the ancient Romans built the Colosseum

2. In groups of three or four students, brainstorm the topics above. Each student must contribute his or her ideas. After the conversation, write freely in your journal for at least ten minutes on any of the subjects. All group members are to read these freewritings aloud. Choose one or two of the best ideas to emerge. Individually or in collaboration, write a thesis statement using the group's best ideas.

3. Record the changing contents of your kitchen refrigerator. List everything on a daily basis; hypothesize why certain items, like milk, may be used more quickly than others. Describe the changes, if any, in the composition (shape, size, color, freshness). After one week, write a short essay explaining your findings. Conclude by making an observation no one may have noticed before.

4. Outside of class, observe and record the movements of an insect, or a pet for approximately ten minutes. Consider, as Casey or Ellington did above, how much energy this insect or animal must need in order to perform these movements. Write your experiment scientifically, as if you were Casey or Ellington. Begin with a clear statement of purpose (thesis) and conclude with a unique observation that may change the way people think about this behavior.

Recommended Films and eConnections

Best science videos – December 2010. newscientist video. 11 Jan. 2011. YouTube video.

Top 5 Science Conspiracies: Theories and Hoaxes. Discovery Channel. 3 Nov. 2008. YouTube video.

Antarctica: An Adventure of a Different Nature. Dir. John Weiley. Perf. Alex Scott. Heliograph, 1991. Film.

Lorenzo's Oil. Dir. George Miller. Perf. Nick Nolte, Susan Sarandon. Universal, 1992. Film.

Quiz

_____ 1. The thesis statement of "Flight of the Bumblebee" occurs in: (a) the first paragraph; (b) the second paragraph; (c) the third paragraph; (d) the concluding paragraph.

_____ 2. Casey and Ellington measured: (a) the energy it takes for a bumblebee to fly; (b) the oxygen consumption of bumblebees; (c) the speed of a bumblebee in a wind tunnel; (d) none of the above.

_____ 3. Mary Jones' intent in this article is: (a) to portray the steps in Casey and Ellington's experiment; (b) to inform and teach her audience about new research; (c) to encourage the reader to live through the scientific discovery experienced by Casey and Ellington; (d) to argue about the validity of the bumblebee experiment.

_____ 4. As a reader, your primary task should be: (a) to envision; (b) to live through the experience; (c) to learn about bumblebees; (d) to judge whether or not to believe the information given.

_____ 5. In their ability to "hover," bumblebees are similar to: (a) bats; (b) hummingbirds; (c) eagles; (d) both (a) and (b) are correct.

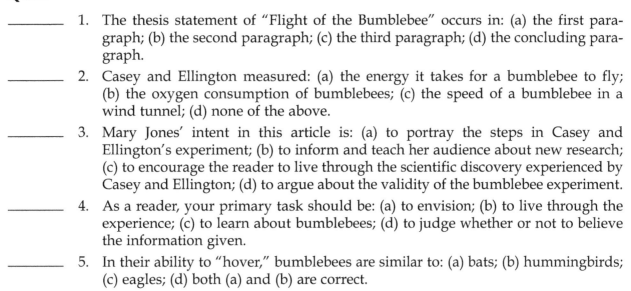

'STAR TREK: INTO DARKNESS' REVIEW

John Hayward

There's no way to review this movie without spoiling it, so, in short: it's got a few laughs and a couple of good action scenes, but it's a warp-speed train wreck of bad writing, vastly inferior to its goofy but fun 2009 predecessor. Fans waited a long time for this movie, and deserved better . . .

"Star Trek: Into Darkness" [is] . . . written by graceless dimwits who can't even be bothered to keep track of where the spaceships are during the battle scenes. . . . This film has a good cast, capable direction, and top-notch production values, but it's betrayed by sloppy writers who bit off far more than they could chew.

This movie seems to see itself as a parable for the War on Terror, a statement against militarism. There's a terrorist who doesn't quite see himself as a terrorist—he's just taking care of his "family." The villain is the latest in a long line of corrupt Starfleet admirals—they turn evil and/or nuts with disturbing frequency, in every era of Trek.

"Into Darkness" is packed full of stupid plot devices, from the forehead-slamming inconsistency of transporter technology ("We can't beam anyone up, but we can beam people down!") to a massive starship, somehow constructed in secret and crewed not by Starfleet officers but rented thugs. . . .

So no . . . it doesn't stand anywhere near the classic Trek episodes that bravely tackled momentous issues of the day. Those scripts were written by people who quoted Shakespeare and Melville. This script quote[s] Star Trek movies from 30 years ago. . . .

If J.J. Abrams and his team of 14-year-old screenwriters can't come up with anything original for the crew of the *Enterprise* to do . . . it's time to give someone else a try.

The Reading Experience: Questions for Reading and Discussion

1. Is it necessary for a reader of this article to have seen the movie in order to completely understand the article? Why or why not?

2. The author, John Hayward, states that the film "Star Trek: Into Darkness" is a "warp-speed train wreck of bad writing." What exactly does that mean? Is there enough information in his review to permit the reader to guess the meaning from its context?

3. Hayward uses the terms "sloppy," "dim-wits," and "stupid" in his review. Is this appropriate language for a published review? What is the effect on you as a reader who has contemplated seeing the film? Has he convinced you that it is not worth your while and your money for a ticket? Why or why not?

4. What kind of film *does* Hayward want to see? What is he looking for? Does he suggest an alternative?

5. Does the author have anything positive to say? Do you think a fair and just film review (or any sort of review—a concert, a play, or a TV show) should provide both good and bad points? Why or why not?

The Writing Experience: Suggestions for Short Papers

1. Rent the movie "Star Trek: Into Darkness." View it with several friends. Discuss the movie in terms of its plot, characters, special effects, dialogue, and the cast. Write your own review. Do you agree or disagree with Hayward?

2. The cinema is an important component of our contemporary culture. Survey your local newspaper for current films. Which are the most successful? What does this list tell you about our society?

3. Write a review of an event you have attended (film, concert, play, or another type of performance). To be even-handed, discuss both its good and bad points. If you really did not enjoy it, explain why, using effective powerful language.

4. Watch one or more episodes of the original *Star Trek* series, written by Gene Roddenberry. Compare the earlier 1980s films with the current film being reviewed. Use specific points to compare and contrast. (The website is provided below.)

Recommended Films and eConnections

Star Trek: The Original Series (Every Episode Tribute). Lawrence Whitehurst. 16 June, 2012. YouTube video.

Tribute to Gene Roddenberry's Star Trek (45 Years). The Star Treker. 24 May 2010.

Star Trek: Into Darkness. Dir. J. J. Abrams. Perf. Chris Pine, Zachary Quinto, Zoe Saldana. Paramount Studios, 2013. Film.

2001: A Space Odyssey. Dir. Stanley Kubrick. Perf. Keir Dullea, Gary Lockwood, Willia Sylvester, Daniel Richter. Metro-Goldwyn-Mayer, 1968. Film.

Quiz

_____ 1. The main idea in this review is: (a) there is no way to review the film without giving away the ending; (b) the lines in the film are stupid and sloppily written; (c) the film is funny and has good action scenes; (d) this film cannot compare to the original *Star Trek* episodes.

_____ 2. The review was written: (a) judiciously; (b) emotionally; (c) objectively; (d) ungrammatically.

_____ 3. The equipment shown in the film demonstrates: (a) technical accuracy; (b) unbelievable transporter technology; (c) credible technological devices; (d) none of the above.

_____ 4. Hayward longs for references to: (a) Melville; (b) Shakespeare; (c) *Star Trek* movies from 30 years ago; (d) both (a) and (b) are correct.

_____ 5. To read this review in the most readerly manner possible, you should: (a) envision the film; (b) try to put yourself in Hayward's place and agree with him; (d) learn what Hayward is trying to explain to the reader; (d) judge the review, and the film, for yourself.

PUTTING IT ALL TOGETHER

You may realize by now that you have definite preferences in writing and reading—have you noticed the ease or comfort you experience with certain types of texts and the labor you go through with certain others? What makes you perform this way? Based upon studies done on the brain, we know that writing and reading behavior is more than attitudinal. To a large degree, it's physiological. The next essay can help you understand how our brains work.

OUR TWO-SIDED BRAIN

John Chaffee

One of the most intriguing areas of scientific and educational exploration concerns the manner in which our brain processes information. It has been known for a long time that the brain is divided into two seemingly identical halves, usually termed the left hemisphere and the right hemisphere. Until recently, it was assumed that these two hemispheres were similar in the way that they operated. However, a variety of current research has shown conclusively that each hemisphere has a distinct "personality," processing information in its own unique way.

From "Our Two-Sided Brain" by John Chaffee, *Thinking Critically,* 10e. © 2012 Wadsworth, a part of Cengage Learning, Inc. Reproduced by permission. www.cengage.com/permissions

The left hemisphere exhibits those qualities that we normally associate with higher intellectual activities. For example, the left hemisphere functions analytically, tending to break things and processes down into component parts, like taking apart an automobile engine in order to diagnose the problem. The left hemisphere is also the seat of most of our verbal activity, decoding and encoding the bulk of our language, mathematical symbols, and musical notations. Finally, the left hemisphere tends to process information in a linear, sequential way, one step at a time. This is consistent with the verbal capacities which it exhibits, since language is spoken/heard/read one word at a time, and the meaning of the words depends in large measure on the order in which the words are placed.

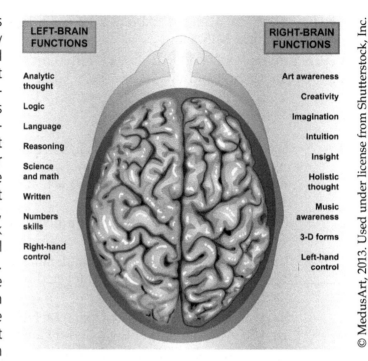

LEFT-BRAIN FUNCTIONS

Analytic thought
Logic
Language
Reasoning
Science and math
Written
Numbers skills
Right-hand control

RIGHT-BRAIN FUNCTIONS

Art awareness
Creativity
Imagination
Intuition
Insight
Holistic thought
Music awareness
3-D forms
Left-hand control

In short, the left hemisphere is similar to a modem digital computer in that its individual operations unfold in an orderly, logical sequence.

The right hemisphere operates in a much different fashion. Instead of analyzing things and processes into component parts, it seeks to synthesize by organizing parts into patterns and wholes-like arranging individual flowers into a floral arrangement. The right hemisphere normally has much less to do with verbal activity. Instead, it is much more visually oriented, focusing on shapes, arrangements, and images. It also processes information based on what we personally experience with all of our senses (including touch). So, for example, while the left hemisphere might enable us to remember someone by their name, the right hemisphere might enable us to recognize them by their face of the feel of their handshake. Finally, rather than processing information in a linear, sequential fashion, the right hemisphere tends to organize information into patterns and relationships which are experienced as a whole. For instance, in listening to music, the right hemisphere focuses on the overall melody rather than the individual notes, or on the pattern of play on the chessboard rather than the individual pieces. While we compared the linear functioning of the left hemisphere to a digital computer, we might compare the functioning of the right hemisphere to a kaleidoscope, as it continually works to organize information into meaningful shapes and patterns.

The modern research into how our brain functions has significant implications for human learning. Much of our education is structured for left hemisphere thinking-analytical, verbal, logical, and sequential. Yet much of our understanding about the world is based on the activities of right hemisphere-synthesizing, visual, experiential, and pattern-seeking. If education is to become as effective as it can be, it must introduce teaching methods that address the right hemisphere as well as the left hemisphere.

THE WRITING/READING EXPERIENCE

Sandra G. Brown

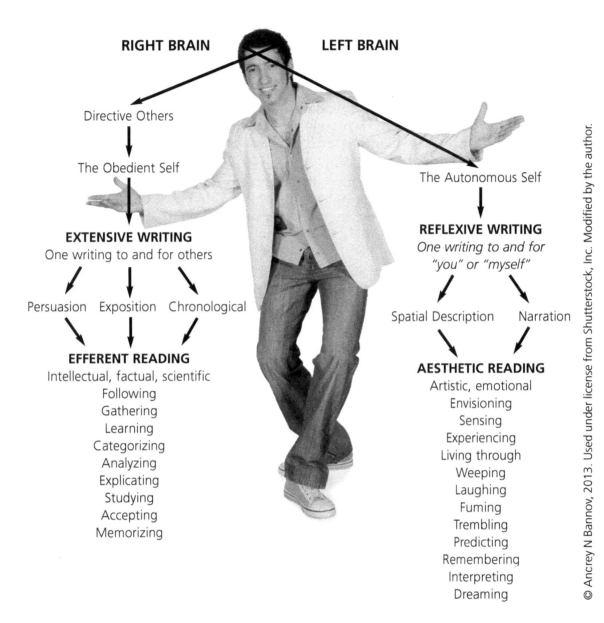

RIGHT BRAIN   **LEFT BRAIN**

Directive Others

The Obedient Self

The Autonomous Self

EXTENSIVE WRITING
One writing to and for others

REFLEXIVE WRITING
One writing to and for
"you" or "myself"

Persuasion Exposition Chronological

Spatial Description   Narration

EFFERENT READING
Intellectual, factual, scientific
Following
Gathering
Learning
Categorizing
Analyzing
Explicating
Studying
Accepting
Memorizing

AESTHETIC READING
Artistic, emotional
Envisioning
Sensing
Experiencing
Living through
Weeping
Laughing
Fuming
Trembling
Predicting
Remembering
Interpreting
Dreaming

If we connect this information about the brain with the knowledge we have about reading and writing, we can begin to understand ourselves as scholars. Remember that the left hemisphere controls functions on the right side of the body; the right hemisphere controls the left. Looking at the illustration, consider first the functions of each side of the brain. Then, examine the way these functions match the ways *writers* express ideas and feelings. Move on to observe how each of these writing modes are usually *read*. Then, think of your own way of experiencing writing and reading. Which combination seems to match your own preferences? How does this illustration explain your past reading and writing experiences? Can you begin now to modify the way you have always written and read? Record your changes in your journal. You'll be on your way!

The Reading Experience: Questions for Reading and Discussion

1. Did you know any information about the brain before reading Chaffee's article? If so, what details in the article add to your knowledge? Importantly, how does his article connect with the reading/writing experience as shown in Brown's illustration? Do these connections help you to make more sense about your writing habits and your reading preferences?

2. Consider how you learned to read and write. Throughout elementary school, were the books you read simple, with easy vocabulary? Were you taught to write only the answers to questions that tested your knowledge of grammar? Did you learn phonics? In what grade did you do your best writing and reading? What was the best essay you ever wrote about? When did you write it? Have you ever written a poem? If not, why not? Would you like to try? What words would you use to describe your reading and writing ability?

3. Do you recognize yourself in Chaffee's description? Are you left-brained? Are you organized, neat, logical? Do you need directions from a teacher or employer in doing an assignment or a job? Or are you right-brained? Are you messy, but the kind of person who knows where you put everything in your jumbled room? Would you rather work things through for yourself? Would you prefer online assignments, virtually a classroom without a teacher?

4. Consider paragraph 2 in "Our Two-sided Brain." The author states that "decoding and encoding" (reading and writing) letters, "mathematical symbols, and musical notations" requires analytic thought. Do you think that joyful, self-sponsored writing (encoding) like writing a love letter, fits this definition? While solving difficult math homework problems surely stimulates left-brain activity, do you think that someone like Pythagoras, who was so delighted when he discovered his famous theorem $a^2 + b^2 = c^2$. that he sacrificed an ox, stimulated only the left side of his brain?

5. Consider the right brain's academic activity, as explained near the model's left hand. In which college courses might an autonomous learner shine? (You may want to consult the college catalogue or schedule of courses to help you answer.) Is answering this question a right- or left-brained activity?

The Writing Experience: Suggestions for Short Papers

1. Try these simple experiments, and then try to connect them with the materials in this chapter.

   First, look at your thumbnails. Which is wider? Studies claim that the wider nail corresponds to the opposite hemisphere of your brain, indicating that kind of dominance. So, if your right thumbnail is wider, it may be an indication that you are more strongly left-brained. Check the chart! Look back at Chaffee's essay.

   Try covering one eye when looking at the moon. Does your image of the moon jump when you uncover the eye? That indicates that the other eye is dominant.

   Write your name in script, using the opposite hand that you do not prefer. Is your hand-writing fairly legible, or is it impossible to read?

   Write a short essay explaining how your experiments and your observation of the Reading/Writing illustration point to your physiological makeup and help to explain your academic success.

2. Write a short comparison and contrast essay, contrasting your responses to Reading Question #5 above with a list of academic courses that would fit the characteristics near the model's right hand, activities that are ascribed to the left hemisphere of the brain.

3. In his groundbreaking 1983 book *Frames of Mind: The Theory of Multiple Intelligences*, Howard Gardner explained how there are a wide range of 'intelligences'—musical, verbal, logical, bodily-kinesthetic, and spiritual—to name a few. His work is widely respected in education today. Can you name and explain one way that you think you are intelligent? Write a short definition of one type of intelligence that you know you have and give examples from your daily activities or past life experiences (even when you were a young child). As a conclusion, tie this together with the information given by Chaffee or Brown in the previous selections.

4. Has the information in this chapter, especially the articles on the right and left brain, changed your ideas about the way you read and write? Can you see a new way to approach learning? Explain in a short essay.

Recommended Films and eConnections

Howard Gardner of the Multiple Intelligence Theory.<edutopia.org> LENCharlotte. 7 Nov. 2009, YouTube video.

How Exercise Rewires Your Brain. DNews 9 July 2013. YouTube video.

Good Will Hunting. Dir. Gus Van Sant. Perf. Matt Damon, Robin Williams, Ben Affleck, Minnie Driver. A Band Apart and Lawrence Bender Productions, 1997. Film.

Music of the Heart. Dir. Wes Craven. Perf. Meryl Streep, Angela Bassett, Aidan Quinn, Gloria Estefan. Craven-Maddalena and Mirimax, 1999.

Quiz

_____ 1. An example of left-brained activity is demonstrated in the following: (a) a musician plays the guitar with such passion that he continues jamming on stage long after the concert is over; (b) a carpenter is following a floor plan for building a staircase; (c) a florist is arranging a display in the shop window; (d) an actor cries on stage when he enacts an emotional scene.

_____ 2. An example of right-brained activity is demonstrated in the following: (a) a talented chef prepares one of his signature dishes, mixing, adding, and tasting to make it better than it ever was before; (b) an art student taking a course in geometric drawing maps out how the light falls from a high window on a bowl of fruit on a nearby table; (c) an art student given an entire wall to fill with her concept for a mural symbolizing the creation of the world stands back and looks at her space; (d) an audience laughs hysterically at a new comic's routine.

_____ 3. John Chaffee believes that: (a) education is making strides year by year; (b) education must be individualized; (c) education must incorporate collaborative activities; (d) education must introduce teaching methods that address the right hemisphere as well as the left hemisphere.

_____ 4. Sandra Brown's graphic infers that: (a) one side of the brain shows more intelligence than the other; (b) men have different capabilities than women do; (c) students' preferred modes of writing and reading can be connected to one's inherited brain dominance; (d) none of the above.

_____ 5. At the college level, students can: (a) learn that they need to change some of the strategies that have not previously been successful; (b) recognize that an understanding of their preferred modes of writing and reading can help them focus on altering their learning behaviors; (c) understand that becoming aware of their multiple intelligences can help them make informed course choices; (d) all of the above.

COLLABORATION SENSATION: JOURNAL JAM—A PARTNER PROJECT IN EVALUATING STUDENT JOURNALS

- Review the criteria for keeping a triple-entry journal.
- Divide the class into groups of four students.

Phase I

- At the instructor's signal, students will begin to freewrite on a limited number of topics the teacher will put on the chalkboard. Topics should be chosen from the readings in Chapter 1. Choose from the following or create original categories:

    homelessness

    guns

    war

    stereotypes

    feral children

    breaking the racial barrier

    science experiments

    sci fi

    the brain

- Continue writing for five minutes. Do not stop until signaled.
- Students are to read their entries aloud to others in their group.

Phase II

- Students read aloud earlier entries from Part I of their daily journals, agreeing on an individual day (for example, the second day of the first week of class; the first day of the third week of class; etc.).
- Discuss how these entries differ from each other and from Phase I above.

Phase III

- Each student passes his/her journal to the student at the right.
- Students are to read these silently and write brief comments in each journal after they have read enough to see its merits and weaknesses.
- Stop when all students have read from all students' journals.

Phase IV

- Each group of students chooses the best journal in its group, based on criteria they establish themselves.
- A spokesperson reads aloud to the class one of the best entries from the chosen journal.
- The instructor may offer advice throughout, but not choose the winner.
- Afterward, students are to write journal entries evaluating the class activity.

CHAPTER 2

DESCRIPTIVE VOICES

The First Message of Intent—What's Happening?

THE WRITER'S INTENTION TO PORTRAY

To describe is to present an image, as a camera or an artist's brush does, but instead of film or paints, to use simple words to do so. The most important element of descriptive discourse is clarity. The best way to accomplish this is to provide detail, detail, and more detail!

Spatial and Chronological Description

There are two types of description, spatial and chronological. The first focuses on how people, places, or things appear to the senses in the space around us. The second focuses on how objects are created or how events transpire in time. For example, spatial description can give the contours, dimensions, decoration, and setting of a luxurious home, while chronological description can tell how to build it. Spatial description can present the memory of grandmother's freshly baked bread, evoking the smell and taste of that bygone experience, while chronological description can present the recipe for the bread, allowing anyone who so chooses to make it. Spatial description can recreate in words the quality of sound of a magnificent piano concert and its effect on the audience, while chronological description can provide instructions and sheet music for piano students who want to learn and practice that music. Spatial description can take the form of a map of your community, while chronological description can take the form of verbal or printed directions to your house, across those very streets. Spatial description can be as factual as a poster for a missing child, or as fantastic as your dreams, but chronological description must be precise, so that another will be able to follow the sequence properly.

The Simplest Type of Discourse

An author speaking descriptively tells the reader what's happening, or what it's like at the moment she perceives something. The descriptive voice is generally easy to understand. In fact, it is the simplest or least complex type of discourse to write and read. For this reason, description is often used to make the other writing modes—narration, exposition, and persuasion/argument—more vivid and easier to read.

Newborns learn about the world through their five senses: sight, hearing, touch, smell, and taste. They form impressions easily and naturally through the presentation of stimuli—brightly colored toys that jingle and rattle, soft blankets, fragrant baby powder and lotion, and sweet milk. All of these become associated with the mother and father or other primary caretakers, beginning the network of cognitive and affective responses which will serve the new little person as a model for his ever-expanding world.

Use Your Five Senses

The processes of coming-to-know and coming-to-expect continue throughout our lives. Reading is an extremely important way of knowing, for it can move the mind from the concrete, here-and-now to the imagined, extended universe of thought. Basic sensory experience, portrayed through the living medium of language can be recreated if we envision and are presented stimuli, using our own experiences. What is known can extend to what can be known, even if we will never actually be there. We need to picture, to listen, with an inner ear, to try to feel, and to sense through our own memories odors and fragrances, sweetnesses and pungencies, and all shades in-between.

Do more than look at descriptive words. Take off your jacket, and your shoes, too. Wiggle your toes. Get ready to feel those words. Expand your world to include the writer's. Reading spatial description requires the participation of the reader. Put yourself into it and let go! This is *aesthetic* reading.

STARS

Sara Teasdale

Alone in the night
On a dark hill
With pines around me
Spicy and still,

And a heaven full of stars
Over my head,
White and topaz
And misty red;

From "Stars" by Sara Teasdale, *Collected Poems of Sara Teasdale,* 1920. Published by Macmillan Publishing Co. / Simon & Schuster, Inc.

Myriads with beating
  Hearts of fire
That aeons
  Cannot vex or tire;

Up the dome of heaven
  Like a great hill,
I watch them marching
  Stately and still,

And I know that I
  Am honored to be
Witness
  Of so much majesty.

The Reading Experience: Questions for Reading and Discussion

1. Who is "alone in the night"? Why is it important to know this? Would the poem be different if there were two or three people there? Explain.

2. The word "still"—which illustrates the sense of hearing—is mentioned twice: "spicy and *still*" and "stately and *still*." The author repeats the word, as well as its complementary rhyme, *hill*, twice. Perhaps they are doubly important? The setting is very, very quiet. In the first stanza, we can see in this silent setting a "dark" hill—the real hill (dark perhaps because it is night; in the daytime it probably is green— perhaps with colorful flowers or animals somewhere). But later on, in the fourth stanza, the poet tells us about "the dome of heaven" which is "like a *great* hill." Now we have two hills. Do you think by using a *simile* the poet wants us to compare them? Is there any more *auditory imagery*? Why is the sense of hearing so important here? With a partner, find other examples of sensory imagery in the poem. Explain what they ask the reader to perceive.

3. Can you think of a reason for Teasdale's choice of the words "topaz" and "misty red" instead of *yellow* and simple, unmodified *red*? How many different ways can you think of to describe blue, green, or other colors? How are they different from each other?

4. How does the phrase "beating / Hearts of fire" affect your perception of Teasdale's stars? How does she feel about the stars? Why do you think she feels this way? Consider the last stanza.

5. Last, make a simple sketch of this poem in your journal. Where is the speaker in relationship to the stars? How large or small will you draw the speaker of the poem? Why did you draw it this way? Share your sketch by putting it on the chalkboard. Compare as many sketches as possible. How are they similar? How different? What does this mean?

The Writing Experience: Suggestions for Short Papers

1. In class, take notes about the student sketches on the chalkboard. Who did what? Use your notes to write an interpretive essay on the significance of each student's drawing. What does this tell you about reading poetry? How does it connect to what you know now about aesthetic reading?

2. Using the second discussion question above, write a short essay explaining how sight, hearing, smell, touch, and taste are used in the poem.

3. Write a short essay (approximately 250–500 words) discussing how a person with a sensory disability might perceive the scene in "Stars." What metaphors or similes would she choose?

4. Sit quietly in your backyard or on your front steps well after dark. Bring a flashlight, a pad, and a pencil. Record the sights and sounds of the night. Explain how you feel while you are writing there.

   Recopy and edit afterward, striving for perhaps a poem either using a rhyme scheme like Teasdale's, or blank verse. And don't forget to use some mosquito repellent!

Recommended Films and eConnections

Introduction to Poetry by Billy Collins. nada yas. 28 Feb. 2011. YouTube video.

SHS Singing Sailors MPA's – Stars I Shall Find by Sara Teasdale. Delena Chau. 29 Apr. 2013. YouTube video.

The Dead Poets Society. Dir. Peter Weir. Perf. Robin Williams, Robert Sean Leonard, Ethan Hawk. Touchstone Pictures and Silver Screen Partners IV, 1989.

Slam. Dir. Marc Levin. Perf. Saul Williams, Sonja Sohn. Trimark Pictures, 1998. Film.

Quiz

_____ 1. Which one of the following phrases specifically uses visual sensory imagery? (a) witness of so much majesty; (b) hearts of fire; (c) white and topaz and misty red; (d) aeons cannot vex or tire.

_____ 2. The primary purpose of the first two stanzas is: (a) to convey the perspective of the scene to the reader; (b) to explain the feelings of the poet; (c) to introduce the season and its weather to the reader; (d) to evoke a sense of fear and mystery.

_____ 3. The primary purpose of the third and fourth stanzas is: (a) to emphasize the superiority of stars over humankind; (b) to emphasize the superiority of humankind over the stars; (c) to provide an explanation of the stars' stamina; (d) to provide illustrations and examples of the main idea.

_____ 4. The primary purpose of the last stanza is: (a) to conclude with a generalization; (b) to reinforce the visual imagery of the poem; (c) to emphasize the superiority of humankind over the stars; (d) to portray the feelings of the speaker of the poem, as she stands on the dark hill.

_____ 5. As a reader, your primary task is: (a) to predict the unfolding events in the poem; (b) to picture images and sensations portrayed in the poem; (c) to study and memorize the information given; (d) to evaluate the poem.

Map of the Middle East

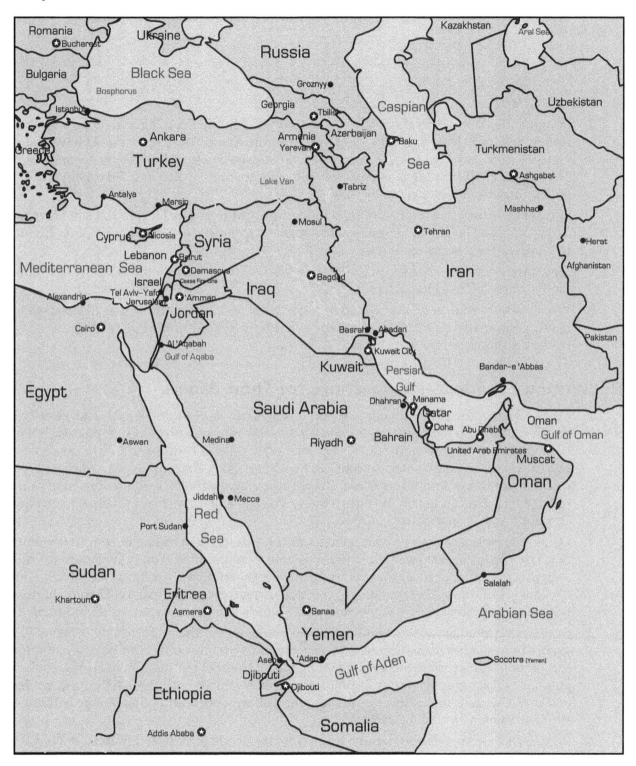

© Olinchuk, 2013. Used under license from Shutterstock, Inc.

The Reading Experience: Questions for Reading and Discussion

1. What body/bodies of water or country/countries border Saudi Arabia on the

   North? _____

   South? _____

   East? _____

   West? _____

2. Imagine the floor of this classroom is a map of the Middle East. The instructor's desk is somewhere near Russia. How would you get from Saudi Arabia to Israel? How would you get from Israel to Iraq? First, write your answers using the proper terminology. Then, with another student as your travelling companion, walk from "Saudia Arabia to Israel," and from there, go on to "Iraq."

3. Syria is to Turkey as which pair of the following locations? The Florida Keys to Havana, Cuba; Naples, Florida, to Miami Beach; Fort Pierce, Florida, to Lake Okeechobee; Miami to Hialeah. How is the relationship similar?

4. How many countries border on the Persian Gulf? Can you list them? Why do you think the Persian Gulf is so important?

5. Which side of your brain and which of your five senses do you think is utilized most in reading the spatial description of a map? What is the most appropriate reading stance in reading a map, efferent or aesthetic?

The Writing Experience: Suggestions for Short Papers

1. Draw a map showing how you get from your home to your college. Use tagboard or sturdy drawing paper. Indicate major landmarks, intersections, and stoplights. Make sure that you observe traditional map legendry, especially the position occupied by North. Using a step-by-step format, write either: (a) a description of your project's process, or (b) how you travel. Note: Do not rely on narrative to explain your map or its process, nor exposition that includes a thesis statement or a conclusion. This is to be pure chronological, sequential description.

2. Using a pre-printed map of your college campus, describe in sequence your daily journey. Use the map itself as an illustration of your peregrination. You may choose for this assignment a chart or diagram as your format. Begin with your arrival at the parking lot. Designate buildings, classrooms, and courses, using their proper names. Using objective language, describe briefly each location. Use words like first, second, next, and finally.

3. Construct a graphic of the Middle Eastern countries on this map. Using a chart, bar graph, or any other format, show statistics about five features that can be compared for this demographic group. Suggested features to be studied: population, religions, spoken languages, topography (terrain), political systems (tribal, civic, and religious), trades and professions, range of income, health and welfare, sports and other leisure activities. Write an explanation of the categories.

4. Write a short essay (250–500 words) discussing the need for maps today, in an era of navigational devices. Are maps important, needed, relevant? Why or why not?

Recommended Films and eConnections

BBC The Beauty of Maps 3 of 4 City Maps Order Out of Chaos. Tuzbeka Kigyo. 24 Jan. 2013. YouTube video.

BBC.The.Beauty.of.Maps.1 Of 4. Atlas. Maps. Thing Big. Part 2. Tuzbeka Kigyo. 27 Jan. 2013. YouTube video.

Incendies (Scorched). Dir. Denis Villeneuve. Perf. Mustafa Kamel, Mélissa Désormeaux-Pouli, Maxim Gaudette. Micro-scope and TS Productions, 2010. Film.

Football Under Cover. Dir. David Assmann, Ayat Najafi. Perf. Niloofar Basir, Narmila Fathi, Sanna El-Agha. Flying Moon filmproduktion, 2008. Film.

Quiz

_____ 1. Planes flying from Iraq to Iran must proceed in: (a) a northward direction; (b) a southward direction; (c) an eastern direction; (d) a western direction.

_____ 2. Iran is bordered on the north by: (a) the Caspian Sea; (b) Turkmenistan and the Caspian Sea; (c) Turkmenistan, the Caspian Sea, Armenia, and Azerbajian; (d) Turkey, Russia, and the Caspian Sea.

_____ 3. Jidda is: (a) a city in the middle of Saudi Arabia; (b) a port on the Red Sea; (c) a desert in Iran; (d) a mountain range north of the Tropic of Cancer.

_____ 4. (a) Jerusalem is north of the Red Sea; (b) Tel Aviv is west of Amman; (c) Cairo is south of the Mediterranean Sea; (d) all are correct.

_____ 5. Syria is larger than: (a) Saudi Arabia; (b) Iraq; (c) Egypt; (d) Israel.

FIGURATIVE LANGUAGE: DESCRIBING THE INDESCRIBABLE

How do you describe something or someone as "indescribable"? Some of our students at first have said, "You can't!" Others have suggested drawing, while still others recommended "acting it out." First guesses soon gave way to the realization that the "indescribable" person, object, or experience can be compared effectively to a commonly known thing or event. Not all of these qualities may match, but the listener or reader will be able to deduce significantly what the teller means. Another means of describing the indescribable is the use of idioms—expressions that serve a code, or shorthand, for wordy descriptions.

Figurative Language in Everyday Life

These comparisons or figures of speech are used more often than most people would believe. Poetry, song lyrics, and jokes depend upon them. Our daily conversations rely so heavily on them that we readily lose sight of their original meanings. Slang's allure derives from a desire to be fashionable, to be "with it," to be "in." But what is *it*? What do we want to be *with*? And what do we want to be *in*? The expression's popular usage serves to camouflage the actual referent, the word *trend*.

Figurative Language as a Means of Analyzing Culture

Linguists tell us that analogic or figurative language exists in every language, and has done so across centuries. Variations of time and place reveal semantic and syntactic patterns that can provide us with a means of analyzing the culture from which they derive. But that is not our purpose here. We are concerned with identifying figurative language forms as a dimension of spatial description so that we can further enrich our awareness of the aesthetic reading stance. For figurative language, like other forms of sensory description, calls out to our emotions—to our artistic sensibility as well as our sense of humor.

Metaphors

Essentially, it is useful to become aware of several types of figurative language. Metaphors, which can actually encompass *all* the other types, make use of implicit, direct connections. For example, "He is a lion in the courtroom." In that sentence there is no doubt of the man's strength.

To identify a "pure" metaphor, i.e., one that is not also a simile, personification, or an idiom, look first for some form of the linking verb *to be*, which frequently links the subject with its complement. Second, look for a comparison with an unlike object. Third, consider how the characteristic of the unlike object may in some way match the thing being compared.

Similes

Similes are specific types of metaphors which make use of implicit connections. For example, the poet Louis Simpson writes, "The moon is blazing like a sign for beer." In that sentence, the reader knows full well that the moon is not lit by electricity, but it suggests that the brightness coming from it is as radiant as a neon sign on a dark street. It is just a suggestion, not something absolute or apparent. To identify a simile, look first for the words "like" or "as . . . .as" which compare the subject to a limited degree with something else. Second, as with the pure metaphor, look for a comparison with an unlike object. And third, consider how the similarity is limited. The moon is less like a sign for beer than it is *un*like it.

Personification

Personification is another type of figurative language that makes use of analogy between non-human objects or life forms and human beings. This specific type of metaphor endows artifacts in the environment (e.g., machines, sculpture, musical instruments, buildings, computers, paintings), and symbols (e.g., numbers, letters, spoken or written words) as well as things in nature, living or nonliving things (e.g., plants, animals, caves, waterfalls, lakes, oceans, the sun, the moon) with human characteristics (e.g., personality, movement, expression). For example, consider this phrase: "The moon kissed the shore." Here the sea exhibits behavior possible only by human beings. Although an explicit statement, the characteristic of gentleness must be extracted from the sentence through the medium of the reader's imagination.

To identify personification, look for a comparison that involves human attributes. Then imagine how these attributes affect the object compared. Remember: a human being compared to an animal or any nonhuman object is not personification. It must be the other way around!

Idioms

Idioms, when they are used to describe an object, an experience, or a state of mind, can be considered metaphors. What distinguishes them from the other types described is their utter lack of sensible meaning based upon their parts. Idioms take their meaning from use in the culture from which they derive. Plainly, speakers of the language make them up! They often cannot be translated into other languages, because of their word order, meaning, and commonality of context. For example, "He's got me climbing up a wall!" In that sentence, there is no explanation for the acrobatic behavior of the speaker, nor any link to another term in the sentence which would establish a verbal comparison. The reader/listener must participate linguistically in the culture in which this figure of speech is used in order to understand it.

To identify an idiom, first establish that there is no clear link with any other word (person, object, or event) in the sentence. Second, if you can, try to check its usefulness in another language. If it "loses something in the translation," more than likely it is an idiom.

Both figurative language and sensory images are examples of spatial description, requiring the aesthetic stance. However, while ordinary description relies upon the five senses, the figurative dimension calls for a "sixth sense," an understanding of a metalanguage which calls for analysis, as well as emotion.

THE WANING MOON

Percy Bysshe Shelley

> And like a dying lady, lean and pale,
> Who totters forth, wrapt in a gauzy veil,
> Out of her chamber, led by the insane
> And feeble wanderings of her fading brain,
> The moon arose up in the murky East,
> A white and shapeless mass.

From "The Waning Moon" by Percy Bysshe Shelley, 1824.

The Reading Experience: Questions for Reading and Discussion

1. To what does Shelley compare his moon? How does this comparison reflect the culture Shelley experienced? Remember, he lived in England during the Romantic era (1792–1822), when mental illness was considered to be demonic possession. Gothic literature was at its height.

2. The word "like" is a clear clue to a type of figurative language Shelley uses, but the moon certainly is exhibiting behavior possible only by a human being. Therefore, what are the two types used here?

3. Although "The Waning Moon" relies on figures of speech, what *sensory* imagery is used to heighten the description? Consider the adjectives. How do they create and heighten the mood of the poem?

4. Is this poem written extensively or reflexively? Should it be read efferently or aesthetically? Do you think it will be more easily understood by readers with a right or left brain preference?

5. What is the mood of the poem? If it were used for the setting of a scene in a film, what kind of film might it be?

The Writing Experience: Suggestions for Short Papers

1. Shelley's second wife, Mary, is the author of *Frankenstein.* Together, both writers created some of the most vivid gothic prose and poetry in the history of literature. In small writing groups of three or four students, create scenes suitable for a horror film, by using figurative language. For starters, complete these descriptions with horrific similes, metaphors, or vivid examples of personification:

   The forest was as dark as _____. (simile)

   A woman ran out screaming from the lagoon. She was _____. (metaphor)

   The lake at dusk _____. (personification)

   Continue on to compose more fully one or more short scenes, comparing objects in nature to body parts or endowing objects with human personalities.

2. The five-minute video recommended below, *Figurative Language*, leads to a writing assignment based upon figurative language used in popular music. Katy Perry's "Firework," Nikki Menaj's "Super Bass," Cinema's "Skrillex," The Black Eyed Peas' "Boom Boom Pow," and Philip Phillips' "Gone, Gone, Gone" are used as examples. Using this video, write a short essay that discusses either these or five other popular songs of your choice.

3. List as many slang expressions from the past as you can. Today they may mean something entirely different than they did fifty or a hundred years ago, or even may be incomprehensible. Provide their original, literal meanings and when and how they were used. If they have a meaning today, what may that be? Are these metaphors, similes, idioms, or examples of personification? To get started, think of expressions that are used as greetings, designations of sad or happy events, or words of advice. Use slang as the topic for a short essay.

4. Foreign languages provide a clear illustration of how figures of speech work. Try translating as many foreign metaphors, similes, idioms, or examples of personification that are in common use in Spanish, German, Hungarian, Italian, Russian, Polish, Chinese, or any other language. First, write them in the original language (use their own alphabet, if not the Roman alphabet). Next, provide the *transliteration* (phonetic pronunciation) in English. Third, write their *literal* (exact) meaning, word for word. Last, explain what they mean in context. Use your information as the topic for a short essay.

Recommended Films and eConnections

Figurative Language. Laura Touchstone. 9 Apr. 2013. YouTube video.

Phrasal Verbs — Learn English Idioms. EnglishAnyone. 3 Sept. 2011. YouTube video.

Gothic. Dir. Ken Russell. Perf. Julian Sands, Natasha Richardson, Gabriel Byrne. Al Clark and Robert Devereaux, 1986. Film.

Haunted Summer. Dir. Ivan Passer. Perf. Philip Anglim, Laura Dern, Eric Stoltz. Cannon Films, 1988. Film.

Quiz

_____ 1. Shelley's poem is an example of: (a) simile; (b) metaphor; (c) personification; (d) both (a) and (c) are correct.

_____ 2. "Feeble wandering of her fading brain" means: (a) the moon is a weak influence on the earth; (b) the lady is wandering in her chamber; (c) the moon can make you insane; (d) according to Shelley, the moon has a definite shape.

_____ 3. Shelley's use of the moon indicates: (a) a fascination with space; (b) superstition; (c) an attempt to describe the indescribable; (d) devil worship.

_____ 4. Figurative language may be found in all the following forms of writing *except:* (a) Gothic literature; (b) slang of every era; (c) foreign languages; (d) prescription labels.

_____ 5. We commonly use this term to encompass all the rest: (a) metaphoric language; (b) idiomatic language; (c) the language of personification; (d) the language of the simile.

OBJECTIVE AND SUBJECTIVE DESCRIPTION

Writing Objective Description

To what extent can we rely on a writer's or a speaker's description? While everyone has a unique point of view, many descriptions are undoubtedly rooted in fact. An architect's statement that a room is 19½ × 24' is absolute. There can be no quarrel with a yardstick. In fact, any description which can be verified by a measure or a consensus of opinion may be considered to be *objective*. Technical manuals, medical textbooks, police blotters, recipes, labels listing product contents, and travel guides are all examples of objective description. The writer's personal feelings and biases play no part in this type of description.

Writing Subjective Description

Subjective description, on the other hand, is dependent on the mind of the writer or speaker. As we have seen in the previous pieces of writing, it involves memories, feelings, imagination, interpretation, and is an internal phenomenon. A journalist striving for exciting copy may write, "In the heat of late evening, in the steam coming up from the grimy streets, the anger of the inner city people spilled over." In addition to omitting the actual temperature, the writer of this sentence leads the reader to imagine anger arising like steam from streets that he calls "grimy," a loaded word that connotes sordid conditions. In addition, the people's anger is described as "spilling over," an action that relies not upon sensory description, but a metaphor. The author provides not only the view of the scene, but his inner perception of it.

How Objective and Subjective Description Affect Your Reading Stance

Because the desire to provide clear direction and order drives chronological description (a form of extensive writing), it is always factual, or objective. As a reader, your stance should be *efferent*. You are to follow the order as it is given, no questions asked. Because the desire to be vivid guides spatial description—a form of *reflexive* writing—it can be factual, or objective, but is more often subjective. Subjective description calls for the *aesthetic* stance. Try to connect it to your own past experiences. Sense the colors, sounds, textures, odors, tastes, and the mood or tone of the piece, allowing figurative language to stimulate your imagination.

Although the following selection, "Dermatitis," is an example of spatial description, it requires that you read it *efferently*, taking concepts away from the selection and "putting them into YOU" for practical use. Unlike subjective spatial description written from one person's point of view, the following selection is culled from the experiences of more than one writer.

DERMATITIS

Samuel M. Bluefarb, M.D.

Dermatitis (eczema) is inflammation of the skin and one of the commonest reactions occurring in the skin. Dermatitis is the cutaneous pattern to many causative agents.

REACTION PATTERN: The reaction pattern will depend on the stage of reaction and the severity of the injury.

In the acute stage, there is redness (vasodilation of the subpapillary plexus); itching, with release of proteases and/or peptase and/or histamine; moist surface, vesicles and bullae (increase in epidermal fluid either as fluid loculi or intercellular edema [spongiosis]).

In the chronic stage, there is dryness, scaling, thickening of the skin (hyperkeratosis and parakeratosis) and lichenification (ascanthosis and hyperkeratosis).

Source: "Dermatitis" by Samuel M. Bluefarb, *Dermatology,* 1986, p. 6.

The Reading Experience: Questions for Reading and Discussion

1. What are two visual signs of dermatitis in its acute stage? Refer to the selection to answer correctly. Use the language of the text.

2. What are two visual signs of dermatitis in its chronic stage? Refer to the selection to answer correctly. Use the language of the text.

3. How does dermatitis feel? Refer to the selection to answer correctly. (Do not supply your personal response.)

4. Why is dermatitis different in different people? Refer to the selection to answer correctly. Use the precise language of the text.

5. How can this description help a doctor or a nurse recognize dermatitis? Even though technical language predominates in this description, can you picture this medical condition? What makes the description effective?

The Writing Experience: Suggestions for Short Papers

1. In two or three paragraphs, describe as objectively as you can an experience you have had with dermatitis caused by mosquito bites, poison ivy rash, or rashes from food allergies. Use visual and tactile imagery, but be as precise as you can without adding any emotional language. How does your writing match Dr. Bluefarb's description? These descriptions may be shared with other students to see how they compare to each other.

2. Rewrite your experience as if you were a nurse or a physician in a clinic, from their point of view.

   Explain what your diagnosis would be, using the technical language in Dr. Bluefarb's article.

3. The description above is based upon *observation*, not by one doctor, but many, over a long period of time. Use this as a model for your own group observation. In groups of four students, objectively write a collaborative observation of an object, a condition, or a lesson. Avoid personal opinion entirely. Be as specific as possible. Begin with a clear definition of your topic, as does the article above. Then, divide your topic into its component parts. Think about what went into the creation and then the current presentation of the object, condition, or lesson. All students must add sensory details to the description. Suggested topics: (a) the seating arrangement in the class—how it appears, who sits where, how it may change, and why; (b) the weather—what it is; how the media presents it; how it affects the learning environment; (c) a class lecture—how it begins, how it proceeds, how it ends, and how it can affect the listeners.

4. Research either in the library or online a common illness or injury you have experienced—a sore throat, a virus, a swollen ankle, or broken finger, for example. Compare how the clinical description matches your own experience of this medical issue. Write your comparison as objectively as possible. Cite your source carefully.

Recommended Films and eConnections

The Aurora Borealis Viewed from Orbit. <http://www.openbulture.com/2011/09/aurora_borealis_from_orbit.html> Dan Colman. 21 Sept. 2011. Online lesson. YouTube video.

New Photos of Einstein's Brain.<http://video.pbs.org/video2304521197> NOVA science NOW. Air date 15 Nov. 2012. Online lesson. YouTube video.

Universe—Full Length Documentary Movie with William Shatner. Manicmovies.com. 9 Feb. 2013. YouTube video.

BBC Secret Universe: The Hidden Life of the Cell. SchoolHelper 94. 28 Oct. 2012. YouTube video.

Quiz

_____ 1. To describe dermatitis objectively, the writer would have to: (a) experience it personally; (b) observe many patients and consult other medical sources for an accurate description; (c) propose a theory about it; (d) draw conclusions about its impact on society.

_____ 2. Dermatitis: (a) follows a reaction pattern; (b) is an inflammation of the skin; (c) is extremely common; (d) draw conclusions about its impact on society.

_____ 3. The senses utilized in this description are: (a) sight and touch; (b) hearing and smell; (c) taste and touch; (d) sight and hearing.

_____ 4. Thickening of the skin is also known as: (a) eczema; (b) vasodilation of the sub-papillary plexus; (c) hyperkeratosis; (d) acanthosis.

_____ 5. As a reader, your task is: (a) to picture all the details that make up the condition; (b) to challenge the writer; (c) to follow events in the story; (d) to identify the thesis and conclusion.

MUSIC, THERMOMETER, LOST DOG, JOB APPLICATION

Some students believe that once they graduate they may never need to know how to write seriously again. Such an assumption can easily be proven wrong. What would happen if you lost your iPhone or your pet? Of course, you would have to extensively write a clear, objective description of the lost item in order to post it—whether on the Web or the nearest telephone pole. Think of all the descriptions of missing children posted online, on buses, on milk cartons. These need to be composed accurately. The police and the FBI also need to objectively describe a criminal on the loose, but they take the information from those who knew or saw the perpetrator. Objective detail is crucial. In another instance, when applying for a position, your concise, objective résumé must be chronological and/or functional. To accompany it, you will also need to compose a clear cover letter that states your _objective_. Note the word that designates your purpose: _objective_. These descriptions must be factual and perfect.

Reading a poster for a missing child or pet calls for keen efferent skills, so that you can remember the information when you are out and about, keeping your eye peeled for the lost loved one. As an employer, you need to read the information critically, taking away the facts from the resume and cover letter and making the important decision to hire or "file."

Some of the most common instances of reading objective description go unnoticed; in order to know whether you or another person has a fever, you must know how to read a thermometer. The same is true for a ruler, a scale, a clock, or a blood pressure monitor.

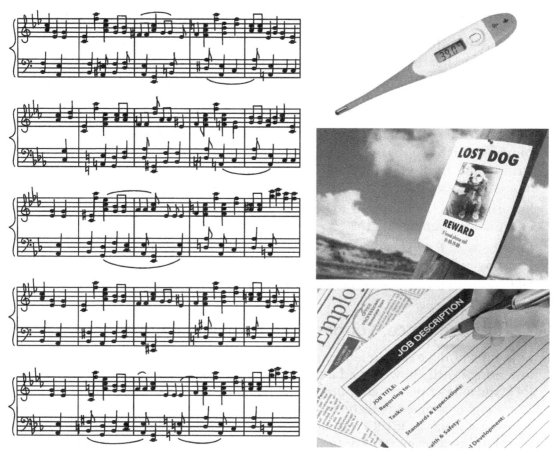

Music: © Annykos, 2013. Used under license from Shutterstock, Inc.; Thermometer: © Lipskiy, 2013. Used under license from Shutterstock, Inc.; Poster: © Fer Gregory, 2013. Used under license from Shutterstock, Inc.; Job Description: © Pixsooz, 2013. Used under license from Shutterstock, Inc.

When you look at the time, do you realize that you are reading? In like manner, reading a graph or chart allows us to comprehend important information about statistics on various topics: demographics, politics, wellness, the stock market, or any other tally. On a lighter note, you are reading objective description when you interpret a poker wheel, a chessboard, or playing cards. Reading music requires the same cognitive process. We bring these to your attention so that you can understand how efferent reading of objective writing is crucial to an advanced, civilized society like our own.

In its own way, each is a symbol system that needs to be decoded, interpreted, and acted upon—but remember that it is first encoded, or written objectively very carefully, by someone, somewhere, who is wide awake and knows what she is doing.

The Reading Experience: Questions for Reading and Discussion

1. How are the objects portrayed as well as those mentioned in the previous explanation examples of the concept of YOU, ME, and IT studied in Chapter 1? Using a "Wanted" poster as an example, YOU = the reader, the citizen looking at the poster; ME = the writer, the FBI agent, or police agency who composed the poster; and IT, of course, = the poster itself.

2. Can you connect standard punctuation — periods, question marks, exclamation points, commas, colons, and semi-colons, as well as dashes, asterisks, and parentheses to the writing and reading of the symbol systems portrayed above? How are these writing tools similar or different from the other graphic items?

3. In each instance, what needs to be read? What needs to be done by the reader after the information is understood?

4. Could any of the items pictured or mentioned in the text above be written subjectively (personally)? Which, and why?

5. Did you read this explanation efferently or aesthetically?

The Writing Experience: Suggestions for Short Papers

1. In groups of three or four students, perform the following tasks in writing: (a) Explain in writing exactly how to read a thermometer, a scale, and a clock (not a digital clock!). (b) Write a description that should be included on the "Lost Dog" poster. Include breed, age, weight, color, body features or special markings, and whether or not the animal is wearing a collar or identifying tag. Will a reward be forthcoming? Add anything else you think is relevant. (c) Try to read the piece of music, even if you have never been given music lessons. For what instrument is it designed? Is the music fast or slow? Do any of the notes repeat? Do you think it is a march, a waltz, or music suitable only for listening? Each student must contribute ideas to these questions. Afterward record your process for (c) in your journal. How did you make your decisions? What sort of questions would you ask a music teacher?

2. With the parents' permission, try to teach a young child how to read a clock with hands. Record your experience as it enfolds. Rewrite this process objectively as a short essay.

3. Write your own resumé. Follow suggestions given on the internet. Remain objective.

4. Assume you are an employer, and need three employees: a clerk, a bookkeeper, and a truck driver. Write three clear job descriptions objectively listing your requirements and the employee's expected duties.

Recommended Films and eConnections

How to Read Music. Waltribreiro. 12 June 2007. YouTube video.

How to Write a Good Resumé. techblueweb. 1 July 2010. YouTube video.

Copying Beethoven. Dir. Agnieszka Holland. Perf. Ed Harris, Diane Kruger. Metro Goldwyn Mayer, 2001. Film.

Call of the Wild — Dog of the Yukon. Dir. Peter Svatek. Perf. Rutger Hauer, Richard Dreyfuss. Kingsborough Greenlight Pictures. 1997. TV Movie.

Quiz

_____ 1. To write a job description effectively, the writer would: (a) have to have held the job himself; (b) have to remain objective and write clearly; (c) have to list the hours and benefits; (d) both (b) and (c) are correct.

_____ 2. To write an effective poster for a lost pet, the owner would: (a) have to offer a reward, provide the number to call to contact the owner; (b) list the location where, and the date when, the animal was lost; (c) describe what the animal looks like; (d) all the above.

_____ 3. To read a thermometer correctly, one must: (a) hold it upside down; (b) put it in cold water first; (c) hold it in the right hand; (d) know whether the thermometer is Fahrenheit or Celsius.

_____ 4. In order to read music, one must: (a) be intuitive; (b) play an instrument; (c) sing with the school chorus; (d) be taught by a musician.

_____ 5. All the above examples require: (a) decoding of a symbol system; (b) efferent reading; (c) attention to objectively written details; (d) all the above.

Compare the subjective descriptions in the two pieces that follow, excerpts from a true experience and a well-known piece of fiction. Both writers rely on their inner perceptions. As a reader, put yourself in their shoes — use all your senses to experience the characters fully. Let yourself go!

JACK LUGGAGE

William J. McGreevy

I encountered him for the first time years ago when I was a newly enrolled business major at St. Peters College.* The serendipitous meeting occurred on one of the antique, tired buses of the Montgomery Street Line. This transit company, whose buses were painted a rather subversive red color, carried many eccentric and exotic passengers along its tortuous route. It is quite conceivable that in order to drive one of the buses, one had to pass an elaborate series of tests designed to insure, shall we say, unusual behavior. These hybrid drivers then conspired to pick up only those passengers who complimented their personalities.

The Montgomery line duplicated a Public Service route, but the fare was less on "Big Red." Of course the rolling stock was less dependable. Riding this line was an adventure equivalent to shooting the rapids on some unchartered river. These buses were usually owner-operated and for some reason seemed to ignore any semblance of scheduling, so they travelled in packs. Like some offshore red tide, they would threateningly swell down Montgomery Street in waves of three or four. Their route from Exchange Place past the main branch of the library also helped to insure a capacity crowd of anomalously unique passengers.

. . . Resigned to our cruel state as pauperized students, we located a seat in the belly of the bus. As the bus wheezed and coughed its way past City Hall, we noticed a heavy set, sloppily dressed man who appeared to be in his mid-thirties sit down directly in front of us. He was not conspicuous because of the grime-edged collar of an an allegedly white shirt; nor because of the egg-stained tie which flapped gratuitously over his left shoulder in a fashion reminiscent of an aviator's nonchalantly flapping scarf. No, what made him really noticeable was the excited manner in which he was engaged in conversation with himself, oblivious to the rest of the humanity swept up within this floating red tide of a bus line.

. . . We dubbed him "Jack Luggage," for he carried an oversized attaché case which was indeed luggage-size. Jack Luggage seemed an appropriate name also because he had an urge to express the primitive as a source for most answers to perplexing dilemmas . . . Jack Luggage's oversized luggage probably contained an oversized lunch to go with his oversized and outlandish notions.

* A private college (now Saint Peter's University) in Jersey City, New Jersey, two miles from New York City.

The Reading Experience: Questions for Reading and Discussion

1. Examine how the author—the first person narrator—prepares the reader by setting up his own point of view: what is stressed is "ME"—the writer. What do "YOU," the reader, find out about him and the time of his life when he met Jack Luggage? How might his perspective and his age influence the story? If he wrote about Jack Luggage then, at the time he first met him, would his experience be different? How?

2. Before we meet the main character in this excerpt from the full story "Jack Luggage," the author provides us with the setting. Where does this story take place? How does the bus appear? What sensory imagery is used? Are there any examples of figurative language? Why is it important for the reader to know the history of the bus line? How do these descriptions set you, the reader, up for the meeting to follow? What do you expect?

3. What is the connection established between the bus, its driver, the other passengers, the author, and Jack Luggage? Does he fit in? How?

4. Is the writing effective? Did you reread any lines or passages as you were reading, or after you were finished? Which ones? Why did you go back to these? Did any passages confuse you?

5. Subjective description, as we have seen, involves memories, feelings, imagination, and interpretation. How do these elements fit the description above? Does McGreevy "tell it like it is," or not?

The Writing Experience: Suggestions for Short Papers

1. Write a description of Jack Luggage from the point of view of: (a) the bus driver; (b) a social worker who knows and has worked with Jack Luggage; (c) an old woman seated across from Jack Luggage, who has far less than he does; (d) Jack Luggage's brother, an affluent corporate executive for a large oil firm in Texas, who has urged him many times to move westward and join him in business.

2. Use an encounter with an unusual person from your past to write a one- or two-paragraph description. Convey to the reader your memories, feelings, imagination, and interpretation of that person.

3. A *raconteur* is an oral storyteller. Using note cards, present orally to the class a portrait of one of the most unforgettable characters you have ever met. You may do a PowerPoint presentation, if you choose, to accompany your talk. Plan to speak for approximately five minutes.

4. Think of Jack Luggage as the character for the basis of a TV sitcom. Who would play the main character? Would the other passengers or the narrator be in the cast? If so, who would play the narrator? Create a story line for one or two episodes.

Recommended Films and eConnections

First Person to Ever Run Around the Whole World. Broadband TVEccentric. 24 Sept. 2008. YouTube video.

The Woman Who Lives in a Shop Window. Broadband TVEccentric. 16 Sept. 2008. YouTube video.

Grumpy Old Men. Dir. Donald Petrie. Perf. Jack Lemmon, Walter Matthau. Warner Bros., 1993. Film.

Being There. Dir. Hal Ashby. Perf. Peter Sellers, Shirley MacLaine. Lorimar, 1979. Film.

Quiz

_____ 1. Jack Luggage was: (a) neatly dressed; (b) sloppily dressed; (c) dressed as a businessman; (d) not described in the story in terms of the way he was dressed.

_____ 2. The description takes place in: (a) London; (b) San Francisco; (c) Jersey City; (d) New York.

_____ 3. "Big Red" buses were: (a) cheaper than other buses; (b) undependable; (c) travelled in packs; (d) all of the above.

_____ 4. Writing subjective description is: (a) an act of *reflexive* writing; (b) an act of *extensive* writing; (c) largely personal; (d) both (a) and (c) are correct.

_____ 5. To read subjective description, one should: (a) take away only the facts, reading *efferently*; (b) put yourself into it and try to imagine the description from the writer's point of view; (c) disconnect yourself from the writing and look at it objectively; (d) none of the above.

THE CASK OF AMONTILLADO

Edgar Alan Poe

The thousand injuries of Fortunato I had borne as best I could, but when he ventured upon insult, I vowed revenge. You, who so well know the nature of my soul, will not suppose, however, that I gave utterance to a threat. AT LENGTH* I would be avenged; this was a point definitely settled . . . I must not only punish, but punish with impunity. . . .

It must be understood that neither by word nor deed had I given Fortunato cause to doubt my good will. I continued, as was my wont, to smile in his face, and he did not perceive that my smile *now* was at the thought of his immolation.

He had a weak point—this Fortunato—although in other regards he was a man to be respected and even feared. He prided himself on his connoisseurship in wine. Few Italians have the true virtuoso spirit. . . . In painting and gemmary, Fortunato, like his countrymen, was a quack—but in the matter of old wines he was sincere. . . .

It was about dusk, one evening during the supreme madness of the carnival season, that I encountered my friend. He accosted me with excessive warmth, for he had been drinking much. The man wore motley. He had on a tight-fitting parti-striped dress, and his head was surmounted by the conical cap and bells. I was so pleased to see him, that I thought I should never have done wringing his hand. . . .

* Poe's narrator uses capital letters for these words, as if he were stressing them in writing or speech.

The Reading Experience: Questions for Reading and Discussion

1. Poe is credited with writing the very first short story. He believed that readers ought to be able to finish an entire tale in one sitting—and that every sentence in that tale should build in intensity toward one idea. In most of his stories, that idea, or theme, was either *fright* or *horror*. How does this description fit the theme of this excerpt from "The Cask of Amontillado"?

2. The element we have called IT (the story) here remains as it does in every piece of writing. Of course, ME is always the writer, and YOU the reader. But here, when the narrator says "I," he means the fictional character who is telling the story—not Poe, the writer, at all. This storyteller has a grudge. In the story's first paragraph, he vows "revenge"; he seeks to "punish" Fortunato, and to punish him "with impunity."[1] YOU, the reader, will never know why. But this narrator (his name, we find out later, is Montresor) is talking to a fictional "you," not YOU the reader. Who is this person? Well, YOU (the reader) will never know who it is, either. But whoever he or she may be, that person is addressed in the second sentence: "You, who so well know the nature of my soul." This fictional listener knows that Montresor will never threaten anyone out loud. No, Montresor will just think of what he will do, silently, to himself.

1. Oddly, *impunity* means "without punishment," or "without pain." The word originates from the Latin prefix *in-* and the root *poena,* meaning pain. Poe intends, of course, to punish him without Fortunato realizing it.

Would YOU (yes, you, the reader) trust this man? Is he a reliable friend, or even a *reliable narrator*?

In the excerpt above, there are emotional words that describe Fortunato, revealing the narrator's dislike. What are some of these words?

3. What are two of Fortunato's hobbies? What does the narrator think of his ability? How does he compare these two hobbies to his favorite study—what Poe calls his "connoisseurship"—"old wines"?

This is the height of subjective description—actually resorting to name calling!

4. Like McGreevy's portrait of Jack Luggage, Poe describes what Fortunato is wearing. What is "motley"? What does it look like? Name the visual details of his outfit. Is it a handsome or stylish outfit? Why is he wearing these clothes? Why might the narrator be happy to see the insulting Fortunato, who had been drinking too much, in this state? Do you think he is really *happy* to see him, as you would be if you saw an old friend?

5. Is the writing effective? Does it give you a good idea of the way the storyteller sees his "friend"? Explain why.

The Writing Experience: Suggestions for Short Papers

1. "The Cask of Amontillado" describes Fortunato very well, but indirectly Poe is describing the narrator, Montresor, as well, by giving clues about his two-faced nature by the things he says. Write a description of a concert, a football or baseball game, or a movie, from an *unreliable narrator's* point of view—a person no reasonable person would trust. This is the essence of subjective description.[2]

2. Describe what you are wearing today. Provide details about color, size, and style; but in particular, include your appraisal of your clothes. Do you like them? Did someone else choose them for you?

3. In small writing groups of three or four students, describe this class, giving your opinions of the following: the room itself, the seating, the instructor, the textbook, the homework, the tests, and anything else you care to say. Include the things you like best and least about the course. If your group disagrees on any point, state by name the students' differences of opinion.

4. Be a literary critic! Write a short essay discussing Edgar Allan Poe's writing. If you have read other stories or poems by Poe, include them by name. Provide reasons for enjoying or not enjoying particular features of his style or his themes. Or compare Poe to another short story writer. Describe features of both authors' work. Which one do you prefer? Give solid reasons for your opinion.

---

2. The recommended 1947 film *Lady in the Lake* is the first film ever to be made from an entirely subjective point of view. The term *subjective camera* was coined at that time to simulate a hand-held camera, making the image appear as if the camera were a person in the film.

Recommended Films and eConnections

The Cask of Amontillado. Sheri Lazare. 25 Oct. 2011. YouTube video.

Edgar Allan Poe. Biography.com. <www.biography.com/people/edgar-allan-poe-9443160/videos> 28 Sept. 2011. YouTube video.

The Raven. Dir. James McTeigue. FilmNation Entertainment and Intrepid Pictures. Perf. John Cusack, Luke Evans, Alice Eve. 2012. Film.

Lady in the Lake. Dir. Robert Montgomery. Perf. Robert Montgomery, Audrey Totter, Lloyd Nolan. Metro Goldwyn Mayer. 1947. Film.

Quiz

_____ 1. "The Cask of Amontillado" is a story of: (a) revenge; (b) friendship; (c) the history of carnivals; (d) good will.

_____ 2. The story is told from the point of view of: (a) an "I" or first person narrator; (b) an unreliable narrator; (c) Montresor, who is mentally unbalanced; (d) all of the above.

_____ 3. The setting is: (a) the dead of winter in Paris; (b) the July 4th weekend in Chicago; (c) Christmas season in New York; (d) carnival season in Italy.

_____ 4. "Motley" refers to: (a) the narrator's personality; (b) Fortunato's personality; (c) the narrator's attire; (d) Fortunato's attire.

_____ 5. The language used to describe Fortunato: (a) is completely objective; (b) is completely subjective; (c) uses metaphor and simile; (d) is written in modern American English.

CHRONOLOGICAL DESCRIPTION

Recognizing Sequences

The Greek word *chromos* means "time." When writers describe experience in chronological order, they arrange the phases of that event in the order of occurrence. To recognize this type of description, a reader needs to look for clue words, such as *first, second, next, then, afterward, at last,* and *finally.* Sometimes, instead of words, numbers or dates are used. Another device is to present the sequence with labels, such as "the Stone Age," "the Iron Age," etc., giving the proper sequence of historical events. In a minute-by-minute description, such as the countdown of an airplane crash or the last quarter of a football game, the chronology is identified in minutes and seconds.

Checking Sequences

Checking the sequence often requires your active participation. To assemble a model airplane or follow an aerobic exercise, a reader has to carry out the directions accurately. In writing such directions, one has to mentally or physically perform the motions. If the writer or reader has been slipshod about representing the time order, the description will not produce the desired result. While reading a chronological description, such as a historical chart, one must check the progress or evolution of one stage into another. Generally, each step builds on the preceding step.

Remembering Sequences

Remembering the sequence calls for various strategies. To remember a continuum, look for gradual development. Try listing each step on a 3 x 5 card, using a symbol on the revere side of each card as a clue. Use these for study and review. See chart on following page.

The Reading Experience: Questions for Reading and Discussion

1. English is the most popularly spoken language in the world. Survey the chart above. Why do you think this is so? Can the explanation come from looking at a chart alone? Which modern languages are closest to Modern English?

2. Languages from the Far East, Middle East, and Africa are not represented here. Originally, three large language groups dominated the world. The others are Hamitic and Semitic. Research these languages to see how and where they developed. What does the name of the original language from which English derived tell you? Although land and water formations, boundaries, and names of countries changed over the tens of thousands of years since the original three languages predominated, in which countries, as we name them today, do you think the earliest form of English was spoken? How did you make your decision?

3. As you can see from the chart, where in Europe did English come from? Does this information surprise you? Why do many scholars attribute English's origin to Latin and Greek?

4. How did Spanish, Portuguese, French, and Romanian develop? Based upon your knowledge of these languages, do you think they are similar? Can you identify any vocabulary items in these languages that sound alike? (Consider the words for *face*, *work*, and *heart*, for example.)

5. What if no one ever had wanted to migrate? What would happen to the language? What language would *you* be speaking today?

The Origins of the English Language
Indo-European: One of Three Major Groups of the Ancient World

INDO-EUROPEAN

- Albanian
- Armenian
- Balto/slavic
  - Baltic
    - Lithuanian, Lettish
  - Old Slavic
    - Russian, Polish, Czech, Bulgarian, Serbo-Croatian, etc.
- Celtic
  - Irish
  - Welsh
  - Breton
  - Gaelic
- Germanic
  - E. Germanic
    - Gothic
  - N. Germanic
    - West Norse
      - Norwegian, Icelandic, Faroese
    - East Norse
      - Swedish, Danish, Gothlandic
  - W. Germanic
    - High German
      - German
      - Yiddish
    - Low German
      - Old Saxon
        - Middle Low German
          - Plattedentsch
      - Low Franconian
        - Middle Dutch
          - Dutch, Flemish
      - Old Fisian
        - Fristian
      - Anglo-Saxxon (Old English)
        - Middle English
          - Modern English
- Hellenic
  - Greek
- Indian
  - Sanskrit
    - Middle Indian
      - Hindustani, Bengali, & other modern Indian languages
- Iranian
  - Avestan
  - Old Persian
    - Persian
- Italic
  - Latin
    - French
    - Provencal
    - Italian
    - Spanish
    - Portuguese
    - Catalan
    - Romanian

The Writing Experience: Suggestions for Short Papers

1. Compose a short essay that addresses this question: What would you do to learn a language other than English? Choose a language on this map and design an ideal plan for its mastery. Include coursework and life experiences as a part of your plan.

2. Write a short essay explaining what language you would be speaking today if your family had decided to remain in the country/countries of your ancestors. Hypothesize about your life, as you imagine it would be.

3. Why is Latin considered to be a "dead" language? How do you think it "died"? Hypothesize in a short essay. No research is needed!

4. Make several lists of English words in use today that come from the following languages: Spanish, German, Russian, Hebrew, French, the African languages, Irish or Gaelic, Arabic, the Scandinavian languages, and Native American. What does this tell you about Modern English? Write a short essay explaining what you found.

Recommended Films and eConnections

How to Speak Proto-Indo-European. Xidnaf. 27 Oct. 2012. YouTube video.

The History of the English Language. Nokia88e1. 27 May 2012. YouTube video

The Adventure of English – Eight Episodes. ITV. Dir. Melvyn Bragg. Perf. Melvyn Bragg. 2003. TV Mini Series.

The Story of English. WNET Channel 13 New York. Dir. William Cran. Perf. John Barton, Richard Bebb, Penny Downie. BBC. 1986. TV Mini Series.

Quiz

_____ 1. According to the chart, English can trace its parentage to which of the following languages? (a) Greek; (b) Italic; (c) Germanic; (d) Latin.

_____ 2. According to the chart, how many stages did English have? (a) one; (b) three; (c) many; (d) the chart does not cite this.

_____ 3. Which of the following groups cannot trace their "parentage" to Germanic? (a) Swedish, Yiddish, Frisian; (b) Danish, Dutch, Icelandic; (c) Swedish, Yiddish, Flemish; (d) Danish, Catalan, Icelandic.

_____ 4. Of the following four, which is not a Celtic language? (a) Welsh; (b) Gaelic; (c) Baltic; (d) Breton.

_____ 5. In spite of the fact that Latin today is considered a "dead" language, it has exerted tremendous linguistic influence through the ages. How many modern languages, according to the chart, trace their "parentage" to Latin? (a) six; (b) eight; (c) seven; (d) an indeterminate number.

RECIPE FOR LEMON CHICKEN

6 boned chicken breasts
3 sliced onions
3 stalks sliced celery
2 cups sliced mushrooms
2 cups sliced carrots
1 cup lemon juice
¼ cup olive oil
Salt and pepper to taste

Brown chicken in oil, 10 minutes, turning occasionally. Drain. Place in pan and cover with onions, celery, mushrooms, and carrots. Pour lemon juice, salt, and pepper over all. Cover with aluminum foil; poke holes in the foil. Bake at 375° for one hour.

The Reading Experience: Questions for Reading and Discussion

1. If you were going to the supermarket to buy the ingredients for this recipe, what item would you buy first? Why?

2. The first step in cooking is to "brown chicken in oil." However, there may be one or more steps that need to be done beforehand. What are they?

3. What might happen to the recipe if the chronology were slightly changed this way, "First, pour lemon juice, salt, and pepper over the chicken; then cover chicken with the vegetables"?

4. Why does a recipe need to be written in strict chronological order?

5. Was this written reflexively, chiefly to express oneself, or extensively, to notify others? To read this purposefully, should you aesthetically "put YOU into the reading," or efferently "put the reading into YOU"?

The Writing Experience: Suggestions for Short Papers

1. Make Lemon Chicken. As you move through the process, record your experience in your triple-entry journal. Afterward, re-craft your experience into a personal essay, complete with an introduction, thesis statement, and a conclusion (by its very nature, the essay will need to describe how your dish turned out). Complete objectivity in this assignment may be impossible, and is not expected. In fact, humor is a plus! What is most important, however, is that your essay recreates the process chronologically, as it is written.

2. Write a fairly complex recipe of your own. List your ingredients in the order of importance, being precise about the measurements. The description must be in perfect chronological order. You may choose to use numbers, letters, or signal words (*first, second, next,*

finally, etc.) when you write the directions. The internet boasts many fine websites that can help you in this assignment, starting with Sara Kate Gillingham-Ryan's "How to Write a Recipe Like a Professional." Consult textbooks you may have at home, as well, as models. As pure chronological description, a recipe does NOT need an introduction, thesis, or conclusion.

3. Write a sequential plan for constructing an object you have had success in building in the past, such as a tree house, a sand sculpture, a campfire, or even a Lego castle. Set out your materials first and proceed in strict chronological order. Your choice of words must be completely objective. Here, also, as this writing project is not a typical essay, an introduction, thesis, and conclusion are NOT necessary, but the plan must be stated clearly at the outset.

4. If you are a chemistry or nursing student, write a clear set of directions for a process you have studied. Some examples may be: stitching a wound; performing CPR; analyzing skin or hair samples; distillation of a single solution; making a fog chamber; experiments with soap. Do not experiment with any hazardous materials, and insure that you work in a safe environment. All steps in your process must be itemized.

Recommended Films and eConnections

Easy and Moist Lemon Chicken Recipe. Inspired taste. 25 Mar. 2013. YouTube video.

How to Change a Tire – Step by Step. Howdini Guru. 30 Jan. 2008. YouTube video.

Julie and Julia. Dir. Nora Ephron. Perf. Meryl Streep, Amy Adams, Stanley Tucci. Columbia Pictures, 2009. Film.

Like Water for Chocolate. Dir. Alfonso Arau. Perf. Marco Leonardi, Lumi Cavazos, Regina Torné. Miramax, 1992.

Quiz

_____ 1. Which one of the following steps in the Lemon Chicken recipe is not in chronological order? (a) Brown chicken in oil 10 minutes; (b) Turn occasionally; (c) Place in pan and cover with onions, celery, mushrooms, and carrots; (d) Drain.

_____ 2. The recipe for Lemon Chicken is written for: (a) experienced cooks; (b) women; (c) men; (d) anyone who wants to make it.

_____ 3. This recipe is intended for: (a) one or two people; (b) three to six people; (c) dinner for eight; (d) a large crowd.

_____ 4. Holes should be poked in the foil: (a) before beginning the recipe; (b) after one pours the lemon juice; (c) after covering the pan with the foil; (d) after baking.

_____ 5. Reading a recipe requires: (a) good cooking skills; (b) knowledge of kitchen utensils; (c) awareness of chronological description; (d) none of the above.

Bernard Grun

	A. History, Politics	B. Literature, Theater	C. Religion, Philosophy, Learning
1854 *contd*	Republican Party formed in the U.S. Abbas I, Viceroy of Egypt assassinated; succeeded by Mohammed Said (—1863) Ostend Manifesto advises U.S. to annex Cuba		
1855	Czar Nicholas I of Russia d.; succeeded by Alexander II (—1881) Britain and Afghanistan join against Persia in Treaty of Peshawar Taiping Rebellion ends Russians capitulate at Sebastopol; Allies enter town	Charlotte Bronte d. (b. 1816) Robert Browning: "Men and Women," poems Dickens: "Little Dorrit" (—1857) Dumas fils: "Le Demi-monde" Gustav Freytag: "Soll und Haben," novel Ludwig Ganghofer, Ger. popular novelist, b. (d. 1920) Longfellow: "The Song of Hiawatha" Marie Corelli (Mary Mackay), Eng. novelist, b. (d. 1924) Adam B. Mickiewicz d. (b. 1798) Arthur Wing Pinero, Eng. dramatist, b. (d. 1934) W. H. Prescott: "The History of the Reign of Philip II" (—1858) Tennyson: "Maud," and other poems Anthony Trollope: "The Warden" Turgenev: "Rudin" Walt Whitman: "Leaves of Grass"	Alexander Bain: "Senses and Intellects" Johann Droysen: "History of Prussian Policy" (—1886) Auguste Gratry: "Connaissance de Dieu" Soren Kierkegaard, Dan. philosopher, d. (b. 1813) Henry Milman: "History of Latin Christianity" Pierre Le Play: "Les Ouvriers europeens" (on working-class incomes) Herbert Spencer: "Principles of Psychology"
1856	Queen Victoria institutes the Victoria Cross Britain annexes Oudh, India, and establishes Natal as a Crown Colony Reform edict in Turk. Empire; peace conference in Paris recognizes integrity of Turkey Fr. Prince Imperial, son of Napoleon III, b. (d. 1879) Massacre of Potawatomie Creek, Kansas-slavers murdered by free-staters Aust. amnesty for Hungarian rebels of 1848–49 Anglo-Chin. war begins; Brit. fleet bombards Canton Persia occupies Herat—outbreak of Brit-Persian war James Buchanan wins U.S. presidential election Fr.-Span. frontier defined South African Republic (Transvaal) organized under Mart.hinius Pretorius Woodrow Wilson, future President of the U.S., b. (d. 1924) Britain grants self-government to Tasmania Emperor Francis Joseph visits Lombardy and Venice and appoints his brother Archduke Maximilian governor of the provinces	Edmond About: "Le Roi des montagnes" Flaubert: "Madame Bovary" (—1857) H. Rider Haggard, Eng. novelist, b. (d. 1925) Heinrich Heine d. (b. 1797) Victor Hugo: "Les Contemplations," poems Ibsen: "The Banquet at Solhaug," Norw. play Gottfried Keller: "Die Leute von Seldwyla," short stories M^rike: "Mozart auf der Reise nach Prag," short story Charles Reade: "It Is Never Too Late to Mend" George Bernard Shaw, Anglo-Ir. writer and dramatist, 1925 Nobel Prize, b. (d. 1950) Oscar Wilde, Anglo-Ir. author, b. (d. 1900)	J. A. Froude: "History of England from the Fall of Wolsey to the Defeat of the Armada" (—1870) Theodor Goldstucker: "Sanskrit Dictionary" Rudolf Lotze: "Mikrokosmos" (—1864) J. R. Motley: "Rise of the Dutch Republic" Hippolyte Taine: "Les Philosophes classiques du XIXe siècle en France" Augustin Thierry, Fr. historian, d. (b. 1795) Alexis de Tocqueville: "L'Ancien regime et la revolution"
1857	Peace of Paris ends Anglo-Persian war; shah recognizes independence of Afghanistan James Buchanan inaugurated as 15th President of the U.S. Indian Mutiny against Brit. rule; siege of Delhi begins; Delhi captured; British enter Cawnpore Royal Navy destroys Chin. fleet; relief of Lucknow; Britain and France take Canton Garibaldi forms ItaL National Association for unification of the country William H. Taft, future President of the U.S., b. (d. 1930) Irish Republican Brotherhood (Fenians) founded	George Borrow: "Romany Rye" Charles Baudelaire: "Les Fleurs du mal" Bjornstjerne Bjornson: "Synnove Solbakken" Joseph Conrad (Korzeniowski), Anglo-Pol. novelist, b. (d. 1924) Joseph von Eichendorff; Ger. poet, d. (b. 1788) George Eliot: "Scenes from Clerical Life" Thomas Hughes: "Tom Brown's Schooldays" Dinah Mulock: "John Halifax, Gentleman" Alfred de Musser, Fr. poet, d. (b. 1810) Hendrik von Pontoppidan, Dan. author, 1917 Nobel Prize, b. (d. 1943) Adalbert Stifter: "Nachsommer," Aust. novel	Henry T. Buckle: "History of Civilization in England" (—1861) Auguste Comte, Fr. philosopher, d. (b. 1798) Sir Charles T. Newton (1816–1894) discovers remains of the Mausoleum of Halicarnassus Ernest Renan: "Erudes d'histoire religieuse"

D. Visual Arts	E. Music	F. Science, Technology, Growth	G. Daily Life	
				1854 *contd*
Jakob Bruckhardt "Cicerone," art history Courbet: "Pavillon du Realisme" at Paris World Fair J. B. Isabey, Fr. painter, d. (b. 1767)	Berlioz: "Te Deum," Paris (written 1849) Verdi: "Les Vepres Sicilennes," opera, Paris Wagner conducts a series of orchestral concerts in London	George Audemars takes out first patent for production of rayon Sir Richard Burton: "Pilgrimage to Mecca," travel book Professorship of technology created at Edinburgh University David E. Hughes (1831–1900) invents printing telegraph Aust. engineer Franz Koller develops tungsten steel R. S. Lawrence of Vermont, U.S., constructs turret lathe Livingstone discovers Victoria Falls of Zambezi River Percival Lowell, Amer. astronomer, b. (d. 1916) Matthew Maury: "Physical Geography of the Sea"	First iron Cunard steamer crosses Atlantic (in nine and a half days) Founding of "The Daily Telegraph," London Ferdinand de Lesseps (1805–1894) granted concession by France to construct Suez Canal Electric telegraph between London and Balaklava London sewers modernized after outbreak of cholera Florence Nightingale (1820–1910) introduces hygienic standards into military hospitals during Crimean War Paris World Fair	1855
Hendrikk Petrus Berlage, Dutch architect, b. (d. 1934) Heinrich van Ferstel begins the Votivkirche, Vienna (–1879) Jean A. D. Ingres: "La Source," painting	Karl Bechstein founds his piano factory Alexander Dargomijsky: "Russalka," opera, St. Petersburg Maillart: "Les Dragons de Villars," opera, Paris Robert Schumann d. (b. 1810) Christian Sinding, Norw. composer, b. (d. 1941)	Sir Henry Bessemer (1813–1898) introduces converter in his process for making steel Pure cocaine extract from cocoa beans Sigmund Freud, Aust. neurologist, founder of psychoanalysis, b. (d. 1939) Hermann von Helmholtz: "Manual of Physiological Optics" (–1866) Nikolai I. Labachevsky, Russ. mathematician, d. (b. 1793) Robert E. Peary, Amer. explorer, b. (d. 1920) William H. Perkin prepares first aniline dye Ger. botanist Nathaniel Pringsheim (1823–1894) observes sperm entering ovum in plants Sir William Siemens (1823–1883) makes ductile steel for boiler plating	Baseball: Chicago Unions organized Black Forest railroad with 40 tunnels opened First Australian interstate cricket match: Victoria versus New South Wales Keir Hardie, Brit. socialist leader, b. (d. 1915) Longest bare-knuckle boxing fight in history: James Kelly versus Jack Smith, Melbourne, Australia, 186 rounds lasting 6 hours 15 minutes Neanderthal skull found in Feldhofer Cave near D sseldorf Frederick W. Taylor, Amer. inventor and pioneer in scientific industrial management techniques, b. (d. 1915) "Big Ben," 13.5 ton bell at Brit. Houses of Parliament, cast at Whitechapel Bell Foundry (named after Sir Benjamin Hall, Director of Public Works)	1856
Max Klinger, Ger. sculptor, b. (d. 1920) Miller: "The Gleaners," painting National Portrait Gallery, London, opened Christian D. Rauch, Ger. sculptor, d. (b. 1777) Victoria and Albert Museum, (contd)	Hans von B low marries Cosima Liszt Edward Elgar, Eng. composer, b. (d. 1934) Mikhail J. Glinka, Russ. composer, d. (b. 1803) Charles HallE founds the HallE Concerts in Manchester Wilhelm Kienzl, Aust. composer, (contd)	Emile Coue, Fr. psychologist, b. (d. 1926) Heinrich Hertz, Ger. physicist, b. (d. 1894) Julius Wagner von Jauregg, Aust. neurologist and psychiatrist, 1927 Nobel Prize, b. (d. 1940) Pasteur proves that fermentation is caused by living organisms Ronald Ross, Eng. physician, specialist in tropical diseases, 1902 Nobel Prize, b. (d. 1932)	Alpine Club, London, founded "Atlantic Monthly" founded Robert Baden-Powell, Brit. general, founder of the Boy Scout movement, b. (d. 1941) Financial and economic crisis throughout Europe, caused by speculation in U.S. railroad shares Matrimonial Causes Act in Britain North German Lloyd founded (transatlantic steamship company) American civil engineer E. G. Otis installs first safety elevator Science Museum, South Kensington, (contd)	1857

The Reading Experience: Questions for Reading and Discussion

1. How did you read this chart at first glance, horizontally or vertically? Why? Which is easier? Did you reread any section? Is reading a chart of this type easier or more difficult than reading traditionally arranged paragraphs? Explain.

2. After reading the chart on your own, group yourself with two or three other students. Together: (a) decide upon three sections of the chart that are the most interesting and three the least interesting; (b) choose three events that impact the world most strongly today; (c) list five authors with whom you are familiar; (d) list two musical pieces you would most like to hear; (e) choose three scientific/technological advances that you would like most to study more closely. Give reasons for your choices and explain how you came to your decisions.

3. Why do you think Grun prepared this chart in this manner? How did he decide what would be first (Category A), and in what order did he move to Category G? What may have been his rationale for this order?

4. What are the limits of such a chart? What features of society *could* have been included that Grun left out? What type of events *cannot* be included? Why not?

5. What type of chart could be created about today's society? What labels would you use? What events would you choose to list under these labels?

The Writing Experience: Suggestions for Short Papers

1. Divide your life into three parts, beginning with the specific day of your birth and ending with today's date. Where would you make the cutoffs? How could you label your time periods? Construct a horizontal chart modeled on Grun's above. Identify specific events horizontally across the top of your chart; list inclusive dates (not each year, but the thirds you first identified) vertically to the left.

2. Using any tool on the internet that you choose that explains graphics, construct a schedule of your day. Include activities in and out of school.

3. Using question #4 above, create a Timetable of the twenty-first century. First, sketch out your ideas. Then, combine your ideas with one or two partners.

4. Write a short essay explaining what you have learned by reading Bernard Grun's timetable. Include a discussion of the chart's form as well as its content.

Recommended Films and eConnections

The Voice of Florence Nightengale. transformingArt. 21 Oct. 2008. You Tube video.

Livingstone – Victoria Falls – Zambia. Livingstonesadv. 16 Oct. 2011. YouTube video.

Florence Nightengale – Full. Dir. Daryl Duke. Perf. Claire Bloom, Timothy Dalton, Jaclyn Smith. 1985. TV Film on YouTube.

A Dangerous Method. Dir. David Cronenberg. Perf. Keira Knightly, Viggo Mortensen, Michael Fassbender. Recorded Picture Company and Telefilm Canada. 2011. Film.

Quiz

_____ 1. Sigmund Freud died in: (a) 1863; (b) 1939; (c) 1934; (d) 1915.

_____ 2. The fifteenth President of the United States was: (a) Theodore Roosevelt; (b) Woodrow Wilson; (c) William Howard Taft; (d) James Buchanan.

_____ 3. A famous Norwegian composer was: (a) Claude Debussy; (b) Robert Schumann; (c) Christian Sinding; (d) Hector Berlioz.

_____ 4. Florence Nightengale introduced: (a) hygienic standards into military hospitals; (b) lived from 1820 to 1910; (c) worked in the Crimean War; (d) all of the above.

_____ 5. In Chicago, baseball was organized into Unions in: (a) 1854; (b) 1855; (c) 1856; (d) 1857.

COLLABORATION SENSATION: HOROSCOPES AND THE ZODIAC

A Partner Project in Description

With a partner, choose one of these signs of the Zodiac:

Aries the Ram

Taurus the Bull

Gemini the Twins

Cancer the Crab

Leo the Lion

Virgo the Virgin

Libra the Balance

Scorpio the Scorpion

Sagittarius the Archer

Capricorn the Goat

Aquarius the Water Bearer

Pisces the Fishes

Share these tasks:

* Draw or illustrate your chosen sign as a cover for your essay
* Describe the etymology of its name by using resources in the library or internet
* Describe its placement in the heavens by drawing the chart of the night sky
* List the features of the human personality attributed to the sign
* List all members of your class and five famous people born under this sign
* Create a horoscope describing what will occur "tomorrow" for people with this sign
* Combine all partners' projects in one spectacular display in the classroom
* After class, include in your triple-entry journal a freely written appraisal of your experience in every phase of the activity
* In your triple-entry journal include another entry that comments upon the "match" between the description of the human personality traits for your Zodiac sign and yourself

NARRATIVE VOICES

The Second Message of Intent—What Happened?

THE WRITER'S INTENTION TO ENTERTAIN

Fictional Narration

What do Ray Romano, William Shakespeare, Garry Trudeau, Quentin Tarantino, Lady Gaga, Giacomo Puccini, E.T.A. Hoffmann, and August Wilson have in common? They all write stories. Some of the stories are sung, some are danced, some are acted, while others are read. Nevertheless, they're all stories. They may appear on TV, on the opera stage, in the Sunday comics, in ballet, on Broadway, on the movie screen, or in Madison Square Garden. But they all tell you something that "happened."

The Four Elements

What makes a story a story, and not a description, an essay, or an argument? Essentially, four elements: plot, setting, characters, and a narrator. Each of these has its own function.

The Plot

The most important element is the *plot* of the story; it relies upon time. The writer must choose the order of events being presented in a way that the reader can follow. The easiest way to create this is to let the order of things in the story match the *chronological* order of life as it is lived. That sounds logical, doesn't it? Why should anyone want to write events any other way?

However, many writers choose to write their stores in an *achronological* manner, which may include flashbacks, dream sequences, or journeys into the mind while the character is awake. These techniques were perfected about a century ago by James Joyce and Virginia Woolf, two of the most outstanding writers in all of literature. Their novels and other stories that use flashbacks, dreams, and the stream of consciousness technique are much harder to follow, since the reader has to understand when the writer is in the past, the present, the future, or simply, in an imaginary time.

In any chosen time order, however, there always is a beginning, a middle, and an end. Every story has a high point—a *climax*—which comes not in the middle of the tale, but closer to its end, when things usually "come to a head." At that point, the main character usually has to make a decision about the problem her or the main character is involved in, a life-threatening situation which will determine her fate, or all the characters are present in one room or one place where they find out the truth about each other, all at the same time.

Once the high point is reached, the story is virtually over; the action spins and plummets rapidly—almost like a twisted cord unraveling—until the ending is reached. This spinning and plummeting, or falling action, is called the *dénouement*, a French term that literally means "an unraveling."

The Setting

The second element, the *setting* of the story, generally is established through the mode of description. The sights, smells, sounds, and sensations of the story are sometimes established at the outset, but often continue to be told throughout the plot. In drama and ballet, the setting includes the time and place of each act and determines the scenery, or dramatic sets, including the lighting, sound effects, and music. Fairy tales historically begin with the phrase "Once upon a time..." which establishes the time and place, but few modern tales plainly announce the setting. The writer needs to use attire and hairstyles, homes and furnishings, modes of transportation and the roads on which they travel, technology (or its lack) and, of course, speech patterns to provide the era and location of the story. Perceptive readers will experience these as the characters themselves do, and put themselves in the described time and place. If the author is successful, they will feel like they are "there."

The Characters

The *characters* in narration make this type of discourse different from description, exposition, or persuasion and argument. For narration is the story of a person or persons; narration tells us what happened to someone. A reader can tell who the main character is (the *hero*, either male or female) by looking for two features: first, who is the main mover of the action? And second, who changes the most from the beginning to the end of the story? There are major characters, minor characters, and those characters who serve merely as background (you can tell who they are, because they usually have nothing to say). The second most important character (if there is one) is the villain; the third most important character (if there is one) is the major support, often taking form as the main character's best friend, wife, husband, lover, co-worker, or sibling. Characters who serve merely as background often stand in the background; in films, these parts are played by "extras."

What makes characters do what they do? What the main character *needs* or *fears* often will govern the plot of the story and move it forward. Consider the motives of each character, but note the hero's needs and fears in every story you experience. If you can figure these out, you can probably predict what will happen. However, the very best stories end unpredictably. The ending of a great tale should surprise you!

The Narrator

The *narrator*, the person who tells the story, may do so in the first person, using the words "I," "myself," "me," etc. As you might guess, this is called the *first person narrator* or the "I" narrator.

The *third person narrator* uses pronouns such as "they," "he," "them," but the important distinction is that the third person narrator may see into the minds of all the characters. This all-knowing presence is also known as the *omniscient narrator.*[1] Such a narrator may move back and forth in time, using foresight and hindsight. The best narrators will motivate sympathy and recognition in the reader. Their point of view will be clear, and may even be familiar. But not all narrators are reliable. The reader must be the judge of that. The conscientious reader will always think about whether the experiences being related match his or her own experiences, or whether they sound as if they really can happen. This is aesthetic reading.

How the Aesthetic Experience Happens

Aesthetic experience is, by its very nature, an extremely private phenomenon. Perhaps you've heard the saying "I don't know much about art, but I know what I like!" Basically, liking an art form is at the heart of the aesthetic experience.

Do you know how the aesthetic experience happens? First, we encounter something new. We experience it directly. Pow! It knocks us out. Then we begin to think about it. We reflect on all the things that pleased us. We go over it and over it. Next, that reflection takes the shape of a conceptualization—that is, we think about how it stacks up against other things like it. Do we like it as well as others? Is it like something else we know? Does this do more, go further, seem more exciting, tasty, or lovelier? What did the experience do for us? What do we think, anyway? Finally, we think about what we want to do about it, if anything. Shall we copy it, adapt it to ourselves for our own use, recreate it into something new? If it's a story, shall we read it again?[2]

Aesthetic Reading and the PBRI Process

Can this type of reading be taught? Yes, absolutely! If we really adore a film, concert, painting, ballet, or a book, it can take only a moment for us to know it. It can be "love at first sight." We don't need to teach very much in that case. But the very same process we go through to enjoy things we like can work to help us appreciate things we don't like nearly as well. How?

There are actually four phases that can be analyzed, studied, and practiced. These can be coded for easy retention using the first letter of each phase. Unlike many "codes," however,—the very word makes it sound cold and impersonal—this one emphasizes YOU, the reader. Every phase relies on "you." YOU are in the spotlight. Your actions and your judgment are paramount. We can break the process into four phases, labeled for ease in recall, PBRI:

1. **Predict**
2. **Build**
3. **Review**
4. **Interpret**

Here's how the process works:

Before Reading
- Consider the title
- Guess what the story will be about

---

1. The prefix *omni-* in Latin means "all"; *scientia* means "knowledge."
2. The explanation of the aesthetic experience here is based largely upon David Kolb's well-known experiential learning theory, as expressed in his earliest work with Roger Fry. The ELM (Experiential Learning Model) appears in *The Theories of Group Process*, C. Cooper (ed.), London: John Wiley, 1975.

During Reading
- **Predict** what will happen
- **Build** meaning

After Reading
- **Review** the whole
- **Interpret** the meaning

After you have completed the first part of the checklist above, *Before Reading*, begin to read and follow the PBRI formula this way:

1. **Predict**. Who is the main character? How is this character changing? What does the character need? How will s/he get it? What does the character fear? How will this fear affect the character's actions? Use these clues to predict what will happen to the main character.

2. **Build** meaning. Piece the story together as you read. Is it arranged chronologically? What days or months can you assign to specific events? Are there any flashbacks or dream sequences? Where do they occur in the chronology of the plot? How does one event lead to another?

   Does the character "think aloud," allowing the reader to see into his "stream of consciousness"? Do the experiences of the main character seem credible? Do the events match things that you have known to happen?

   Do you trust the narrator? Is s/he reliable? Does the narrator's voice inspire sympathy?

   What do you think the events and the narrator's comments mean? Put two and two together.

3. **Review** the whole. Chart the sequence of the story. Sketch the major events. Which section of the story seems to be the turning point? Analyze the patterns in the story. Is an action scene followed by a quiet scene? Is any character the opposite of any other?

   Review the four elements of narration: *plot, setting, characters*, and the *narrator*. Jot down your ideas in your journal.

4. **Interpret.** Analyze what the story means to you. Think of other stories you have read that remind you of this one. Think of how the words are used. Are there any rhymes or repetitions? How do they contribute to the story? What does the ending mean? Did it come as a surprise? Is the story "finished," or is the outcome left "up to you"? Why did it end this way? What did the story value? Is there any "moral" to the story? Was it shocking, boring, heartwarming, frightening, revealing?

   Did it succeed?

   As you read the following story, write in either the margins or in your journal after each paragraph. Predict what will happen. When some new information is revealed, write down your "Aha!" moment. Save your notes and review them later. Your own reading process may surprise you!

THE STORY OF AN HOUR

Kate Chopin

Knowing that Mrs. Mallard was afflicted with heart trouble, great care was taken to break to her as gently as possible the news of her husband's death.

It was her sister Josephine who told her, in broken sentences; veiled hints that revealed in half concealing. Her husband's friend Richards was there, too, near her. It was he who had been in the newspaper office when intelligence of the railroad disaster was received, with Brently Mallard's name leading the list of "killed." He had only taken the time to assure himself of its truth by a second telegram, and had hastened to forestall any less careful, less tender friend in hearing the sad message.

She did not hear the story as many women have heard the same, with a paralyzed inability to accept its significance. She wept at once, with sudden, wild abandonment, in her sister's arms. When the storm of grief had spent itself she went away, to her room alone. She would have no one follow her.

There stood, facing the open window, a comfortable, roomy armchair. In to this she sank, pressed down by a physical exhaustion that haunted her body and seemed to reach into her soul.

She could see in the open square before her house the tops of trees that were all aquiver with the new spring life. The delicious breath of rain was in the air. In the street below a peddler was crying in his wares. The notes of a distant song which some one was singing reached her faintly, and countless sparrows were twittering in the eaves.

There were patches of blue sky showing here and there through the clouds that had met and piled one above the other in the west facing her window.

She sat with her head thrown back upon the cushion of the chair, quite motionless, except when a sob came up into her throat and shook her, as a child who has cried itself to sleep continues to sob in its dreams.

She was young, with a fair, calm face, whose lines bespoke repression and even a certain strength. But now there was a dull stare in her eyes, whose gaze was fixed away off yonder on one of those patches of blue sky. It was not a glance of reflection, but rather indicated a suspension of intelligent thought.

There was something coming to her and she was waiting for it, fearfully. What was it? She did not know, it was too subtle and elusive to name. But she felt it, creeping out of the sky, reaching toward her through the sounds, the scents, the color that filled the air.

Now her bosom rose and fell tumultuously. She was beginning to recognize this thing that was approaching to possess her, and she was striving to beat it back with her will—as powerless as her two white slender hands would have been.

When she abandoned herself a little whispered word escaped her slightly parted lips. She said it over and over under her breath: "free, free, free!" The vacant stare and the look of terror that had followed it went from her eyes. They stayed keen and bright. Her pulses beat fast, and the coursing blood warmed and relaxed every inch of her body.

She did not stop to ask if it were or were not a monstrous joy that held her. A clear and exalted perception enabled her to dismiss the suggestion as trivial.

She knew that she would weep again when she saw the kind, tender hands folded in death, the face that had never looked save with love upon her, fixed ad gray and dead. But she saw beyond the bitter moment a long procession of years to come that would belong to her absolutely. And she opened and spread her arms out to them in welcome.

From "The Story of an Hour" by Kate Chopin, April 19, 1894. First published in *Vogue* December 6, 1894, under the title "The Dream of an Hour."

There would be no one to live for her during those coming years, she would live for herself. There would be no powerful will bending hers in that blind persistence with which men and women believe they have a right to impose a private will upon a fellow creature. A kind intention or a cruel intention made the act seem no less a crime as she looked upon it in that brief moment of illumination.

And yet she had loved him—sometimes. Often she had not. What did it matter! What could love, the unsolved mystery, count for in the face of this possession of self-assertion which she suddenly recognized as the strongest impulse of her being!

"Free! Body and soul free!" she kept whispering. Josephine was kneeling before the closed door with her lips to the keyhole, imploring for admission, "Louise, open the door! I beg; open the door—you will make yourself ill. What are you doing, Louise? For heaven's sake open the door."

"Go away. I am not making myself ill." No, she was drinking in a very elixir of life through that open window.

Her fancy was running riot along those days ahead of her. Spring days, arid summer days, and all sorts of days that would be her own. She breathed a quick prayer that life might be long. It was only yesterday she had thought with a shudder that life might be long.

She arose at length and opened the door to her sister's importunities. There was a feverish triumph in her eyes, and she carried herself unwittingly like a goddess of victory. She clasped her sister's waist, and together they descended the stairs. Richards stood waiting for them at the bottom.

Someone was opening the front door with a latchkey. It was Brently Mallard who entered, a little travel-stained, composedly carrying his gripsack and umbrella. He had been far from the scene of the accident, and did not even know there had been one. He stood amazed at Josephine's piercing cry, at Richards' quick motion to screen him from the view of his wife.

But Richards was too late.

When the doctors came they said she had died of heart disease—of joy that kills.

The Reading Experience: Questions for Reading and Discussion

1. A great deal of information is given to the reader in the first sentence in terms of the background we need to know to understand the story and the kernel of action that is the core of the plot. How much information did you get from this sentence?

2. As you read the story did you *predict* what would happen? How did you *build* the meaning of the story? Did you write notes as you read, following the PBRI formula? Now that you've finished the story, reread your notes. Did you anticipate the ending? Compare your thoughts with other students in the class.

3. Where does the climax of the story occur? Is there a *denouement*? Why did Louise Mallard die of heart failure? Do you agree with her doctors? Why or why not?

4. Consider the other characters, Josephine and Richards. What do they contribute to the story? Are they similar or different? Why does Richards try to "screen" her husband, Brently, from her view?

5. What is the point of view of the narrator? Is the narrator impartial or biased? Provide reasons for your answer.

The Writing Experience: Suggestions for Short Papers

1. Review the chronological order of events by preparing a timeline. Since this is "the story of an hour" how long do you think each segment takes? Prepare a "schedule" as one would when retrieving a black box from a plane crash. For example: "9:36 a.m.: The Yazoo Line Train crashes into the Mandeville Station, killing dozens of passengers." Include events leading up to the railroad disaster, as well as the time Mrs. Mallard spends in her room after receiving the news by telegram. The "hour" should end at the conclusion of the story.

2. Write an obituary for Louise Mallard. Include biographical details of your own choosing, based upon her family, hobbies, personality, and health. State the time and place of the funeral, as well as any donations that may be made. Consult your local newspaper as well as the internet for the correct form.

3. Write a letter from one of the characters to a family member or close friend from out of town, explaining the events from that character's point of view. Be sure to include their personal insights, based on their involvement and closeness to Louise and Brently Mallard. You may choose to write a letter from Louise Mallard herself as she sat in her armchair, or from Brently after his wife's demise.

4. Kate Chopin is one of several women who wrote outstanding fiction in the nineteenth century, including the Brontë sisters (Anne, Charlotte, and Emily), Jane Austin, and Mary Shelley. Using your professor's references or the internet, find out as much information as you can about the writing lives of any Victorian women you choose. Write a short essay discussing the difficulties they faced in publishing and the problems they had finding the time to write.

Recommended Films and eConnections

Kate Chopin's "The Story of an Hour." uwsclassof2012. 20 Apr. 2009. YouTube video.

Kate Chopin. 4everSaddleseatRider. 16 May 2011. YouTube video.

Kate Chopin: The Joy That Kills. Rathborne Productions. Dir. Tina Rathborrne. Perf. Frances Conroy, Jeffrey DeMunn, Patrick Hogan. Films On Demand. Digital Education Video. 1984. Film.

Jane Austen's Sense and Sensibility. Dir. John Alexander. Perf. Hattie Morahan, Charity Wakefield. BBC, PBS. TV Mini Series. 2008.

Quiz

_____ 1. Mrs. Mallard was: (a) young; (b) middle-aged; (c) elderly; (d) no reference to her age is given.

_____ 2. When she heard the news: (a) she was paralyzed because she could not accept it; (b) she wept at once; (c) she sank into the nearest armchair; (d) she stared at the sky filled with clouds with patches of blue.

_____ 3. "There would be no one to live for her during those coming years; she would live for herself." This sentence from Chopin's story indicates: (a) the main character would miss her husband's company very much; (b) the main character was happy to be alone; (c) the main character feared making her own decision; (d) the main character was beginning to worry about her heart condition.

4. Chopin's story uses: (a) a first-person narrator; (b) an omniscient narrator; (c) a shifting narrator; (d) no narrator.

5. "The Story of an Hour" is: (a) a flashback; (b) written in chronological order; (c) a dream sequence; (d) written in achronological order, using "the stream of consciousness" technique.

ELMIRA

Richard Brautigan

I return as if in the dream of a young American duck hunting prince to Elmira and I am standing again on the bridge across the Long Tom River. It is always late December and the river is high and muddy and stirs dark leafless branches from its cold depths.

Sometimes it is raining on the bridge and I'm looking downstream to where the river flows into the lake. There is always a marshy field in my dream surrounded by an old black wooden fence and an ancient shed showing light through the walls and the roof.

Source: "Elmira" by Richard Brautigan, *Revenge of the Lawn,* 1971, p. 34.

The Reading Experience: Questions for Reading and Discussion

1. Many features of this excerpt from Brautigan's story are designed to produce an eerie, surrealistic effect. The words "as if" in the first sentence immediately obfuscates! Discuss the following questions in groups of three or four students and then share your responses with other groups in the class.

   (a) Is the speaker the first person narrator in the dream, or isn't he?

   (b) If he is in the dream, is he there *as if* he were a prince?

   (c) The river "stirs branches from its depths." Are the branches coming out of the water? How is this possible?

   (d) An ancient shed is "showing light through the walls and the roof." How does the writer see the light—from what point of view? Is he inside the shed looking out and up, or outside the shed looking in?

2. The passage is full of repetitions. Underline as many of these as you can find. Look for clue words, like "again" or "always" that signal the repetitions. Then predict what will happen next—will something new happen or will the basic story be repeated? Will he come back to the bridge again?

3. Consider the tense of each verb in this passage. This is an example of the *historical present tense,* which is used to tell something that has already happened, but continues to occur. The same tense is used in writing scripts for films and plays, when giving stage directions ("Richard enters"). Why? Why do you think Brautigan uses it here?

4. What does this passage tell you about the narrator? What can you infer about the type of person who is speaking (age, hobbies, gender, personality, etc.)?

5. Compare the content of this dream sequence with the story "Chains" found later in this chapter. How are they different?

The Writing Experience: Suggestions for Short Papers

1. Change all the verbs in "Elmira" to the past tense. Rewrite it as the first two paragraphs of a short essay. Compare and contrast the two versions in a short essay to explain the difference in meaning, and in effect. Which is more dramatic? Why?

2. Write a dream you have had or create a fictional dream, using the historical present tense.

3. Read and report on another story by Richard Brautigan. Suggested works include *Trout Fishing in America*, and *Revenge of the Lawn*. What makes his writing so unusual? What is his point of view? Does he follow a traditional plot line? Are his characters believable?

4. "Elmira" is a fragment, not a complete story. Using this dreamer as your main character, continue the story. Include another character or two; bring your story to a climax, follow with a denouement, and then quickly end. Aim for a surprise ending.

Recommended Films and eConnections

Spellbound – Dalí Dream Sequence. draniline. 25 July 2012. YouTube video.

Shutter Island Dream Sequence. allmightyganesh. 11 July 2010. YouTube video.

Spellbound. Dir. Alfred Hitchcock. Perf. Gregory Peck, Ingrid Bergman. United Artists, 1945. Film.

Un Chien Andalou. Dir. Luis Buñuel. Perf. Pierre Batcheff, Simone Mareuil. Les Grandes Films Classiques (France). 1929. Film.

Quiz

_____ 1. The Long Tom River is: (a) high and muddy; (b) cold and deep; (c) filled with dark leafless branches; (d) all of the above.

_____ 2. This story is told by: (a) an omniscient narrator; (b) a first-person narrator; (c) two narrators; (d) no narrator at all; the speaker is asleep.

_____ 3. This excerpt, "Elmira," from the novel *Revenge of the Lawn*, illustrates a literary technique known as: (a) the stream of consciousness; (b) a dream sequence; (c) a flashback: (d) a chronological narrative.

_____ 4. The ancient shed is: (a) inside the black fence; (b) outside the black fence; (c) filled with light; (d) not clearly explained.

_____ 5. "Elmira" uses: (a) confusing images; (b) the historical present tense; (c) repetitious actions; (d) all the above.

FAHRENHEIT 451

Ray Bradbury

One drop of rain. Clarisse. Another drop. Mildred. A third. The uncle. A fourth. The fire tonight. One, Clarisse. Two, Mildred. Three, uncle. Four, fire. One, Mildred, two, Clarisse. One, two, three, four, five, Clarisse, Mildred, uncle, fire, sleeping tablets, men, disposable tissue, coattails, blow, wad, flush. Clarisse, Mildred, uncle, fire, tablets, tissues, blow, wad, flush. One, two, three, one, two three! Rain. The storm. The uncle laughing. Thunder falling downstairs. The whole world pouring down. The fire gushing up in a volcano. All rushing on down around in a spouting roar and rivering stream toward morning.

"I don't know anything anymore," he said, and let a sleep-lozenge dissolve on his tongue.

Source: "Fahrenheit 451" by Ray Bradbury, 1953, p. 16.

The Reading Experience: Questions for Reading and Discussion

1. How has the "sleep lozenge" affected the speaker's thought patterns? Is the speaker asleep yet, or is he still awake? Explain your answer.

2. Describe the setting, in your own words. Where is the narrator? What time of day is it? What's the weather like?

3. How does Bradbury demonstrate the speaker's level of consciousness, in terms of writing technique? Name as many features of this passage as you can that differ from traditional grammatical and syntactic patterns. Which part of this selection does use traditional grammatical and syntactic patterns? Why do you think Bradbury combines the two types of writing?

4. What kind of day has the narrator had? What were some of the activities that took place? Who were some of the people that he met or thought about? What might be his relationship to these people?

5. Although this passage is taken out of context from a novel, you can still try to predict what will happen next. Using the "pieces of the puzzle," build a scenario which may foretell the next phase of the plot.

The Writing Experience: Suggestions for Short Papers[3]

1. Write a paragraph or two of your thoughts using this situation as a stimulus and background: You are sitting in a dentist's chair as he drills your teeth under novocaine. You have a drain and some cotton in your mouth; you cannot speak. Disregard in this section of your narrative the ironbound rule for avoiding sentence fragments, using Bradbury as your model. Write freely! As a final paragraph, write a completely grammatical conversation as you exit the dentist's office.

---

3. For internet help with these four writing suggestions, see "Writing Dialogue: The 5 Best Ways to make your Characters' Conversations Seem Real." Scott Francis. *Writer's Digest.* http://www.writersdigest.com 14 Feb. 2012.

2. Write a paragraph of your thoughts using this situation as a stimulus and background: You are sitting on a noisy train and watching the landscape move by. You see your face in the glass as well as the outside scenery; you hear the wheels and whistles of the train. You have just left someone you love. Disregard in this section of your narrative the ironbound rule for avoiding sentence fragments, using Bradbury as your model. Write freely! As a final paragraph, write a completely grammatical conversation as you hand the conductor your ticket.

3. Write a paragraph or two of your thoughts using this situation as a stimulus and background: You are lying on a sunny beach with your eyes closed, the noise of the gulls and the surf in the background. You may be listening to your favorite music. Disregard in this section of your narrative the ironbound rule for avoiding sentence fragments, using Bradbury as your model. Write freely! As a final paragraph, write a completely grammatical conversation with a friend who has just come out of the water.

4. Not every piece of writing that uses the stream of consciousness is ungrammatical. Many films (such as *Father of the Bride,* recommended below) use this technique, employing a "voice-over" to show the character's thoughts. As in writings that abolish traditional grammatical and syntactic patterns, no one else in the story/film knows what is being thought. That is the province of the thinker, and, of course, YOU, the reader or viewer! Write a paragraph or two of your thoughts, as you sit in class while the professor is giving a lecture.

Recommended Films and eConnections

Father of the Bride – Wedding. Blue9819. 24 July 2007. YouTube video.

How to Use Stream of Consciousness. K. M. Weiland. 16 Apr. 2013. YouTube video.

Fahrenheit 451. Dir. François Truffaut. Perf. Oskar Werner, Julie Christie. Universal. 1966. Film.

The Wonderful Ice Cream Suit. Dir. Stuart Gordon. Perf. Clifton Collins, Jr. Joe Montegna, Gregory Sierra, Edward James Olmos. Touchstone, 1998. Film.

Quiz

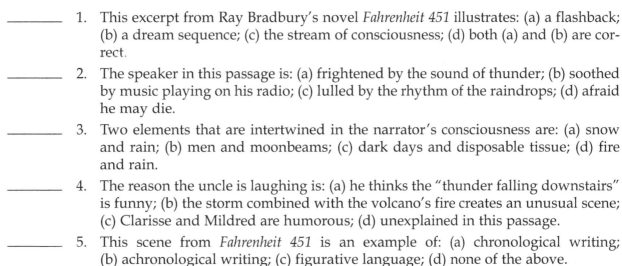

_____ 1. This excerpt from Ray Bradbury's novel *Fahrenheit 451* illustrates: (a) a flashback; (b) a dream sequence; (c) the stream of consciousness; (d) both (a) and (b) are correct.

_____ 2. The speaker in this passage is: (a) frightened by the sound of thunder; (b) soothed by music playing on his radio; (c) lulled by the rhythm of the raindrops; (d) afraid he may die.

_____ 3. Two elements that are intertwined in the narrator's consciousness are: (a) snow and rain; (b) men and moonbeams; (c) dark days and disposable tissue; (d) fire and rain.

_____ 4. The reason the uncle is laughing is: (a) he thinks the "thunder falling downstairs" is funny; (b) the storm combined with the volcano's fire creates an unusual scene; (c) Clarisse and Mildred are humorous; (d) unexplained in this passage.

_____ 5. This scene from *Fahrenheit 451* is an example of: (a) chronological writing; (b) achronological writing; (c) figurative language; (d) none of the above.

FACTUAL NARRATION

Narration is not always fiction. It is commonly used in correspondence, biography, autobiography, eye witness reporting, court testimony, speeches, historical writing, journalism, and the composition of logs, diaries, and personal journals. We use narration every day of our lives. When a member of our family asks us, "What did you do today?" Our answer takes the form of narration. Narration tells *what happened*, whether fiction or fact.

The Writer's Intention: To Report

While the writer's intention in writing literature or other forms of fictional narration is to entertain, when writers write factual happenings in a narrative way, their purpose is more often *to report*. Reportage strives to be interesting and emotionally engaging, but unlike fiction, its goal is not to surprise or shock the reader. The masks are off: tabloids that subscribe to sensationalism ("Princess Gives Birth Under Hypnosis"), or "yellow journalism," are simply substandard works of fiction. Biographies that sentimentalize their subjects also fall short of their goal. The best factual narratives "tell it like it is."

While journalism, biography, and autobiography are the chief forms of factual narration, there are many other types found in writing. Did any of your elementary school teachers write comments on the back of your report cards, explaining to your parents how you had progressed as a student that marking period? That tells the story of you, the student. Have you ever belonged to a club or organization? If you had a club secretary, he probably took "minutes." When these minutes are read at the next meeting, the club members are listening to a form of factual narration.

Characteristics of Factual Narration

Factual narration, like fictional narration, tells what happened. But unlike fiction, there is no plot. Instead we have merely a series of events. There is no cast of characters, just people—all of whom may be very important to the telling of the story. Therefore, we do not refer to the subject of a biography or the cover story of a newspaper or magazine as "the main character." Sometimes the person simply is referred to as "the subject"; in journalistic terms, he or she is "featured." Also, we do not refer to the writer as the narrator. He or she is simply the writer, the biographer, or the journalist.

The Five Ws and an H: Literal, Inferential, and Applied Processes

What is important in reading factual narration is to consider what has been called "the journalist's questions, the five Ws and an H": *Who*, *What*, *When*, *Where*, *Why*, and *How*. To write an article for the school or local paper, a magazine, or even an internet article, the reporter needs to include significant details that will answer each of these questions.

To read for the first four out of the five Ws—that is, learning who the article is about, finding out what happened, noting when it happened, and seeing where it happened is to read for the facts. These questions call for a *literal* answer. There is no guesswork involved. Reading literally means to take away facts from the material—to read *efferently*. (The left side of your brain is hard at work!) Noting what is said by the writer, quoting from the text, or carefully paraphrasing what the writer relates is to take the article literally. To read for the fifth W, *why*, is to try to read between the lines—to *infer*. This is more than guesswork; it involves your own logical interpretation. However, *inferential* reading does not necessarily yield the absolute truth. Here you are trying to figure out what the writer himself does not really know. To read for answers to the question *how?*—the sixth letter in this "formula" involves what we call *applied* reading. Here, you are going beyond the words in the article or book and applying the information either to your own life or to the society around you.

To read for answers to all five "Ws and an H," a reader needs to identify *causes* and *effects*. For example, these questions might be asked: What caused this event to happen? What will be its effect? What can it lead to? An informed reader needs to be able to perform actively all three levels of reading. The reader must be a participant in the material, as fully as the reporter, biographer, historian, or diarist was when s/he wrote it.

Point of View

Every writer, no matter how truthful and objective he or she may strive to be, has a *point of view*. The same events may be reported differently by various people who were there. Even the very same person may tell a story differently soon after it happened and years later. Generally, the closer an event is to its telling, the more accurate the telling will be. Memory is selective; we all tend to forget details that are not important to us. Over a period of time, without meaning to, we may emphasize certain items and minimize others, creating a distorted view of a past experience.

A reader of factual narration will want to do two things: judge the reputation of the writer, and judge the reputation of the publication. What has the writer written before? Does the writer sound logical? Does the newspaper or publishing company have a good reputation? The fact is that not all of what passes for factual narration is, in fact, factual!

Efferent and Aesthetic Reading: A Delicate Balance

Ultimately, the reading of journalism, biography, and autobiography requires your judgment. You need to follow the sequence of events, as you do with fiction, but you must decide on their validity before you become emotionally involved. The writer's artistic ability to craft a keen and sensitive piece of writing will encourage the aesthetic response. The process of taking information from the text to comprehend its logic, i.e., efferent reading, should precede that response. This delicate balance of the efferent and aesthetic stances when reading gruesome stories provides a bridge between the voice of narration, ordinarily a reflexively written mode of discourse, and the voice of exposition, an extensively written mode of discourse, which this textbook will examine in its next chapter.

CHAINS
1942

Fanny Tillman Trueherz and Sandra G. Brown

It is about four a.m. when again I wake in the familiar sweat. As always, it is raining. For the thousandth time, I dream that I cannot leave the truck.

That day, after a funeral, I followed the river, hoping to find a pace to hide. I took refuse with an old woman. Her one-room cabin was very comfortable. During the day I stayed in the back of the chicken coop. To see me one had to walk past chickens, droppings, feathers. The coop looked something like the inside of a paperweight. I always wanted to turn it upside down to see the play of the feathers going the other way.

At night I would come out and go into the house to eat and sleep. She made me a *paille** by the fireplace. I remember that her dog would bark if anyone passed nearby, and so I felt safe.

But my favorite time came when supper and the dishes were done. Madame Millot sat by the fireplace, sang me old songs, and told me stories about when she was young. I couldn't imagine her ever having been young. There was a lot of dirt in her wrinkles and nostrils and she had only two teeth left. When she laughed, the mouth looked like a cavern with one stalagmite, one stalactite. She looked so good old.

I loved it there. One morning all this ended.

When the old woman left with the dog to graze her goats on the hill, I heard a truck in the distance. Even as it came closer, I wasn't worried, for no one knew I was there.

Then I saw the gendarmes.* They jumped out of the truck, came straight to the coop and ordered me out. I came out covered with feathers and droppings. They dutifully kicked me and shouted, "On the truck!" There, steel-chained to its floor, were people covered with manure or straw that told where they had been hiding. They were very quiet. I too.

I contracted the sound of those chains, my chains.

When the truck took off and my chain rattled, I noticed that its lock had sprung open. I furtively wiggled to the side of the truck to hide it. The next stop was to be a farmhouse where they picked up two young boys and their grandmother. They stacked them in front of me. The truck was full.

Back to the village for delivery, but first a stop at the *auberge.*** A deep drink, a *salut.**** I quietly left the truck. All the eyes in the truck protected me, covering for me. The grandmother took her skirt, covered my chain, and sat on it.

I walked to the river to wash and reassemble my thoughts. The sound of a bus made me hurry to the main road. Clean, I looked like all the other girls in those parts.

The bus stopped. I got on and observed the driver. His way with the wheel was firm but gentle. His rapid glances from the windshield to rearview mirror showed a kind face. His lips were even and relaxed. I asked for a ticket to the next train stop.

When we arrived at the train stop, everyone got off.

I was the last to leave. I asked him point blank, "When do the gendarmes leave the platform?"

* the French police
** tavern
*** a toast literally meaning "health"—something like our toast, "Cheers!"

"After the trains leave. Two trains a day. One going to Limoges in the morning, and one coming back at night."

"And the bus? Is there a bus to Limoges?"

"No."

I just stood still. Very still. I could not hear myself breathe. I looked at the creases in his face, waiting for them to go Yes or No. I could taste the gasoline. In the distance I heard faint hammering.

"But I have to deliver coffins today. You may come."

His words ricocheted in my head.

"We will pass a railroad crossing. There's a short train stop there. No gendarmes. You can get on safely and buy your ticket on the train. I'm going to pick up the coffins now. I'll meet you at the church in an hour. Here, put my kerchief on your head." He removed it from his neck and gave it to me. "A bit sweaty," he apologized.

The church was quiet, cool, and safe. I wet my fingers, crossed myself, and kneeled at the altar. At that moment, more *fidels*[*] came for the Angelus. They prayed, some in silence, some in lament.

After the rites, everyone began to leave, lazily, lingeringly, as if to prolong the moment. So did I, but instead, I remained behind. When I saw the curé[**] stroll over to the parish house, I darted into the confessional and stayed there until I heard the sweet and gentle shriek of my bus.

As I closed the door behind me, the bus sputtered around to the back of the church. I went around the other way. There, I hopped on. The man insistently pointed his finger downward. I climbed into a fresh pine coffin with gleaming silver nails.

Sitting in the train later that day, I slid the kerchief off my hair and left it knotted around my neck.

I put on my raincoat and galoshes, take my dog, and I go into the garden. I unhook the swings. For in an astonishing moment of clearness, I realize that the sound of the swing's chains is the same as the sound on that truck.

[*] worshippers; literally, "the faithful"
[**] priest

The Reading Experience: Questions for Reading and Discussion

1. This story is a *flashback* – another form of achronological narrative – often used in a memoir. In this type of narrative, the story generally begins in the present, moves back to a past point in time, and returns to the present. This type of story is often referred to as a *framework* story. The beginning and ending (sections of the story that generally take place in the present) comprise the "frame." The recalled event that makes up the bulk of the story is the "picture" in the "frame." In "Chains," where is the girl at the beginning and end of the story? Do you think she is still in France?

2. The full meaning of the story depends upon the reader's knowledge of world history. What was happening in France in 1942? Does the date in the subtitle refer to the frame of the story or the flashback? How much time has passed between the framework of the story and the story itself? What triggers the flashback?

3. How old is the girl that "looked like all the girls in those parts"? Why is she not with "all the girls"? How is she different and alone, without friends and family? Clearly, her life is in jeopardy. Why does she have to hide?

4. Non-Jewish French citizens were threatened with death or imprisonment for hiding their Jewish neighbors. In addition, monetary rewards were given for turning Jews in to the authorities. What, then, motivates the bus driver to safe the girl? What are his values? Contrast him with the old woman. Do you think she turned the girl in? Explain the circumstances.

5. In retelling this true story from her life, Trueherz vividly remembers the detail of the sweaty kerchief. Can you guess why?

The Writing Experience: Suggestions for Short Papers

1. Use a sensory experience as the trigger for a memory from the past; it may be your own, or perhaps a memory that may actually belong to your parent or grandparent. If you choose not to use your own memory, interview someone and suggest a "trigger" to see what will result. Write the flashback using the frame of the present time of the interview, modeling your tale on the form used in "Chains." Suggestions for a trigger: (a) Listen to a "golden oldie"; (b) taste a food eaten in childhood; (c) take a deep breath of a perfume used by your mother or grandmother; (d) look at the internet to find examples of comic books you read as a child; (e) visit an old camping ground or school you knew well as a youngster.

2. Think of "Chains" as a screenplay. You are the director. Who would you cast in the roles? Where would the story be filmed, on location or in a studio? What sort of costumes would the cast wear? Would any scenes be omitted or changed? What scene is the climax of your film? How would your film end? Add other details as you see fit.

3. Research the history of the WWII era, in particular, France in the year 1942. Write or present orally a short report that explains the events behind the story.

4. Explain your reading process using the PBRI formula. What did you predict the story would be about at the beginning? How did you build its meaning? What did you think was happening when the narrator tells you that she spent her days in a chicken coop? What was your first impression of the old woman? Did any part of the story surprise you? Did you anticipate the ending? Review each of these elements, as applicable to a true story (remember, the terms plot, setting, characters and narrator do *not* apply): the sequence of events, the different settings, the people in the story, and the writer, as the teller of a true personal experience. Now that you have read it fully, can you interpret the events?

Recommended Films and eConnections

France Remembers WWII Jewish Deportation. AFP. 16 July 2012. 17 July 2012. YouTube video.

Jewish Children in France during Holocaust: Survivors Tell Stories. JewishNewsOne. 3 July 2012. YouTube video.

La Rafle (*The Roundup*). Dir. Rose Bosch. Perf. Jean Reno, Mèlanie Laurent, Gad Elmaleh. Gaumont Film Company. 2010. Film.

Miracle at Moreaux. Dir. Paul Shapiro. Perf. Loretta Swit, Genviève Appleton, Milan Cheylov. Atlantis Films. TV Movie. 1986. TV Movie.

Quiz

_____ 1. This story exemplifies: (a) a stream of consciousness story; (b) a dream sequence; (c) a strictly chronological story; (d) a flashback story.

_____ 2. The main character is: (a) the bus driver; (b) the old woman; (c) the narrator; (d) the gendarmes.

_____ 3. The gendarmes found the girl because: (a) the dog led them to the chicken coop; (b) Madame Millot may have informed them; (c) they followed her trail from the river; (d) a passerby notified them to collect the reward.

_____ 4. The coffin: (a) suffocates the girl; (b) silences the girl; (c) saves the girl; (d) symbolizes death.

_____ 5. To appreciate this story fully: (a) readers should know about the history of the era; (b) readers should put themselves into the story, living through the girl's experience; (c) closely follow the achronology of the story to understand its sequence; (d) all of the above.

MAO'S LAST DANCER

Li Cunxin

. . . Next morning we started at eight o'clock. Teacher Song called out our names one by one from her roll book and we all obediently answered, *"Ze!"* Then she picked out the boys and mixed us in with the girls, which I thought was cruel, because I had chosen a spot at the back with two of my best friends. Now I was sandwiched between two girls I didn't even know.

Teacher Song handed out our textbooks. "Students. Welcome to your first official lesson." She paused. "Do you know who this person is?" She pointed to Mao's picture on the wall.

"Chairman Mao, Chairman Mao!" we all shouted excitedly.

"Yes, our beloved Chairman Mao. Before we start our first class each day, we will bow to Chairman Mao in all sincerity. We should wish him a long long life, because we wouldn't be here if it wasn't for him. He is our savior, our sun, our moon. Without him we'd still be in a dark world of suffering. We will also wish his successor, our second most important leader, our Vice Chairman Lin Biao, good health, forever good health. Now, let's all get up and bow to Chairman Mao with your heart full of love and appreciation!"

We all stood up, took our hats off, bowed to Mao's picture and shouted, "Long, long live Chairman Mao! Vice Chairman Lin, good health, forever good health!"

"Before you sit down," Teacher Song continued, "we need to perform one more school rule: I'll say, 'Good morning, students,' to you and you will say, 'Good morning, Teacher,' in reply. Now, let's have a practice. Good morning students!"

"Good morning, Teacher!" we replied in unison.

"Good! Now sit down." She smiled. "Raise your hand if you have Chairman Mao's Red Book."

Most of us raised our hands.

From "Chairman Mao's Classroom," by Li Cunxin, *Mao's Last Dancer,* pp. 84–86. © 2004 by Qingdao Investments Pty Ltd. Used by permission of G. P. Putnam's Sons, a division of Penguin Group USA, LLC, and by Penguin Group (Australia).

"Those who don't have one, please ask your parent to buy you one from town. I want you to have them tomorrow. This is very important. We should follow Vice Chairman Lin's example and never go anywhere without Chairman Mao's Red Book. The Red Book will give us guidance in our lives. Without it we will be lost souls." We placed our Red Books on the left-hand side of our workbenches, as instructed.

"I'll be your teacher for both Chinese and math," Teacher Song continued. "You will learn how to read and write. Raise your hand if you can already read or write."

I looked around. Very few students raised their hands: mostly girls, and I was relieved. I, for one, couldn't recognize a single word in my textbook.

"Good, we have a few smart kids here. Now, please open the first page of your textbook," Teacher Song instructed.

A big colored picture of Chairman Mao stared out at me, occupying half the page, with shooting stars surrounding his face, as though Mao's round head was the sun. The bottom half of the page had words on it, which just looked like a field of messy grass to me. Whoever invented them must have been a peasant, I thought.

"Can anyone read the words on this page?" the teacher asked. The same girls raised their hands again.

"What does the first line mean?" Teacher Song asked the girl sitting to my right.

"Long, long live Chairman Mao!" replied the girl in a proud voice.

"Good, very good!" Teacher Song paused. She glanced over the class. "Yes, we want to wish Chairman Mao a long long life, because our great leader saved us. I'm sure your parents have told you many stories about the cruel life they lived under Chiang Kaishek's Guomindang regime. They were cold, dark days indeed. That government only cared for the rich. Children like you couldn't even dream of sitting here, but Chairman Mao made it possible for everyone in China to have this privilege. Today, I'll teach you how to write 'Long, long live Chairman Mao, I love Chairman Mao, you love Chairman Mao, we all love Chairman Mao.' I'll now write them on the blackboard. Pay special attention to the sequence of the strokes." She turned to the blackboard and wrote several lines with furious pace.

I was stunned. I didn't get the sequence of strokes at all! I turned to look at one of my friends. He just drew a circle around his neck with his right hand and pulled upward, his eyes rolling and tongue hanging out, as though he were being hanged.

"Okay, now I want you to repeat each phrase after me." The teacher pointed to the first line of words with her yard-long stick. "Long, long live chairman Mao," she read.

"Long, long live Chairman Mao!" we repeated.

"I love Chairman Mao!" she read.

"I love Chairman Mao!" we replied.

We repeated the phrases again and again until we had memorized them for life.

The Reading Experience: Questions for Reading and Discussion

Without knowing anything about Li Cunxin's background, try to answer the following questions to the best of your ability.

1. What is Li Cunxin's image of himself as a student? How does he feel about not being able to read? Does this class encourage self-expression, or strive toward building a positive self-image? What are the goals of this class?

2. Why do you think Teacher Song conducts class in this manner? By your standards, is she a good teacher? What do you think of her methods? Does she actually teach the children to read and write?

3. What do you think the learning objective of this lesson may be? What are the students expected to learn, and why? Do you think there will be any behavioral issues in this class? Why or why not?

   If education is designed to mold children into responsible adults, what sort of behavior will this school produce in these children? What sort of knowledge base will these students acquire? Do you think they will become lifelong readers and writers?

4. What is the effect of memorizing Mao's Little Red Book? Do the children appear to have any other textbooks? Why does the class not question Teacher Song? What is the role of memorization in learning? Did you have to memorize any poems or songs in school?

5. Knowing that Cunxin is writing his autobiography in English, what can you predict may happen to him? Use the title as a clue to help you guess the outcome. (Do this before reading further!)

On this first day that Li Cunxin attended school, he was seven years old. Second to the youngest of seven sons, Cunxin along with his brothers worked on the family plot of land, helping his peasant father and mother earn a meager living. Like most of the other peasants in China at that time, his parents could not read or write; indeed, they barely had enough to eat. In a 2010 interview with Julie Bloom for Arts Beat, *Cunxin tells of the 35–38 million Chinese who died of starvation in the four years prior to his birth in 1961. Under these conditions, he felt almost blessed to be able to attend the school portrayed in this excerpt. Four years later Cunxin was randomly chosen to attend ballet school. As an exchange student he was sent to the United States, where he defected and became one of the principal dancers in the United States, later moving to Australia where he was named Artistic Director of the Queensland Ballet.*

The Writing Experience: Suggestions for Short Papers

1. Write a short 250–500 word personal essay about your first recollection of school. Include your classmates, the first teacher you ever had, the classroom itself, and the experience of leaving home.

2. Research the history of the era of Mao Zedong's long reign of power, 1949–1976, beginning with his founding of The People's Republic of China. Include his most well-known programs, especially the Great Leap Forward. Explain the origin and use of his famous Little Red Book. Explain as well how knowing this information may have changed the way you read this selection.

3. Watch a video of the postmodern opera *Nixon in China*, by the American composer John Adams, and discuss how the policies of Mao Zedong are portrayed not only in its vocal music, but in terms of dance, as well, which are spectacularly choreographed by Mark Morris. (Several scenes may be found on YouTube. One is recommended below.)

4. Conduct an interview about early childhood education with someone from another country. Find out how his or her school was run, what materials were taught, the size of classes, and the general teaching strategies. Include any personal stories your interviewee is willing to share.

Recommended Films and eConnections

"Flesh Rebels" from Nixon in China. MetropolitanOpera. 1 Feb 2011. YouTube video.

Andie Lovegrove Interviews Li Cunxin. Darryllovegrove1. 16 July 2012. YouTube video.

Mao's Last Dancer. Dir. Bruce Beresford. Perf. Chi Cao, Bruce Greenwood, Kyle MacLachlan, Joan Chen. Samuel Goldwyn Films. 2009. Film.

To Live. Dir. Zhang Yimou. Perf. Ge You, Gong Li, Niu Ben. Shanghai Film Studio and ERA International. (China) 1994.

Quiz

_____ 1. The excerpt from Mao's Last Dancer is: (a) a factual narrative; (b) an autobiography; (c) written subjectively in the first person; (d) all of the above.

_____ 2. The scene above takes place: (a) in a Hollywood film studio; (b) in a village classroom in China; (c) in Cunxin's dream sequence; (d) none of the above.

_____ 3. The story reveals that the boy: (a) has never been to school; (b) does not know how to read or write; (c) obediently accepts whatever Teacher Song dictates, even though he thinks at first that she is cruel; (d) all of the above.

_____ 4. The repetition of the phrases "Long long live Chairman Mao" and the insistence that students repeat "I love Chairman Mao" indicate that: (a) Teacher Song loves Chairman Mao; (b) Teacher Song is obediently doing her job; (c) the children are being brainwashed; (d) both (b) and (c) are correct.

_____ 5. To appreciate this story fully: (a) readers should know about the history of the era in China; (b) readers should put themselves into the story, living through the boy's experience and building the meaning as they move through the story; (c) interpret the story afterward to understand its significance in not only the author's life, but to compare it with the reader's own experience; (d) all of the above.

HOW A NEW ENGLAND LEGEND CAME TO BE

Alan Ferguson

Ice sheathed the inside of the dory and had to be broken up and pitched overboard. A hard routine developed: pound ice, bail, watch the stealthy seas, row, row, row.

Welch did his part right up to his last gasp, and brave men have long paid tribute of sorrow to this humble hero. All the hardships of those sub-Arctic waters could not subdue his manhood. He fought to the very last, but the combination of evil things was just too much to bear. He slowly froze to death at his post of duty. He died on the third night and lay, an ice-shrouded passenger, on the dory's bottom. Thereafter, Blackburn fought alone.

By this time, he was conscious that his feet were frozen and that his utmost efforts to keep life in his stiffening hands were unavailing. Then, with a new and desperate urgency, death seemed to tap him on the shoulder. If a man could not close his hands around his oar-handles, how could he row?

His solution of this problem was as characteristic as it was direct. Here is what he said later about this phase of his martyrdom.

"My fingers are getting whiter and stiffer. I think too late now to stop 'em freezing. I knew that if my fingers froze straight and stiff I couldn't keep on rowing after they froze. So I made up my mind there was nothing else to do. If my fingers were bound to freeze, I'd make 'em freeze in such a shape as to be of some use afterwards.

"So I curled 'em around the handles of the oars while they wa'nt too stiff and I sat there without moving while they froze around the handles of the oars."

And so he rowed—hands frozen, feet frozen, no sleep, no food, no water, and with a dead man as his silent passenger.

He finally raised the Newfoundland coast and landed in a tiny inlet.

Howard Blackburn's saga occurred in the winter of 1883 but Blackburn, without hands, lived many years into this century—running a restaurant in Gloucester, Massachusetts, crossing the Atlantic several times single-handedly (voluntarily), and generally enjoying his status as a New England legend.

The Reading Experience: Questions for Reading and Discussion

1. This factual narrative reports the harrowing tale of a stranded fisherman, but does not fully observe the 5 Ws and an H—the journalist's questions. *Who* were Welch and Blackburn? All we have are their surnames. The reader does know what happened, but *how? How* did they get there? *Why* were Welch and Blackburn there? *What* were they doing? *Where* exactly in the "Arctic waters" were these men? The article itself does not explain *when* this took place, either; we need to read the information Ferguson provides afterward, in an endnote. Is this good reporting? Probably not, but the mysterious way in which this is told makes a good, suspenseful story. How do you, the reader, envision/ explain this event? Can you "fill in the blanks"? Do you want to discuss various interpretations with other students? Do you think everyone will interpret this story in the same way?

2. Note the transcription of Blackburn's speech. We can perhaps hear with our "inner ear" the New England inflections of his dialect based upon the non-standard spelling and punctuation transcribed on the printed page. Transpose the following back into standard spelling: "I curled 'em around the handles of the oars while they wan't too stiff..." How does dialect make the story more authentic? Can you name other stories that use dialect?

3. Predict what happened to Blackburn after he landed "in a tiny inlet" in Newfoundland. We know from Ferguson's note that he later opened a restaurant. But what happened immediately after his five-day trauma without food, water, or sleep? Who saved him? Where did he go when he got out of the boat?

4. From what point of view is this story told? Does the writer demonstrate emotion when retelling the tale? Do you, as a reader, detect feelings of sympathy, awe, shock, or disgust? Explain.

5. Did you read this true story efferently (primarily for its informational content), aesthetically (with emotion), or a combination of the two? Explain. How would the story have been presented if it were deliberately intended to evoke shock or disgust? What details could have been added? How would the material have been presented if it were intended as a case study, a cautionary tale giving advice in a travel guidebook, or an objective medical description of extreme frostbite?

The Writing Experience: Suggestions for Short Papers

1. Write a short paper on the pronunciation of words in various dialects, perhaps using examples from Mark Twain's *Huckleberry Finn*, Zora Neale Hurston's *Their Eyes Were Watching God*, or any other piece with which you are familiar. Use specific examples of dialect from the work you choose, and then "translate" them into standard English. Explain how the use of dialect makes the work seem more authentic.

2. Regional dialect can include not only differences in pronunciation, but entirely different words for common objects. Use some of these as starters: "bag" / "sack"; "U-turn" / "jughandle"; "knee-baby" / "youngest in the family." Prepare a list of approximately ten terms or expressions that vary from one area of the United States to another. Why do you think there is such variation?

3. Write two paragraphs that respond to questions in #5 above in this manner:

   ¶ 1: How would the story have been presented if it were deliberately intended to evoke shock or disgust? What details could have been added?

   ¶ 2: How would the material have been presented if it were intended as a cautionary tale giving advice in a travel guidebook *or* an objective medical description of extreme frostbite? (Choose one.)

4. Have you ever done anything adventurous? Adventure stories are a *genre* (a particular style or topic that follows a format with features in common, like the Western, the horror story, etc.) that involves risk-taking and survival. Adventure stories generally end on a happy note. Write a short story detailing your experiences—the risk you faced, and how you coped with it. End by answering this question, generally used as part of *the adventure genre*: if you had known ahead of time how perilous your adventure would be, what would you have done differently?

Recommended Films and eConnections

Cheating Death: 15 Incredible Survival Stories—Part 12. P3p3fr3sh. 2 Jul. 2009. YouTube video.

Cheating Death: 15 Incredible Survival Stories—Part 5. P3p3fr3sh. 2 Jul. 2009. YouTube video.

127 Hours. Dir. Danny Boyle. Perf. James Franco, Amber Tamblyn, Kate Mara. Fox Searchlight Pictures, 2010. Film.

Cast Away. Dir. Robert Zemeckis. Perf. Tom Hanks, Helen Hunt. 20th Century Fox and DreamWorks. 2000. Film.

DEATH IN THE ORCHARD

Edward Brown

The bodies, both shot through the head, were found in an orchard across the river from New Brunswick by a couple of youngsters out looking for mushrooms. The man was identified as the Reverend Edward W. Hall, Rector of the largest church in New Brunswick. The woman's body was that of Mrs. Eleanor Mills, a member of the church who sang in the choir and often assisted the minister in his visits to the sick and the poor. But now they were both dead, lying side by side in a lonely orchard. It was early fall, 1922.

The clues were few, and the police were baffled. There was no weapon found with the bodies, although a number of people said they heard cries and shots coming from the orchard the night before. What the police did find was a litter of paper around the bodies, including some notes written by Mrs. Mills which seemed to show that the choir singer was in love with the minister.

They raised a very difficult and delicate question. Perhaps Mrs. Hall, the minister's wife, or Mr. Mills, the choir singer's husband, had a motive for the murder? The police questioned them both, but found no evidence to support that theory, or any other theory. In fact, after a while, there weren't any more theories and puzzled police went down one blind alley after another in the case.

The unsolved murders became a national sensation. Even *The New York Times*, probably the most important newspaper in the country, got into the act. It suggested that powerful politicians and wealthy community leaders were deliberately covering up evidence in the crime.

Then, two months after the killings, Clifton Hayes, 18, was arrested and charged with the crime on the evidence of a man named Raymond Schneider. Schneider said that Hayes had confessed to him that he had mistaken the two victims for another couple—his girlfriend and someone else—and had killed them in a jealous rage.

But Schneider fell apart under police questioning and soon admitted he'd made up the whole story. He got two years in prison for perjury as a result.

Four years later, something else: Arthur S. Reihl claimed that when his wife had been a maid at the Hall home, she had been paid off to stay quiet about "what she knew about the killing."

She denied this, and police were again at a dead end in the Hall/Mills murder case.

Then, in 1926, Mrs. Hall was finally arrested and charged with the murder of her husband and Mrs. Mills. But nothing came of this, and the case remained open.

That was over half a century ago.* The mystery of the two bodies in the orchard is still unsolved. Who did it? A jealous wife or husband? A hired killer? Was the fate of these two simply the result of an unlucky meeting with an armed maniac who had murder on his mind?

Nobody knows, except the killer, if he's still around a lifetime later. He—or she—got away with it.

*As this book goes to press, make that 88 years ago!

The Reading Experience: Questions for Reading and Discussion

1. The first paragraph tells the reader who, what, when, where, and how. The unanswered question is: **Why**? Provide the answers to four of the Ws and an H. Are the levels of these questions literal, inferential, or applied?

2. Why did the unsolved murders become a "national sensation"? Does the selection above provide any real reasons?

3. Who were Raymond Schneider and Arthur S. Reihl? What are their roles—and Reihl's wife's role—in the story? Are their positions credible? Why or why not?

4. Why were the police unable to solve the mystery of the murders? What evidence were they able to examine? Why do you think the crime is still an unsolved mystery?

5. Who do you think did it? Provide reasons for your theory.

The Writing Experience: Suggestions for Short Papers

1. Sleuth it yourself! After the class discussion, respond in a short, but substantive one- or two-page essay to question #5 above. Include quotations from "Death in the Orchard" as well as any class notes taken in your journal. Additional research is not necessary for this paper, but if you wish to include the opinions of students in this class, obtain their permission to use their names.

2. Write a short research paper on the Hall-Mills murder. Using resources from your college and local libraries as well as the internet, find primary sources—essentially newspaper articles and photographs—from 1922 to 1926 that discuss the crime. Note the points of view of the reportage. Consider how the information you find adds to Edward Brown's version of the event. Do your articles use the 5Ws and an H, the "journalist's questions"?

3. The police found "a litter of paper around the bodies, including some notes written by Mrs. Mills which seemed to show that the choir singer was in love with the minister" (Brown). Write your version of these notes, expressing your ideas about what they contained.

4. The Hall-Mills criminal investigation was deeply flawed. Cite violations pertaining to the collection of evidence that would not be permitted today. What methods are now used in gathering evidence at a crime scene that were not available in 1922? (Compare the three videos recommended below.) How would witnesses be questioned? Would the trial proceed differently? How would it be publicized?

Recommended Films and eConnections

FBI: You Can't Get Away With It—1936 Educational Documentary. Ella73TV2. 6 Oct. 2012. YouTube video.

What are the techniques used to gather crime scene evidence? Reelgirlsmedia. 10 May 2007. YouTube video.

Crime Scene Forensics. S010E01. Hertfordshire and Bedfordshire Police Scene of Crime Officers. PSNLounge. 4 May 2013. YouTube video.

Dial M for Murder. Dir. Alfred Hitchcock. Perf. Grace Kelly, Ray Milland, Robert Cummings. Warner Brothers. 1954. Film.

Quiz

_____ 1. Eleanor Mills: (a) was not a member of the church; (b) sang in the choir; (c) did not sing in the choir; (d) killed the Reverend Hall.

_____ 2. The newspaper which suggested that powerful politicians and wealthy community leaders were involved was: (a) *The Daily News*; (b) *The Enquirer*; (c) *The Washington Post*; (d) *The New York Times.*

_____ 3. Clifton Hayes: (a) was a reporter for the newspaper; (b) was the chief detective for the New Brunswick police department; (c) was a minister in a neighboring church; (d) was arrested and charged with the killings.

_____ 4. In this story, the murderer: (a) was Clifton Hayes; (b) was sentenced to 50 years in prison; (c) was a maniacal killer; (d) apparently got away with the crime.

_____ 5. In 1926, Mrs. Hall: (a) was also murdered; (b) was arrested and charged with the murders; (c) died a natural death; (d) was convicted of arson.

COLLABORATION SENSATION: THREE WRITERS WRITING/THREE READERS READING: A PARTNER PROJECT IN PLOT AND POINT OF VIEW

Part I: The Writing

- Select a magazine photo of a person and share it with two others.

- Each student will write five sentences.

- Student "A" will write as the character in the photo. "A" will explain why s/he had to do something shocking or sensational in the recent past or has to do something in the present; e.g., "I had to get away fast!"

- Student "B" will write as "A's" mother, father, child, lover, or best friend. "B" will explain "A" by providing some details about his/her past, childhood, present qualities, or something that would provide a personal anecdote about "A"; e.g., "He was such a good boy."

- Student "C" will write as the omniscient narrator, talking about "A" as from a distance, in the future. "C" may reflect town gossip and provide hindsight needed to make a point about what "A" did, or perhaps what "B" says about "A"; e.g., "Little did the town of Smithville know at that time that . . ."

- When you have finished the writing, proceed to Part II.

This exercise derives from a poem by Bruce Andrews, "Love Song No. 23" in *None of the Above: New Poets of the USA*, Michael Lally, ed. Trumansburg, New York: The Crossing Press, 1976.

From "Three Writers Writing—Three Readers Reading" by Sandra Brown, *Ideas Plus, Book Eight.* Copyright © 1990. Reprinted by permission of the National Council of Teachers of English (NCTE), Urbana, IL.

Part II: The Reading

- This reading is for voices "A," "B," and "C." The readers will stand or sit in a triangle, thus:

A

B   C

- The reading will take about three to five minutes.
- The readers may say their five phrases any time during this period.
- Readers may read consecutively, all together, backward, or may repeat any line or lines they choose.
- Readers may whisper, sing, or shout their lines.
- The group may stop before time is up, as it chooses.
- Groups may show others what they have done or read only for themselves.
- After class, include in your triple-entry journal, the Reflection Section (Part 3), a freely written appraisal of what you experienced while writing and reading, and afterward. How did the experiences affect the members of your group?

CHAPTER 4

EXPOSITORY VOICES

The Third Message of Intent—What Usually Happens?

THE WRITER'S INTENTION TO TEACH

Are you a student who has chosen to major in business, mathematics, or biological science? You may have read Chapter 2 in this book and said to yourself, "Hey, this is for English majors!" Your reaction can be the result of the way your education was constructed for you. Most schools label education "the arts and the sciences," as if they were the only two, and quite separate, ways of knowing about the world.

Do we perceive the universe through only two frameworks? Or are there many? And if multiple frameworks exist, is each one mutually exclusive to an individual adult learner? That is, once you have decided upon your major, can it be possible that all other ways of knowing become closed to you?

All Ways of Knowing Are Open to You

The entire spectrum of knowledge about the world remains accessible to everyone. In other words, the world is yours! The last chapter is designed not for English majors, but especially for "non-English" majors to ease access to different forms of narrative writing, uncommon in science and technology textbooks. However, English majors of course may benefit from newly examining in this course what many have been learned in others!

Expository Writing

This chapter, on the other hand, moves the reader into an entirely different cognitive process. Here, the goal is to ease access to *exposition* – the preferred form of writing used for business, math, history, and science textbooks. Essays, reports, research papers, and nationally given tests of knowledge, particularly reading tests, all use exposition. Students who score highly on standardized tests can read literal information—exposition—very well. Most college writing is expository. Its purpose is to inform or teach, as well as to demonstrate what you know. Basic writing courses focus almost exclusively on expository writing. This chapter is not designed exclusively for majors in the sciences and social sciences, who generally find expository writing more comfortable. Quite the opposite! If you prefer creative writing and have found exposition daunting, this chapter should give you a new perspective on how it's done.

Expository Reading

While the purpose of expository *writing* is to demonstrate what you have learned, to inform or to teach someone else what you know, the purpose of expository *reading* is to learn. If you can't read exposition effectively, you just can't be a successful college student. Right now, that's your job. This chapter intends to help students who prefer reflexive writing and aesthetic reading to be successful extensive writers and efferent readers. Of course, the material presented on the following pages will improve the chances of academic success — for everyone!

The Third Voice of Discourse

Exposition is the third most difficult voice of discourse. Why? Because it is often combined with description, the simplest mode, and narration, second in the line of complexity. Exposition may include spatial description that uses one or more of your senses, chronological description (time order), to crystallize the information and/or an illustrative anecdote to introduce or highlight the information. This is serious, not recreational writing and reading. To write it well, you need to know its patterns and you need a plan to carry them out. To read it well, you need to recognize its patterns, and to plan to read these in a special way. However, as you may know from your life experiences with following patterns, while the process may be difficult at first, once you've got it down pat, you'll never forget it, and it will become second nature to you.

Exposition and the Thesis Statement

Exposition intends to *expose* information in a piece of writing we call an *essay*. To do so clearly, the essay must state what it will say, generally, near the beginning. However, obviously, the essay (IT) does not write itself. The IT does not speak, the writer (ME) speaks. The writer creates IT, the essay. All writers (like ME) will have a reason, or purpose for writing. The writer must inform the reader (YOU) *what* he or she is writing about, and suggest *why*. This statement of purpose is called a *thesis statement*.

Practice writing a few thesis statements. Begin very plainly. For example, "The purpose of this essay is to discuss my favorite Italian dishes, chicken Parmesan, ravioli, and pizza. I always have a hard time choosing number one." In the essay to come, one paragraph will be devoted to chicken Parmesan, the next to ravioli, and the next to pizza. The last paragraph may conclude which one is the favorite. Try your own topic. Fill in this blank:

"The purpose of the present essay is to explain _the topic_ because _(reason for writing)_ ."

For a more sophisticated sentence, leave out the first nine words. Just begin with a sentence about the topic. Then add your *focus*, the direction your topic will take. Practice writing a few in this form:

> "(The topic) may _(do what?)_ , bringing (joy/relief/pain/frustration/new knowledge)
> to the (reader/millions/the world)."

The thesis statement usually appears somewhere near the beginning of the essay, perhaps toward the end of the first paragraph or at the beginning of the second paragraph. Note the clarity of this thesis statement in the opening paragraph from Janet Emig's essay "Hand, Eye, Brain: Some 'Basics' in the Writing Process:"

> The purpose of this chapter is to speculate about the role or roles each [the hand, the eye and the brain] may play in the writing process and to suggest hypotheses, with appropriate methodologies, to assess their contributions, as well as to determine the likely forms orchestration and interplay may take.[1]

Can you guess how the essay to follow will be written? If you said that there will be one internal paragraph on the hand, one on the eye, and one on the brain, you would be right!

Exposition Generalizes

Basically, all forms of exposition are organized through some form of *classification*. When we create classifications, we use general ideas that our life experiences form for us. We tend to see common features. That is how infants begin to learn about the world. For example, as children, we see that all dogs bark and have four legs. Later, we call the various breeds "canines" and put them into classes. We can write about canines, using a general statement, the *thesis statement*, as part of our introduction. The thesis statement is followed in the essay by specific details — perhaps the various breeds of canines. The specific details, or *support statements*, which form the body or internal paragraphs of the essay, must relate to the topic stated in the *thesis statement*.

Writing an essay requires a plan designed around a focus, or central issue. No unrelated issues or examples belong. If you are discussing dogs, you can't add something about cats, or kings, or hairbrushes.

The thesis and related support statements finally come to a *conclusion*. In a successful, well-constructed essay, the thesis statement, taken together with the conclusion, provides the *main idea* of the essay.

Exposition, then, generalizes and tells us "what happens when …," emphasizing what generally or usually happens. To do this, it "speaks" in patterns. These are some of the most common patterns. Sometimes an essay will combine more than one, but all the patterns always focus on the chosen topic.

Writing and Reading Comparison and Contrast

The most familiar pattern of all is *comparison and contrast* (C/C). Comparison means looking at how two things are the same. Contrast means looking at how two things are different. Sometimes, however, they are used to achieve the same purpose. Note the following two sentences. Both could be a thesis statement. Which meaning is clearer to you?

- In comparison with the Japanese and Germans, the U.S. work force suffers from substandard math ability.
- In contrast to the Japanese and Germans, the U.S. work force suffers from substandard math ability.

Often, the words *comparison* and *contrast* are not used, but the comparison is stated. For example:

- Physical and mental health are both necessary for championship in athletics.

---

1. Published in *Research on Composing: Points of Departure*, ed. Charles R. Cooper and Lee Odell. NCTE, 1978.

Try writing several comparison/contrast thesis statements. Use countries, foods, brands of jeans, ice cream flavors, academic subjects, sports, or movies.

Writing and Reading Cause and Effect

The *cause and effect* pattern is used often in science and social science textbooks. These may be arranged in two ways: either beginning with various causes and ending with the effect (conditions that can lead to pneumonia, global warming, or union strikes) or beginning with the effect and looking back at the causes (a tsunami, overcrowding in the cities, internet invasion of privacy). Note the following:

- A rabbit's foot may not improve luck on an exam, but it can calm test anxiety.
- Fluorescent ink was created over 80 years ago by two boys, Bob and Joe Switzer, playing with paint and supplies from their father's pharmacy.

Try writing several cause and effect thesis statements. Use diet, exercise, sleep, cell phones, politics, education, smoking, or good parenting.

Writing and Reading Definition and Example

Exposition can begin with a *definition* and then continue by explaining that definition with clear *examples*. Unabridged dictionaries and encyclopedias are the primary vehicles for this pattern, but it may be found anywhere. Consider these examples, taken from a magazine and a textbook:

- Entertainment in the small villages of India consists of age-old amusements such as dancing bears, snake charmers, and high wire artists and contortionists.
- An essay is one example of expository writing.

Try writing a few definitions and example thesis statements. Use patriotism, holidays, love, jealousy, intelligence, faith, birds, reptiles, war, peace, miracles, justice.

Writing and Reading Analysis

Analysis consists of breaking a whole into parts. When using analysis, a writer looks at all the distinctive qualities that make up the physical or mental state of a living creature; all the components of an organic or man-made object; or all the sections of some type of construction, whether it be an idea, concept, theory, or physical building. All academic topics—indeed, all things on earth—can be analyzed. Consider the following sentences from pharmaceutical and literary texts:

- Aspirin has several beneficial qualities: it relives pain; it is nonsteroidal; it is anti-inflammatory; and it does not produce physical dependence.
- Upon close inspection, the writings of William Shakespeare reveal a combination of characteristics that can be attributed to no other writer.

Try writing several statements using the analysis pattern in your thesis statement. For example, use as topics the following: grades of gasoline; pure blue-white diamonds; schizophrenia; the *Harry Potter* series; political leadership; a mathematical equation.

Writing and Reading Sequence or Chronology

Sequence in exposition is often confused with chronological description. However, like all other forms of expository writing, essays using sequence contain a thesis statement and a conclusion. Simple chronological description needs neither, as we may see in a horoscope chart, a table of contents, or a bus schedule. Sequential exposition is most commonly used in history texts, but may be found in the many bios posted on the Web, or in discussing the origin of a product or a social custom. Sequence (aka the chronology pattern) may be shown in the following fuller examples:

- The evolution of Egyptian art is a fascinating study. Akhenaten (c. 1373–1362 BCE) was the first Egyptian monarch to encourage artists to depict scenes from nature. Unfortunately, much of their work was destroyed after his death. Archaeologists found the fragments utilized years later to build a temple for Ramses II (c. 1304–1237 BCE).
- As a Hungarian peasant boy, my father heard stories about America from his Uncle Morris, who had settled in New Brunswick, New Jersey. The wondrous stories and presents his uncle brought for the whole family on infrequent, glorified visits seem in retrospect to be an emblem of the tremendous immigration movement from Eastern Europe that occurred around the turn of the century. My father was one of millions who sought a better life.

Try writing a few thesis statements using the sequence or chronology pattern. Use the evolution of the Equal Rights Amendment; the handshake; weddings; your own childhood, adolescence, and maturity; the "invention" of money; or the history of product development, like cleats, the electric guitar, meat thermometers, turnstiles, Band Aids, or frozen waffles; how you write an essay.

You can see how each topic, whether it be math ability, entertainment in India, test anxiety, Shakespeare's work, or immigration, is *generalized* through its expository pattern.

The following essay explains, using two expository patterns, *analysis* and *sequence*, an efficient and effective way to find *the main idea* in a piece of writing.

HOW TO ASSAY AN ESSAY

Carmen Collins

An *assay* is a test made on a metal to analyze its composition and measure or extract its valuable metallic content. As readers, we examine a piece of writing in much the same manner as a metallurgist assays a metal. We analyze an essay for its thesis, concluding statement, and related ideas. We weigh and measure its content and form until we can extract the precious portion—its meaning. Until we analyze to understand its meaning, we cannot write critically or clearly about an author's work. The assaying of an essay is one way of extracting meaning for the purposes of clear understanding and critical writing. Read through the assay procedure which follows, and visualize yourself completing each step.

Preparation

Read the title and author's name.

Reflect briefly on both title and author.

Write freely, describing your expectations of the essay.

1. What does the title reveal?
2. Try to predict or anticipate some of the information that might be included in the essay.

From "How to Assay an Essay" by Carmen Collins, *Read, Reflect, Write* 1e, ©1984, pp. 47–49; 60–61, Prentice Hall. Reprinted by permission of Pearson Education, Inc. Upper Saddle River, NJ.

3. What does the author's name or background (if known) suggest?
4. Try to predict the author's point of view or "slant" on the subject.

Step One: Recognizing the Thesis

Read the essay until you come to the author's thesis: the *this is what I am going to say* statement.

Reflect: A thesis tells what the essay will be about. You may have to read one or more paragraphs to find it, but often it follows the introduction. Sometimes it is implied rather than stated. In that case, you may have to infer, or state the thesis in your own words, based on the author's statements.

1. Does the thesis you found tell what the essay will be about?
2. Does the thesis reveal something of the author's viewpoint, feeling, or attitude toward the subject?

Write down the thesis statement. Use the author's words if the thesis is stated; use your own words if it is implied.

If, in the first two paragraphs, there are no clues to the author's thesis, continue with the *assay* then, when you have completed step three, reread and complete step one.

Step Two: Recognizing the Conclusion

Read the last paragraph of the essay for the author's concluding statement: *this is what I have said.*

Reflect: If the last paragraph does not reveal the summary or conclusion, read a paragraph or two before it until you find the concluding statement.

1. Does the statement summarize, conclude, or tell something about what was said?
2. Does the statement include the author's viewpoint or attitude toward the subject?

Write down the concluding statement. Use the author's words if the conclusion is explicit; use your own words if it is implied or suggested.

If, in the last two paragraphs, there are no clues to the author's conclusion, continue with the *assay* then, when you have completed step three, reread and complete this section.

Reread the thesis and the concluding statement.

Reflect. Is there a relationship between the two statements? Are they compatible or in agreement? Or, do they seem unrelated? Do they contain opposing or incompatible ideas?

If the statements seem to be unrelated or not complementary, reread the opening and closing paragraphs to reconsider your choices of thesis and conclusion. At this point, you may wish to choose another sentence for either the thesis or the conclusion. You may decide to change one or the other, or you may conclude that your original choices were best.

Write: If you have chosen or inferred another statement for the thesis or conclusion, write down your final choices.

Step Three: Recognizing Smaller, Related Ideas

Read the first sentence of each paragraph.

Reflect briefly on the sentence and its relationship to the thesis.

Write each of the sentences in the order of appearance, leaving four or five spaces on your paper between each sentence.

If you have not already done so, look up all words you do not understand or for which you cannot get meaning from the context of the sentences in which they appear.

Write one sentence in your own words to summarize or tell what the essay is about. *Remember, the summary will be written from the information included in the thesis, conclusion, and first sentences of each paragraph.*

If you have not, as yet, determined the author's thesis and/or conclusion, study the extracted sentences then reread and complete steps one and two.

Steps one through three of "How to Assay an Essay" provide an overview of an essay. Skimming the surface or reading only key portions gives a firm sense of an essay's thesis and related ideas. By reflecting, writing, and predicting, you add an even deeper dimension to the analysis of an author's work. As a reader, after completing an *assay,* you know what the piece is about, where the author begins, how far he or she develops the topic, and what he or she concludes. In fact, you will know enough about the essay to assure that later, at closer inspection, your familiarity with theme and central thoughts will increase immeasurably your overall understanding of the material. As a writer, your experience of the assay approach leads directly to an effective and proven strategy for developing an original topic, but before thinking about an original topic, apply the *assay* to another author's work.

How to Assay a Textbook Chapter

Textbook chapters make up the bulk of academic reading; therefore, you need a proven method for getting key ideas quickly before taking a closer look at details. Studies have shown that prereading for central concepts increases overall comprehension of a text. Furthermore, the combination of skimming and free writing can have an even more powerful effect on your understanding of a chapter. With minor modifications, the *assay* is readily adapted to chapter reading.

Chapters differ from essays in length, degrees of technicality, and form. Generally, a chapter is longer and contains more technical material than an essay. The form or structure of a chapter, however, varies. At first glance certain chapters in the social sciences might be indistinguishable from essays. But on closer inspection, the large amount of factual material, the lack of opinion, and the impersonal style clearly identify the chapter.

Other differences include purpose, audience, and tone. The purpose of a chapter is to instruct, and it is written for a specific audience—students. Although they may also instruct, essays more often inform or entertain and can be written either for particular audiences or the general reader. An essay's tone may vary from high humor to dead seriousness, while a chapter's tone tends to be more formal and objective. Yet it too may vary in its degree of formality. These differences, while not startling, demand a slightly different prereading approach.

Preparation

Read the chapter's title, subtitles, and headings. Glance at charts and diagrams; read their titles or headings.

Reflect on what you have read.

Write one sentence in which you anticipate or *predict* what the chapter will be about.

Step One: Recognizing the Chapter's Purpose

Read the beginning paragraph(s) for a statement of purpose or thesis (this is what the chapter will be about).

Reflect: Is there a statement that tells what the chapter is about?

Write down the statement, or use your own words.
  If a statement of purpose is not evident, go to step two.

Step Two: Recognizing the Conclusion

Read the last paragraph or two for a concluding statement; read the end-of-chapter questions or exercises.

Reflect on the questions; this is the information you are to recall.

Write the conclusion or summary statement as written, or in your own words.
  If a conclusion is not evident, go to step three.

Step Three: Recognizing Smaller, Related ideas

Read headings and first sentences of each paragraph.

Reflect briefly on the relationship of heading to first sentences.

Write headings and first sentences in order of appearance. Indent first sentences and leave four or five spaces between each.
  If you have not done so, look up all words you do not understand or for which you cannot get meaning from the context. Check the textbook glossary before looking in the dictionary.
  Write two or three sentences to summarize or tell what the chapter is about.
  If purpose statement and/or conclusion have not been determined, study the extracted sentences. Then reread and complete steps one and two.

The Reading Experience: Questions for Reading and Discussion

1. Sit with two or three other students in the classroom. Try this method now by choosing an essay in one of your other textbooks or a full article in a magazine. Underline the sentences as explained. Work individually, but share your responses with other students.

    Collins' method has been used successfully by hundreds of thousands of students over the years. To help you perform it easily, follow these abbreviated steps:

    First, read the beginning until you come to the thesis statement. Underline it.

    Second, read the last paragraph until you come to the conclusion. Underline it.

    Put these two sentences together and you will see the MAIN IDEA, in a nutshell.

    Third, go back and underline the first sentence in each internal paragraph.

    A fairly accurate outline of the article will appear, almost magically.

    The beauty of this method is that it is precise, and it is a time-saver, especially if you did not have the opportunity to finish your reading homework! This can be done quickly just before a class. Of course, it does not substitute for full reading—but it can greatly improve your chances to grasp the most important idea that will be taught.

An assay can—and should—be used before attempting to read a long assignment. Then, when the entire article is read more slowly, you will be able to move through it with recognition, anticipating and reinforcing what you already know about it.

This short method works well 99% of the time. How successful was your group? Record your responses to this exercise in your journal.

2. Would this message be appropriate for narration? Look back at the selections in Chapter 3. Could the assay work with any of those stories? Why or why not?

3. For decades, instructing students to *skim* and *scan* essays and textbook chapters in order to improve their reading speed meant to quickly skip over the material. However, most of the published methods had no precise plan for doing this. Often, the title, subheadings, italicized words, or boldfaced print were suggested as important things to look at. Many students underlined too much; yellow highlighter marks were all over the page! As a result, although they finished quickly (and were often timed with a stopwatch to check reading speed, as if this were a relay race) students were left with an incomplete overview of the material, resulting in mistaken perceptions about the main idea and the important support statements. Compare the *assay* method to traditional methods of skimming and scanning. Which provides a fuller idea of the purpose of the essay? Which provides a clearer undertanding of the author's conclusion? Which presents the major divisions of each topic? Which method is actually the quickest?

4. When is scanning a good idea? Check the following, marking each as Yes or No:
   • phone directory and address book
   • websites for research purposes
   • table of contents
   • book index
   • essay
   • textbook chapter

5. How can the assay technique for reading help a beginning *writer*? Can you spin it around to work for you when you sit down to begin an essay? Can you do this with old-fashioned skimming and scanning?

   Explain why or why not.

The Writing Experience: Suggestions for Short Papers

1. Write the results of your group work, as suggested in question #1 above.

2. Using the sequence pattern, put in essay format a method for using the assay techniqe to write an essay, in answer to question #5 above.

3. Explain your difficulties and breakthroughs in the past in reading textbooks for courses like history, biology, geography, or science. How did you approach your assignments? How long did it take you to complete the readings? Were you able to concentrate on what you were reading all the way through the material? What was your level of retention afterward?

4. Write a short essay that explores your own goals for becoming a better reader and writer. What do you hope to be able to accomplish?

Recommended Films and eConnections

How to Detect Gold Nuggets. ThatAussieFamily. 22 Sept. 2011. YouTubevideo.

Main Idea Song from Reading Learning Upgrade. LearningUpgrade. 24 Oct. 2006. YouTubevideo.

We Are the People We've Been Waiting For. Dir. Darryl Goodrich. Independent Documentary. Perf. Ken Robinson, Tony Blair, Richard Branson, Bill Clinton, Natasha Cooper, Germaine Greer, Henry Winkler. 2009. Film.

Why Reading Matters. Dir. Rita Carter. Perf. Rita Carter. BBC. 2009. Film.

Quiz

_____ 1. An ASSAY is: (a) a test to find the precious content in rock or ore; (b) a good way to find the main idea in a paragraph; (c) an easy way to determine the main idea of a textbook chapter; (d) all the above.

_____ 2. The first step in an assay requires that: (a) you skim the entire essay before you begin; (b) you look at the headings, the subheadings in bold print, the pictures and their captions, the questions at the end of the chapter, and any charts, maps, or diagrams; (c) read the essay until you come to the author's thesis and then either underline it or rewrite it; (d) underline all the most important ideas.

_____ 3. The second step in an assay requires that: (a) you select the most important sentences within the essay or textbook chapter; (b) you write a summary of the essay in your own words; (c) you jot down all the difficult vocabulary words as you read quickly through the essay; (d) you read the final paragraph of the essay, find the conclusion and underline it, comparing it to the thesis statement at the beginning.

_____ 4. The third step in an assay requires that: (a) you go back and read only the first sentence in each internal, or body paragraph, underlining as you go; (b) you read the conclusion of the essay; (c) scan the essay and highlight with yellow marker all the difficult vocabulary words, italicized words, and words in bold print; (d) read the conclusion and rephrase it in your own words.

_____ 5. When you are finished with the assay: (a) you can see the main idea in a nutshell; (b) you will have a topic sentence outline of the entire essay; (c) you will be ready to attend class and speak about the most important ideas in your assignment without guessing; (d) all of the above.

MODELS OF AMERICAN HEROISM

Gerald A. Pomper and Marlene Michels Pomper

From childhood on, we sing folk songs and recite poetry, watch films or read stories that evoke heroic images. From Casey Jones, who immortalized our railroad trains, to Casey at the Bat, who immortalized baseball; from Joe Hill, whose ghost reminded us of the fight for organized unions, to Joan Baez, whose songs protested U.S. participation in Vietnam,

From "Models of American Heroism" by Marlene Michels Pomper in Gerald M. Pomper (ed)., *Ordinary Heroes and American Democracy,* pp. 12–13; 19–25. Copyright © 2004 by Yale University. All rights reserved. Reprinted by permission.

we learn what our citizens value. As befits our multiracial, multicultural nation, our heroes may be women or men, black like Harriet Tubman, Martin Luther King Jr., or Malcolm X, or white like Abraham Lincoln, Franklin Delano Roosevelt, and Ronald Reagan. They may be Native Americans such as Sacajawea, or Asian Americans such as the senator and decorated veteran Daniel Inouye, or Hispanic Americans such as César Chávez. They may even live beyond our shores, as did Anne Frank and Mother Teresa. They may be as distant as space walkers or as close as our parents.

In American discourse, heroes abound in such numbers and such variety that we may find it difficult to see heroism clearly. The problem becomes even more complicated when we seek to understand the concept within American democratic institutions. To focus our attention, I first examine the diverse ways heroism is defined in American popular culture, generating seven archetypes. I will then narrow the discussion to the particular character of heroism in politics and the ways in which it is shaped by the institutions of American democracy.

Heroic Archetypes

A search of the Internet yielded millions of citations of heroes. Although naturally each of these persons is unique, in these almost numberless American heroes we can identify seven categories, or archetypes. These archetypes differ as to the relative importance placed on individual characteristics and their relative degree of involvement in the general community, particularly its political life. Some heroes are honored principally for their personal character and achievements. They act as admirable individuals, rather than as participants in a political process. Building on the common American focus on individual personalities, these heroes of popular culture typically achieve their honored status in relative isolation. They can be described in terms of three archetypes.

Champions of Adversity. We honor some people because they have overcome enormous personal handicaps. Helen Keller was blind and deaf from childhood, yet she spoke and wrote eloquently. Other champions of adversity include the actors Christopher Reeve and Michael J. Fox, who have used devastating injury and grave illness as opportunities to promote public awareness of, and gain research funding for, spinal cord damage and Parkinson's disease. Even the most renowned political figures may be admired as much for their battles against personal adversity as for their public actions. Franklin Delano Roosevelt was able to lead his country despite being crippled by polio, and former president Ronald Reagan bravely revealed that he was afflicted with Alzheimer's disease, thereby spurring public support for investigations into its causes and treatment.

Trailblazers. Be they explorers, scientists, entrepreneurs, artists, or athletes, trailblazers have the courage, imagination, and talent to accomplish what others have not dared to try. Like Champions of Adversity, they are considered heroes primarily on account of their individual achievements, rather than their direct involvement in the community. Our schoolbooks are filled with tales of their exploits. The explorers who sailed to the New World on Viking, Spanish, and English ships were trailblazers, as were the pioneers who crossed America by horseback, covered wagon, and canoe. Meriwether Lewis and William Clark, with the help of their guide, Sacajawea, opened up the West after the Louisiana Purchase. Their travel journals inspired others to seek adventure and fortune in the newly acquired land.

Trailblazers also are found in more civilized settings. "In the modern world," write two admirers of the entrepreneurial spirit, "the wealth creators—the entrepreneurs—actually travel the heroic path and are every bit as bold and daring as the mythical heroes who fought dragons and overcame evil." These entrepreneurs are risk-taking, creative individuals who strive to turn their dreams into reality. By way of illustration, Andrew Carnegie, in the nineteenth century, and Bill Gates, in the twentieth, have contributed vastly to American industry and technology, thereby fostering economic growth. Americans also value as heroes those who mark new trails in the natural world. Benjamin Franklin and Thomas Edison are honored for their practical inventions, Albert Einstein for working out the theoretical underpinnings of atomic physics and space travel, and Jonas Salk for the development of a vaccine that ended epidemics of polio. Medical researchers who will eventually discover new cures through gene therapy will likely be the heroes of coming decades.

Similarly, American artists and performers put their talent and dedication to use in creating new art forms. From George Gershwin to Isadora Duncan to Bessie Smith, we value our composers, dancers, and singers. In the paintings of Jackson Pollack and Georgia O'Keeffe, we honor our artists. In studios and on stage, they served as trailblazers, intent on breaking away from established styles and expanding artistic horizons. Athletes, too, have captured our imagination because of their record-breaking achievements. Young and old have made heroes of such figures as Babe Ruth, Jackie Robinson, Gertrude Ederle, and Mia Hamm—figures whose heroic appeal is often underscored by their successful efforts to overcome poverty, racism, or sexism.

Nurturers. In contrast to the two preceding archetypes, heroes of this category are not noted for extraordinary personal achievements. Their heroism instead comes in their service to others, usually in intimate settings. They are individuals who take their personal responsibilities seriously: dutiful parents and spouses, dedicated workers and providers of hope and comfort. Their selflessness and nurturance, in homes, schools, hospitals, churches, and the workplace, enables others to thrive. As one champion of such "anonymous heroism" puts it: "The bravest things we do in our lives are usually known only to ourselves. No one throws ticker tape on the man who chose to be faithful to his wife, on the lawyer who didn't take the drug money, or the daughter who held her tongue again and again."

To many, their greatest heroes are their closest relatives, often their mother and father. In a 1985 study at the University of Wisconsin that asked undergraduates to name their top five heroes and heroines, "the students' own parents were the most frequent first choices." From the time their children are toddlers, parents serve as role models, and youngsters try to walk in their shoes. Often, as they patiently care for autistic children and aging parents, their heroism is all but invisible.

Rescuers. The heroes in this and the following group are relatively more involved in community life and politics, although their heroism is still defined by their individual deeds. Even in a public setting, they achieve recognition by means of personal valor, by acting apart from their fellow citizens. Rescuers act courageously in emergencies and in other dangerous situations. Such individual heroism is often associated with military combat. Its features, both admirable and wretched, were ably captured in the award-winning film *Saving Private Ryan.* As one writer commented, the film "reminds us of the flesh and blood that soldiers are made of [and] shows them ultimately possessing the stomach to sec a vital but nasty job through, even at the cost of their lives." It also teaches us "that the men who fought found more ugliness in war than glory, that if they were courageous they were also scared, and that none had to be larger than life to deserve our salute."

Rescuers include volunteers, sometimes anonymous, who suddenly commit themselves to saving threatened lives. One example is Roberto Clemente, a Hall of Fame baseball player. On New Year's Eve of 1972, Clemente was on his way to Nicaragua to aid survivors of an earthquake when his plane crashed. Far more than his athletic skill, the heroic circumstances of his death made him a role model for youth. More broadly, firefighters, police, and emergency medical teams may have saved as many as thirty thousand workers from death by their skilled evacuation of the World Trade Center after the September 11 terrorist attack.

As if to foreshadow that event, heroism was widespread among the hundreds who came to help after one of the worst acts of terrorism in American history. Following the 1995 bombing of a federal office building in Oklahoma City, resulting in 168 deaths, volunteers arrived "from down the street and as far away as New York City—cops, doctors, structural engineers, and firefighters from more than so departments. Oklahoma City officials don't even know how many hundreds of emergency workers, and ordinary citizens, rushed to the bombed out Alfred P. Murrah Federal Building on April 19 to help search for survivors and comfort the grieving over the next grueling days that followed. . . . Together, these brave men and women reassured the nation that there is far more heart than hate in the heartland."

Martyrs. These persons go beyond even Rescuers, sacrificing their lives on behalf of others. Combatants killed in military action are the classic example. In remembering them, we increasingly turn to World War II, as is evident in such books as Tom Brokow's *The Greatest Generation,* which extols the self-sacrifice and integrity of that generation of Americans, and in film dramas, such as *Schindler's List* and *Life Is Beautiful,* that focus on individual altruism. In more recent times, American martyrs include leaders who have been assassinated, such as John F. Kennedy and the Reverend Martin Luther King Jr. and the crews of astronauts on the *Challenger* and *Columbia* missions.

Guardians at the Gates. The final pair of archetypes comprise heroes who are more directly involved in public life. Usually standing outside the established processes of politics, these heroes win their accolades by acting independently—as Ralph Nader put it, by "bucking the system and putting themselves on the line because of their ideals." Guardians at the Gates are highly involved in public life, although they may not be active in formal politics. They warn their fellow citizens of dangers, both in the society generally and within government. When Lincoln Steffens wrote his famous muckraking reports, he alerted the public of the dangers of political and business corruption, just as Robert Woodward and Carl Bernstein would later uncover the Watergate scandal.

Within government, this category includes the "whistleblower," who defends the integrity of political institutions by discovering and opposing malfeasance and criminality among public officials. Marie Ragghianti, for example, was chair of the pardons and paroles board of Tennessee. When she discovered that the office of the governor was selling clemencies to convicted criminals, she initiated a federal investigation. Although she was hastily dismissed from her position, she was ultimately vindicated when three persons were convicted and Governor Ray Blanton was ousted from office (and later sent to prison for other crimes). Ragghianti, whose experiences became the subject of a book and a film, won her own reinstatement and later became the administrator, and in 1999 a member, of the U.S. Parole Commission.

Activists, Protesters, and Reformers. Direct political involvement is particularly evident in this final group. From abolitionists to civil libertarians, from suffragettes to women's liberationists, Americans have admired those who have fought for racial and gender equality. Senator Joseph Biden fittingly described political heroes as those with "the courage to seek change when things go stale." They are valued for their "realism, idealism, tenacity, and the ability to sacrifice." History offers us John Brown, Harriet Beecher Stowe, and Susan B. Anthony as examples of courageous individuals who refused to accept the status quo. As compassionate protesters, they not only empathized with the downtrodden, forgotten, or silenced members of society but reached out to help them. Today's activists may lend their support to gay rights or green parties, to a woman's "right to choose" or an embryo's "right to life," or to the control of environmental pollution.

In recent years, women have become prominent social activists, "passionate leaders in fights against toxic waste dumps, against nuclear power, and against nuclear weapons." Karen Silkwood is one well-known example. A chemical technician at Kerr-McGee plutonium fuels production plant in Crescent, Oklahoma, she was the plant's first woman committee member from Local 5-283 of the Oil, Chemical, and Atomic Workers (OCAW) International Union. In 1974, after having her own levels of radioactive contaminants monitored, she blew the whistle on Kerr-McGee's unsafe practices. After she testified about contaminant dangers at a union meeting, her car was involved in a suspicious accident in which she was killed. Books, as well as the movie Silkwood, subsequently made her a national hero.

The Reading Experience: Questions for Reading and Discussion

1. Using the 5 Ws and an H, identify the content of the chapter "Models of American Heroism."

2. Which pattern of organization predominates in this chapter—Comparison and Contrast, Cause and Effect, Definition and Example, Analysis, or Sequence? Provide reasons for your answer.

3. Together with one or two partners, decide upon which of the seven archetypes identified by the Pompers, would include each of the following people: Abolitionist Sojourner Truth, businessman Oskar Schindler, inventor Thomas Edison, WWII photographer Lee Miller, Missions of Charity founder Mother Teresa, author Elie Wiesel, and social activist Gloria Steinem.

4. How should this reading selection be approached, efferently or aesthetically? Is this article written in the extensive or the reflexive mode? Explain.

5. This excerpt uses a two-part—and two-sentence—thesis statement. Identify one sentence of this two-part thesis statement that announces what the writer will write about in the selection used here. Underline it with a single line. Although the entire chapter "Models of American Heroism" is not printed here, next underline twice the sentence in the thesis statement that will continue the chapter.

The Writing Experience: Suggestions for Short Papers

1. Based upon the seven archetypes identified in this selection, compose a 250–500 word essay that defines the meaning of the word "hero." Use, of course, the definition and example pattern.

2. Are there any major differences between men and women heroes? Using the comparison/contrast pattern, compose a 250–500 word essay that explains how gender does or does not play a role in identifying a hero.

3. Do different cultures have different criteria for their heroes? Using any other nation on earth, discuss some of the characteristics, and examples of heroes in countries abroad in a 250–500 word essay.

4. Write a 250–500 word essay on someone you consider to be a hero.

Recommended Films and eConnections

The Greatest Heroes in History — Hannibal Part 1 of 3. Docmate. 25 July 2009. YouTube video.

Real Life Heroes — Tribute to Heroes. Breakaway2X. 22 Dec. 2012. YouTube video.

Lincoln. Dir. Steven Spielberg. Perf. Daniel Day Lewis, Sally Field, David Straithairn, Tommy Lee Jones. Touchstone and Dreamworks. 2012. Film.

42 — The Jackie Robinson Story. Dir. Brian Helgeland. Perf. Chadwick Boseman, Harrison Ford, Nicole Beharie. Warner Brothers. 2013. Film.

Quiz

_____ 1. "Models of American Heroism" posits that: (a) there are so many heroes that it is difficult to see heroism clearly; (b) it is easy to identify heroism in past history, but not as simple today; (c) the definition of heroism is constantly shifting; (d) none of the above.

_____ 2. Heroes include all of the following *except*: (a) martyrs ; (b) artists; (c) average citizens that perform service to others; (d) meteorologists.

_____ 3. The chapter "Models of American Heroism" follows the expository pattern known as: (a) analysis; (b) comparison and contrast; (c) sequence; (d) cause and effect.

_____ 4. The most appropriate way to approach this reading is: (a) to take the efferent stance; (b) to take the aesthetic stance; (c) to skim the selection for important terms; (d) to scan the selection quickly.

_____ 5. The authors' intent is: (a) to describe heroism using visual details; (b) to narrate heroic stories for entertainment purposes; (c) to inform and teach the reader about morality, reverence for the law, and those who succeeded in life by living by these principles; (d) to persuade the reader to await extraordinary men and women to lead and defend us.

THE ONLY ENGLISH KING TO BE BEHEADED

Bruce Felton

Well mannered and devoted to his family, Charles I was nonetheless an insufferable elitist who believed in the divine right of kings and had only contempt for the House of Commons.

Crowned in 1625, he was doomed from the start. He waged an illegal war against Spain and France, ran up the national debt, ailed his enemies without trial, and totally antagonized parliament. When civil war broke out, Charles fled to Scotland.

The fugitive king was taken prisoner in 1648 and accused of "high treason and other high crimes against the realm of England." He refused to testify on his own behalf, archly insisting that "a king cannot be tried by any superior jurisdiction on earth."

Have it your way, king, the tribunal responded. Charles was tried, convicted and, before a large crowd in London on the morning of January 30, 1649, relieved of his head.

A postscript: When Charles II was restored to the throne in 1660, plans were made to transfer his father's body from Windsor Castle to a more fitting crypt in Westminster Abbey. But somewhere between Windsor and London, the royal remains vanished.

In 1813 workmen at Windsor inadvertently poked a hole in the burial vault known to contain Henry VIII's coffin and also found one marked "Charles I." The lid was pried open, revealing a body and severed head, badly decomposed, but with enough hair and facial tissue to leave no doubt it was Charles. Probing deeper, the royal surgeon, Sir Henry Halford, determined that the head had been lopped off with a sharp blow that sliced through the fourth cervical vertebra.

The remains were placed back in the coffin, which was resealed in the vault. However, Sir Henry kept the vertebra, using it for years as a saltshaker and dinner table tchotchke.* Eventually his heirs, who found the relic distasteful, gave it to the Prince of Wales, who arranged for it to be returned to its rightful place in the king's spinal column.

*Now in fairly common use, tchotchka is a Yiddish expression meaning "knick-knack."

The Reading Experience: Questions for Reading and Discussion

1. This *cause and effect* essay explains why Charles I was beheaded. List five facts which contributed to the need for a trial.

2. How did Charles's attitude and behavior at the trial lead to his conviction?

3. How did the royal surgeon, Henry Halford, determine that the decomposed body and head belonged to Charles I?

4. Consider the *tone* of the essay. Is it somber, disrespectful, serious, or lighthearted? Supply adjectives of your own and explain why you chose them.

5. What can we learn about human behavior from the actions of Charles I? Sir Henry Halford? Charles I's heirs? The Prince of Wales?

The Writing Experience: Suggestions for Short Papers

1. Imagine the following. You are a workman at Windsor in 1813. Your job is to move and clean King Henry VIII's burial vault. Accidentally, you poke a hole in it and find another coffin inside. Your supervisor orders you to open it. Describe your experience, in accordance with the information provided in this essay.

2. Write an introductory paragraph for a hypothetical *cause and effect* essay which sets out your intention to explain at least one of the following situations. In your thesis statement, include your reason for choosing this subject.

   • The eruption of a volcano (Mount Etna, Mount Saint Helen's, or another)
   • The crowning of fifteen-year-old Queen Eleanor, the only woman to be queen of both England and France
   • Thomas Edison's discovery of the lightbulb

3. Research information in either the college library or on the internet about Charles I. What information is not included in the essay above? Write a short essay that includes Charles' youth, marriage, and other personal information that may have led to his character and future actions as King.

4. King Charles's execution was a gruesome event. Yet Fulton writes about it with humor. Is this appropriate, or disrespectful? How does humor in a historical essay affect the reader? Can it make the material easier to understand, or less so? Explain the passages where Fulton uses humor and the effect on you, the reader.

Recommended Films and eConnections

The Trial and Execution of King Charles I from "The Devil's Whore" nicnoc1976. 16 Mar. 2012. YouTube video.

Windsor Castle. iMonarchy. 5 Apr. 2009. YouTube video.

Great Kings of England: King Charles I. n. d. n. p. Kultur Films, Inc. DVD. 2006. Film.

The Three Musketeers. Dir. Stephen Herek. Perf. Charlie Sheen, Kiefer Sutherland, Chris O'Donnell, Oliver Platt, Tim Curry. Walt Disney Pictures and Carvan Pictures. 1993. Film.

Quiz

_____ 1. The main idea in this essay is: (a) Charles I was well-mannered and devoted to his family. (b) Charles I fled to Scotland. (c) Doomed from the start of his reign, Charles I was convicted of high treason and beheaded for his crimes. (d) The Prince of Wales arranged for a proper burial for King Charles I.

_____ 2. Sir Henry Halford used as a salt shaker: (a) the lock from Charles I's burial vault; (b) Charles I's fourth cervical vertebra; (c) a precious gem from Charles I's crown; (d) a miniature House of Commons.

_____ 3. Charles I's body: (a) was lost in its extended transfer to Windsor Abbey; (b) was found by workmen 152 years later; (c) shared a vault with King Henry VIII; (d) all of the above.

_____ 4. Charles I: (a) had respect for the House of Commons; (b) was poorly mannered and showed contempt for his family; (c) actively defended himself at the tribunal; (d) was the only English King to be beheaded.

_____ 5. In contrast to the sobriety of the historical events, the tone of Fulton's essay is: (a) sad; (b) hilarious; (c) lighthearted; (d) ridiculous.

THE WEAKER SEX

Maggie Jones

From nursery to nursing home, men face daunting odds.

Men start out ahead: 115 males are conceived for every 100 females. But it's downhill from there.

- The male fetus is at greater risk of miscarriage and stillbirth.

- Male births slightly outnumber female births (about 105 to 100), but boys have a higher death rate if born premature: 22 percent compared with 15 percent for girls.

- Overall, more newborn males die than females (5 to 4).
- Sudden infant death syndrome is one and a half times as common in boys as in girls.
- Boys are three to four times as likely to be autistic.
- Boys are three times as likely to have Tourette's syndrome.
- Mental retardation afflicts one and a half times as many boys as girls.
- Dyslexia is diagnosed two to three times as often in boys as girls.
- As teenagers, boys die at twice the rate of girls.
- Boys ages 15–19 are five times as likely to die in a homicide.
- Boys ages 15–19 are almost 11 times as likely to die by drowning.
- Boys ages 16–19 are nearly twice as likely to die from a car accident.
- Men are 16 times as likely as women to be colorblind.
- Men suffer hearing loss at twice the rate of women.
- Though women attempt suicide two to three times as often as men, four times as many men actually kill themselves.
- The male hormone testosterone is linked to elevations of LDL, the bad cholesterol, as well as declines in HDL, the good cholesterol.
- Men have fewer infection-fighting T-cells and are thought to have weaker immune systems than women.
- Men have a higher death rate from pneumonia and influenza than women.
- By the age of 36, women outnumber men.
- Men ages 55–64 are twice as likely as women to die in car accidents.
- Men ages 55–74 are twice as likely as women to die of heart disease.
- In the United States, men are twice as likely to die from parasite-related diseases (in part, some speculate, because their greater average size may offer parasites a bigger target).
- Among people 65 and older, men account for 84 percent of suicides.
- Stroke, cancer, diabetes, heart disease and accidents—all among the top causes of death—kill men at a higher rate than women.
- American men typically die almost six years before women do.
- By the age of 100, women outnumber men eight to one.
- The good news? Men who live to be 100 tend to be in better shape than their centenarian female counterparts.

The Reading Experience: Questions for Reading and Discussion

1. Who is the weaker sex? What does Jones mean by the term "weaker"? What do *you* mean by this term? Does the date of the research—over ten years ago in 2003—have an impact on the definition of the term "weaker"? If a researcher compiled statistics 100 years ago, would these facts have been known?

2. Although this is written in columns, with bullets for each item, it is a piece of exposition. Identify the thesis statement and the conclusion. What is its expository pattern?

3. Is there actually a competition? What do you think was Maggie Jones' motive to write this article?

4. Would this article be more or less effective if it were written in fully developed paragraphs?

5. Do you agree or disagree with Jones that men are the weaker sex?

The Writing Experience: Suggestions for Short Papers

1. Compile a list of traits that indicate that men are the stronger sex. Research statistics, as Jones did for this article. The choice of traits is yours, but here are a few suggestions for starters: health (specific diseases, types of injury); sports (endurance, records set); and mental abilities (number of scholarships or prizes awarded, grade point averages). Keep your choices to facets of life that can be objectively reported. Begin and end your list with a statement of thesis and a conclusion, using Jones as your model.

2. Compare and contrast the following in a two-paragraph essay, keeping in mind that objectivity here is more persuasive than subjectivity.
   - Online courses/On campus courses
   - Winter sports/Summer sports
   - Keeping secrets/Being transparent

3. Write a short essay investigating how lists that rank objects, people, or trends, are compiled, especially "most popular" lists. Are all lists objective? How is "#1" determined? What purpose do they serve?

4. In 1883, Mark Twain wrote a famous essay titled "Two Ways of Seeing a River." He compared and contrasted the river as seen through the fresh eyes of youth and the experienced eyes of age. Compare an experience you had when you were younger which excited and thrilled you, like going to a favorite playground or theme park, with that same experience today, after seeing much more of the world, or having gone to the place so often that it no longer holds the same interest.

Recommended Films and eConnections

Comparison/Contrast Essay. LoveYour Pencil. 27 Nov. 2011. YouTube video.

Deleted Scenes: Being a Twin – Our America with Lisa Ling. OWNTV. 11 Nov. 2011. YouTube video.

Twins. Dir. Ivan Reitman. Perf. Danny DeVito, Arnold Schwartzenegger, Kelly Preston. Universal Pictures, 1988. Film.

Two Countries, One Street. Dir. Jean Palardy. Perf. Robert Anderson. Office of National Films and National Film Board (Canada). 1955. Film.

Quiz

_____ 1. The projected reason why men are likely to die from a parasite-related disease is: (a) the "bad" men are larger, and offer a bigger target; (b) male births outnumber female births; (c) an organism that grows on another organism is reliant on the generosity of its host; (d) none of the above.

_____ 2. All of the following are true *except*: (a) dyslexia is diagnosed two to three times as often in boys than girls; (b) women live longer than men do; (c) women lose their hearing just as often and as quickly as men do; (d) men die of cancer and heart disease at higher rates than women.

_____ 3. Men face daunting odds, as supported by the evidence in Jones's article. Given that evidence, one can understand that the word "daunting" means: (a) discouraging; (b) brave; (c) particular; (d) hopeful.

_____ 4. There is a popular myth that women are poor drivers, but according to Jones's research: (a) men ages 55–64 are twice as likely as women to die in car accidents; (b) boys ages 16–19 are nearly twice as likely to die from a car accident; (c) as teenagers, boys die at twice the rate of girls; (d) all the above are correct.

_____ 5. The good news for men is: (a) boys rarely drown; (b) men have stronger immune systems than women; (c) men who live to be 100 are in better shape than women at that age; (d) men outnumber women by the age of 100 eight to one.

DOLLIE AND JOHNNIE

William Safire

This is the story of a poignant romance between a couple of science students, recently revealed in a trove of letters that bear some lessons for us today.

She was 21, comely, and signed her letters "Dollie"; he was 17, cut a dashing figure with his curly hair and a mustache, and often signed his passionate missives "Johnnie."

Because she was the only woman at the school pursuing advanced mathematics, she was isolated for her uppitiness, and responded to that prejudice with iciness and impudence.

Not toward Johnnie, though; she found him respectful, exciting, and an intellectual soulmate. Planning a secret weekend in the mountains, he wrote: "I can already imagine the fun we'll have. And then we'll start in on Helmholtz's electro-magnetic theory of light."

His parents, when they discovered the affair, angrily disapproved. She was of a lower social station, of Serbian origin, and an older woman: "by the time you're 30, she'll be an old witch," his mother railed, which he merrily reported to his love. But the opposition from home, source of his financial support at school, grew with the years: "My parents weep for me," he wrote Dollie, "almost as if I had died. Again and again they complain that I have brought misfortune upon myself by my devotion to you. . . ."

She became pregnant. Neither she nor her young lover had any prospects of making enough money to marry and rear a child until after graduation, more than a year ahead. "I received a letter from home today" she wrote, "that has made me lose all desire, not only for having fun, but for life itself." He wrote: "If only I could give you some of my happiness so you could never be sad and pensive again."

"About our future I've decided the following," he added, "I'll look for a position immediately, no matter how modest. As soon as I have such a position I'll marry you . . . and then no one can cast a stone upon your dear head, and woe unto him who dares to set himself against you."

Cut off his studies and take a menial job? She wouldn't hear of it: "You shouldn't take a really bad position, darling; that would make me feel terrible and I couldn't live with it." She left school, at a great cost to her own career, and secretly bore a child they called Lieserl.

"It's such a shame that our dear Lieserl must be introduced to the world this way!" he wrote. "I wouldn't want to have to give her up." He offered nursing advice: "She shouldn't be stuffed with cow milk, because it might make her stupid. (Yours would be more nourishing, right?)"

They decided, after all, it would be best to give up the child for adoption. When he emerged from school he landed a job that allowed him to pursue his theoretical work, and married Dollie. They had two sons; it is probable that with her training she provided a sounding board for his revolutionary ideas.

Three years after their marriage, Albert Einstein—no longer signing his name "Johnnie"—produced, at age 26, three papers that changed the course of history. Within one month, human minds were opened to the quantum theory of light, an explanation of the laws of motion and the fourth-dimensional special theory of relativity. Not before or since has there been such a leap forward in humanity's understanding of space and time.

How do the love letters of Einstein and Mileva Maric, recently published by Princeton University Press, help us understand our personal space and time?

1. The lives of people of great power and influence often contain anguished secrets unknown to their contemporaries, suggesting that our moralizing judgments be tempered by the rarity of moral paragons.
2. The path of honor of — "doing the right thing" — can have consequences beyond calculation. The father of relativity was no moral relativist, and Mileva Maric's topping his offer of sacrifice with her own career sacrifice permitted the flowering of the greatest mind of the age.
3. Endings are not always happy, after 11 years, the marriage broke up.

What became of Lieserl, the daughter carried to term and given up? Nobody knows; she would be 90 now. We can presume she grew up to have a family of her own, and that humanity has been enriched by the propagation of the genes of a genius.

The Reading Experience: Questions for Reading and Discussion

1. Did you wonder who the two lovers were before you reached paragraph 11? Who did you guess they were? How did you feel when you discovered Johnnie's true identity?
2. Why did Johnnie's parents disapprove of his sweetheart? Have you any experience, either in literature or life, with the disapproval of a son's or daughter's romantic choice in this way?

3. What do you think of Dollie's decision to leave school? Do you think she would make the same decision today? Explain.

4. If private letters of famous figures in history are found, as these were, should they be kept private, or made public? Consider your feelings, as well as the laws of public disclosure in this matter.

5. This piece might have been considered a *narrative*, if it had ended after the eleventh paragraph. In fact, Safire begins by claiming that "this is [a] story." However, in paragraph 12 he continues and shifts what seems like his initial writing "intent," to entertain, to become a lesson, when he asks, "How do the love letters . . . . help us understand our personal space and time?" Which mode of discourse is he actually using now? What is his new, or true, intent in writing? Does he have a thesis statement? If so, where is it? Discuss this interesting format, and comment on the effectiveness of Safire's technique.

The Writing Experience: Suggestions for Short Papers

1. Shakespeare's magnificent play *Romeo and Juliet*, the famous myth of Pyramus and Thisbe, and the long-running Broadway play *The Fantastiks* written by Tom Jones and Harvey Schmidt, all deal with the same theme. Write a comparison and contrast essay that points out the similarities and differences between the story of Albert Einstein ("Johnnie") and Mileva Maric ("Dollie") and one of these extraordinary literary masterpieces. Use the following elements:
   - their love for each other
   - the two families' attitudes
   - the outcome of their conflict

2. Research the career of Albert Einstein. List in chronological order his major achievements. At what point(s) in his life did his romance and relationship to Mileva Maric occur?

3. Assume that "Dollie" and "Johnnie's" two sons were to appear on a TV talk show to discuss their search for their missing sister. Write their interview, using dialogue. Present the questions the host would ask and their responses.

4. Does the world today have different moral values than it did when Einstein and Maric were young? Write an essay discussing the situations today of women and education, parental attitudes toward their children's relationships, and the question of raising children inside and outside of marriage.

Recommended Films and eConnections

Mileva Maric. Nico Tesla. 1 May 2012. YouTube video.

Albert Einstein: How I See the World. Nam Ngo. 19 Aug. 2011. PBS. YouTube video.

Albert Einstein Biography — HD. History Channel Documentary. YouTube video.

Einstein's Big Idea. Dir. Gary Johnstone. Perf. John Lithgow, Aidan McArdle, Shirley Henderson. PBS-NOVA, 1999. TV Documentary.

Quiz

_____ 1. The story of Dollie and Johnnie: (a) was found written by Mileva Maric, and hidden in an old trunk; (b) is fiction; (c) is a story of a poignant romance between two science students found in a trove of letters; (d) is from a recent movie.

_____ 2. The story of Dollie and Johnnie shows that: (a) we should be more open to understanding that even great men and women of power and influence can keep anguished secrets; (b) "doing the right thing" sometimes may not be the right thing to do; (c) unlike fairy tales, endings in real life are not always happy; (d) all of the above.

_____ 3. Johnnie was in reality: (a) Albert Einstein; (b) Mileva Maric; (c) William Safire; (d) none of the above.

_____ 4. Three years after their marriage, Johnnie: (a) abandoned his wife; (b) lost his job; (c) cut off his studies; (d) produced three papers that changed the course of history.

_____ 5. The story of Dollie and Johnnie: (a) is an example of the way narration can be used in exposition; (b) is an essay that uses spatial description; (c) is an argument that tries to change the reader's point of view; (d) is an example of the way exposition can be used to introduce narration.

THE HISTORY OF SURNAMES

Sandra G. Brown

How did surnames begin? What do they mean? To answer these questions, consider these facts: first, surnames—last names—are a rare possession all over the world. In many countries, a last name is kept secret, because to know and use it might mean that the speaker would gain power over that person! Many go through life using a nickname (aka a "byname"), the true surname known only to a select few. Even very civilized countries often do not use surnames. This is particularly true in Asia and Africa.

In ancient Rome, citizens generally had three names. First came the _praenomen_, which corresponded to our forename, or first name. It was followed by the _gens_, the clan or race name. Last of all came the _cognomen_, or surname. The man we call "Julius Caesar" actually had three names. Julius was not his first name, but the name of his clan. His actual forename (first name) was Gaius! It was rarely used, saved only for formal accounts of his life.

The Greeks, however, had nothing corresponding to our surnames at all. They were happy with the familiar "son of" or _patronymic_ method (the first method described below) of explaining their relationships.

During the dark ages of western Europe, after the breakdown of the Roman Empire, the Roman system of nomenclature was lost. It was only gradually, during the later Middle Ages, from the thirteenth century onward, that surnames became the common civilized usage. What may be the most amazing global feature of all is that surnames fall into one of only four categories! Besides patronymics, we have place names, occupation names, and nicknames. Into what category does _your_ last name fall?

As you survey the following names, use a dictionary (print or online) to check the various meanings of names from languages other than English. They may surprise you!

MEANINGS OF SURNAMES
THE BYNAMES INTRODUCED BETWEEN 1100 & 1400 CAME FROM VARIOUS SOURCES. SOME WERE LINKS WITH CHRISTIAN NAMES: EG HUGHES FROM HUGH, JOHNSON FROM JOHN, PEARSON FROM PETER. SOME DESCRIBED THE BEARER'S JOB EG FISHER, HUNTER, LEECH (A DOCTOR) KELLOGG (LITERALLY KILL HOG OR SLAUGHTERER) SOME DESCRIBED THE BEARER'S HOME EG WOODS, FIELDS, CLAYTON. SOME DESCRIBED THE BEARER HIMSELF EG BIGGS (SON OF A BIG MAN), CRUIKSHANK (WITH CROOKED LEGS), GIDDY (A MAD MAN), BELL (A HANDSOME MAN), GULLIVER (A GLUTTON)

© Timhunkin

The Four Groups of Surnames

Patronymics

The names below all signify the "son of." Often, the prefix (O, Mc, Mac, Di, De, D', Ben, Bin, Fitz) drops away, leaving a name like Meg Ryan, rather than O'Ryan. And just as often the suffix drops away too, leaving a name like Julia Roberts, Serena Williams, or Michael Phelps (Phelps derives from the English surname Philip – Philip's son). The final "s" is a clue that there was once the suffix–son in place. So what is a patronymic? Why "the name of the father," of course! *Patra* means father, in Greek.

Jackie Robinson	John McEnroe	F. Scott Fitzgerald
John McCain	Tim O'Brien	David Ben Gurion
LeBron James	Benjamin Franklin	Robert De Niro
Katy Perry	Marilyn Monroe	Claus Von Bulow
Martin Van Buren	Steve Martin	Scarlett Johannssen

Place Names

The names below signify cities, towns, buildings, ranges; actually, any feature of the ground. Colors, which also can describe a ground feature (brown, mud; white, snow; green, grass; etc.) may have once designated specific ethnic neighborhoods (e.g., *barrios* or *shetls*) as well as industrial communities owned by a particular company. These cover a multitude of names.

Winston Churchill	Gloria Arroyo ("stream")	Jeremy Lin ("forest")
Tiger Woods	Joe Montana ("mountain")	Ben Blue
Giuseppe Verdi ("green")	George W. Bush	Whitney Houston
Irving Berlin	Enrique Iglesias ("churches")	Betty White
Barbara Eden	Barry Atwater	Jonah Hill

Trade or Occupation Names

Since time immemorial, trade names have fallen into two classes: those which belonged to the true working class people and those taken from the "upper" classes—the clergy and the royal families. Although we certainly have no class system in the United States, which of these do you think belong in the working class, and which in the "upper" class?

Will Smith	Anita Baker
Willie Shoemaker	Rebecca Nurse
Lawrence Taylor	William Faulkner ("falconer")
Dick Chamberlain	Reggie Miller
Samuel Barber	Judas Priest
Dr. Martin Luther King	Anne Sexton
Elizabeth Taylor	Janet Emig ("industrious ruler")
Harold Prince	Geraldine Ferraro ("iron maker")

SMITH

THE NAME SMITH HAS COMMON EQUIVALENTS IN MANY COUNTRIES: SCHMIDT (GERMAN) LEFEVRE (FRANCE), GOUAN (GAELIC), FABER (LATIN), HADDAD (SYRIAN), SAPPANEN (FINNISH), KOVACS (HUNGARIAN), KUZNETSOV (RUSSIAN) KOWALSKY (UKRAINIAN). IN AMERICA THERE IS A JIM SMITH SOCIETY. PROUD OF THEIR WIDESPREAD NAME, THEY HOLD ANNUAL GATHERINGS & COLLECT INFORMATION ABOUT HEROIC DEEDS PERFORMED BY JIM SMITHS.

© Timhunkin

Nicknames

Most modern scholars agree that nicknames are limited. They are the actually the smallest category. Why? Because 99% of the time they are downright nasty! Although some are positive, like the name Justin Beiber, which means "hard worker," most people would hardly want to transmit a "fatso" or "skinny" surname down through the centuries to descendants! And so, uncomplimentary or even cruel names indicating features of the personality and features of the body are very often changed.

Betsy Ross ("red")	Thomas Sweet
Kelly Hu ("mustache" "beard")	Martin Short
Alexander Graham Bell ("handsome")	Louis Armstrong
Christina Pickles	Edith Head
Philip Roth ("red")	Betty White
Louise Rosenblatt ("rose leaf")	Shelley Long
George Meany	Peter Elbow
Shia LaBoef ("beef")	

EMBARRASSING NAMES

IT IS SURPRISING HOW MANY EMBARRASSING NAMES CAME TO BE USED & REMAINED UNTIL THE 19TH CENTURY. BUB, TEATE, HOLDWATER, POOPY, PIDDLE, HONEYBUM & RUMPE ARE EXAMPLES.

© Timhunkin

Where do objects fit in—names like Pete Rose, Gertrude Stein ("beer mug"), Martín Espada ("sword"), or Bill Gates? How about these? Hundreds of years before public schools enabled us to be literate, pictoral signs were hung outside inns or general stores, indicating items or foods sold there. People who worked there or lived "under the sign"—that is, in the immediate neighborhood—often adopted these as surnames. For example, the Indian surname Ghandi means "candy," while the Vietnamese surname Nguyen signifies a plucked string instrument, like a guitar or a lyre. They therefore can be considered either trade or place names.

Animal/Bird Names

(not a separate category; may be a Nickname or Trade Name)

Jokesters are responsible, too, for either ridiculing or complimenting people ("he's smart as a fox") who looked to them like birds, animals, or objects; therefore giving them nicknames. The famous Chinese American cellist, Yo-Yo Ma's surname means "horse." On the other hand, someone who hunted a certain type of animal, like a lion (think Jeremy Lyons or Rob Lowe) or eagle (think Christina Aguilera) would be classified as having a trade name.

Sheryl Crowe   Alfred Drake ("dragon")
Joe Pesci ("fish")   Larry Bird
Hart Crane   Warner Wolf
Florence Nightingale   Judd Hirsch ("deer")
Benicio Del Toro ("bull") Redd Foxx

HOW TO FIND THE ORIGINAL MEANING OF YOUR NAME

TO FIND THE ORIGIN OF YOUR NAME, GO TO YOUR NEAREST REFERENCE LIBRARY & ASK THE ATTENDANT FOR ONE OF THE STANDARD WORKS LISTING ORIGINS OF SURNAMES.

© Timhunkin

As you consider your own name, think of these four categories. Ask your family for help, for your name may have been changed or spelled differently. Your family probably has valuable information not found in any textbook. Remember—every name you can think of in English has its counterpart in every other language in the world!

The Reading Experience: Questions for Reading and Discussion

1. Students who have names in the same category shall sit together in small groups. All "Questions for Reading and Discussion" should be answered by students in the group. What category does your surname fall into?

2. Women: Will you change your name to your husband's when, and if, you choose to marry? Why or why not? Men: Will you expect your wife to change her name to yours when, and if, you marry? Why or why not? How will you react if she refuses to change it?

3. Do you like your names (all or one)? Do you think your name fits you? If not, what other name would you choose for yourself, if you could? Is your *forename* (first name) biblical? royal? Are you named for someone famous? Is it old or modern? Were you named for a hero or a movie star?

4. Are you first in your family to have your first name? If not, after whom were you named? Can you tell a little about that person? Can you describe that person?

5. Is your surname from a foreign language? What is its precise meaning in that language?

The Writing Experience: Suggestions for a Short Research Paper

This paper will consist of 3–4 pages (650–900 words), neatly typed. The topic is the meaning of both your first and last names. Your middle name is optional.

1. Begin with an interesting opening, following guidelines given elsewhere in this chapter.

2. Include a strong, clearly written thesis statement.

3. Your internal paragraphs will consist of your two names, in either order. (You may use a middle name, if you have one, as well.)

4. Identify your surname as one of the four categories. Fully explain why you put your name into that category.

5. Include DESCRIPTION to make your paper vivid. You may include a genealogy map or other relevant graphic or photos.

6. If possible, include NARRATION to make your paper interesting. Relate an anecdote about your family.

7. All essays must follow MLA style. Include a reference to your research in abbreviated form in the body of your essay. Document all the information you find on the internet or in the library.

8. Include a *Works Cited* page as your very last page. See the Purdue OWL website for help. Google these websites for starters:
   - My Cinnamon Toast Genealogy
   - rsl.rootsweb.ancestry.com
   - House of Names
   - Behindthename.com

Recommended Films and eConnections

History of Surnames. Guy Briand99. 5 May 2012. YouTube video.

How to Find the Meaning of A Surname. About. 4 Nov. 2011. YouTube video.

Identity Thief. Dir. Seth Gordon. Perf. Jason Bateman, Melissa McCarthy. Relativity Media, Bluegrass Studios, and Scott Stuber Productions. 2013. Film.

Identity Theft – the Michelle Brown Story. Dir. Robert Dornhelm. Perf. Kimberly Williams-Paisley, Carter Burns, Jason London. Lifetime Studio. 2004. TV Movie.

Quiz

_____ 1. The surnames of these personalities—Gertrude Stein, Mahatma Ghandi, and Martín Espada all are: (a) places; (b) objects; (c) patronymics; (d) animals.

_____ 2. Animal names like Sheryl Crowe, Christina Aguilera, Warner Wolf, and Red Foxx may signify an ancestor who: (a) lived near these animals; (b) lived near signs that were illustrated with these animals' pictures, indicating a restaurant or tavern; (c) resembled one of these animals; (d) both (b) and (c) are correct.

_____ 3. Surnames became popular in approximately the: (a) twentieth century; (b) third century BCE; (c) thirteenth century; (d) nineteenth century.

_____ 4. The most popular surname in the world, spelled in different forms, is: (a) Brown; (b) Taylor; (c) Jones; (d) Smith.

_____ 5. Patronymics, the largest category of surnames, are names that: (a) designate a man's first name, a father who passed on his name to his daughter or son; (b) designate a location, like a house, city, or feature of the ground; (c) designate a trade or profession; (d) designate a feature of the body or the personality.

COLLABORATION SENSATION: MYTHICAL FIGURES—A PARTNER PROJECT IN RESEARCH

This project requires advance planning.

Mythology is an important part of every culture. The following list is a compilation of some figures from Egyptian, Greek, African, Asian, and Native American mythology.

The following project involves an understanding of exposition, emphasizing the patterns of comparison and contrast, definition and example, cause and effect, and analysis.

- Students will work with a partner. Each student will select a character (from different lists).
- Each student researches his or her chosen character in terms of his or her role in mythological history, as well as the god's or goddess's influence on that culture.
- Compare your two figures, using library or online sources. Be sure to cite your source.
- Note cards or written papers may be used to deliver the reports.
- Present your written report to the class. Illustrations, handouts, audio, or PowerPoint addition may (or may not) be used. Each report should take approximately five minutes.
- Speakers are encouraged to involve class members by asking them to participate in their presentation. This may take the form of prepared questions, surveys, or aid in demonstrations.
- Students and the professor may decide whether everyone present will take place in the evaluation, based upon mutually agreed upon criteria.

Afterward, students should comment in their journals about the success of the collaborative project.

EGYPTIAN	GREEK	AFRICAN	ASIAN	NATIVE AMERICAN
Ra	Apollo	Shango	Gautama Buddha (China)	Asdzáá Nádleehé (Navaho)
Nun	Aphrodite	Bumba	Ksitigarbha (China)	Gitche Manitou (Algonquin)
Osiris	Dionysus	Orishas	Amateraso (Japan)	Apistotooki (Blackfoot)
Isis	Poseidon	Eshu	Izanagi (Japan)	Tirawa (Pawnee)
Horus	Zeus	Obatala	Cheonjiwang (Korea)	Hahgwenhdiyu (Iroquoi)
			Queen Baji (Korea)	Eagentci (Seneca)

CHAPTER 5

PERSUASIVE AND ARGUMENTATIVE VOICES

The Fourth Message of Intent—What Should Happen?

THE WRITER'S INTENTION TO CONVINCE

Language Can Change History

Words can change history. Early orators like Socrates and Plato practiced their rhetoric in ancient Greece, where they moved the entire citizenry of their communities to action. As citizens of the United States, we remember Ralph Waldo Emerson's famous line from *The Concord Hymn*: "This was the shot heard round the world." That poem roused the New Englanders to battle in 1775. Taken together with Patrick Henry's powerful declaration, "Give me liberty or give me death!" the colonial population was entirely convinced of the righteousness of revolution.

Every great struggle seems to produce forceful speakers and writers. Abraham Lincoln exhorted a war-weary nation with powerful and convincing language. Winton Churchill rallied a frightened British people through words to withstand a powerful enemy who had in turn been roused by Adolph Hitler's powerful language to make war upon the rest of the civilized world. There can be no doubt that language can and does change the course of events.

Reading the Language of Advertising

The power of language to convince is not limited solely to the geopolitical sphere. Here in the United States, the center of the universe of advertising, we daily are bombarded with ads that tell us that we need to drive a particular car, to condition and color our hair a certain way, to eat in a special fast food restaurant, and to do a myriad number of other things which we originally may never have even wanted to do. Every brand claims to be the best—either the fastest, the safest, the healthiest, the most delicious, luxurious, time-saving, long-lasting, or economical. Financial analysts tell us that currently over 85 billion dollars are spent in the United States annually on print and media advertising. Ads are all around us—on buses, in magazines, sandwiched between radio and TV programs; even interrupting TV movies, becoming more and more intrusive as each plot reaches its climax. But in the words of one ad executive, "eyeballs lead to dollars."

Induction and Deduction

"Pitches" for a product can be either *inductive* or *deductive*. In ads and commercials, *induction* eases the reader or listener into the "pitch" and once s/he is involved, reveals the issue. Commercials often do not show the product at first. We become interested in the scenario presented before we know what it is for. *Deduction*, on the other hand, shows the product at once.

Commercials made around 1950 were more deductive than they are today. They would state the product at once and repeat its name and logo many times. Short songs, or "jingles," as they were called, were sung over and over until they became earworms, playing in endless loops in the consumer's brain. Today's commercials prefer the inductive approach, more like the approaches of Socrates and Plato, withholding not only the name of the product, but often the pitch as well, until the very end.

Successful sales personnel, both on site and on the phone, follow the inductive approach, too. We often hear "Good morning, how are you today? My name is Lucifer, and we're going to be in your neighborhood. . . ." before we know why or what it is they are planning to sell us.

Hearing the Language of Politics

Not only TV commercials, but also newspaper and magazine editorials, roadway posters, and numerous campaign phone calls forcefully try to convince us of the value of a specific political candidate. At times they aim to frighten us. Party symbols and other rhetorical devices abound on leaflets, fliers, banners, hats, t-shirts, and buttons, all intending to manipulate us to accept a preconceived position or belief. On the campaign trail, candidates for public office often use innuendo, biased language, untruths, and even threats. The language used by political party supporters can become nasty and insulting, sometimes even resorting to name-calling.

Harry Truman was one president who refused to become involved in devious ways of persuading the American public. He was open and transparent. He made the deductive approach his own: first, he said what he would do; next, he told how he would do it. Then, he did it. Afterward, he told the American public that he had done it. Many American presidents who followed him emulated his direct, even blunt, approach, which approximated the rhetorical mode of *exposition* more than it did *persuasion and argument*.

Thankfully, most politicians do not resort to smear tactics. Both induction and deduction can be extremely effective, if they are done well; politicians have chosen both routes with success. The response of the public strongly influences how the candidates speak. The "political climate" is set both ways: from speaker to audience, and from audience to speaker.

As we negotiate today's information highway, however, advertising and politicking can overwhelm us. Most of us would like to learn more about how to negotiate our way through it. Is there a way to respond to it all? And what can we learn from it? As a reader, a consumer, and a voter, it behooves us to develop a critical consciousness.

The Importance of Critical Attention

Persuasion and argument (P&A for short) can convince a jury, run up a large bill on our charge cards, make us quit smoking, convince us to sponsor a foster child in a war-torn country, improve our church or synagogue attendance, or lead us down a dark alley. Indeed, sometimes the manipulation can be unscrupulous and designed to push us toward negative ends. Plainly, this type of writing is used both for good or evil. Understanding its rules can help you to discern when you are being manipulated. This is extremely valuable knowledge. On your guard, your critical attention can be raised to its highest degree. If you remain clear-eyed, you will be able to read P&A effectively and act accordingly.

Writing Persuasion and Argument

When used judiciously and carefully by you, the student, P&A can put you in control, encouraging your readers to believe that what you say is right. It constitutes a form of discourse whose intent is to have the reader accept a position, a belief, or to undertake a course of action. Sometimes, as in a persuasive speech, you may want to tap the emotional rather than the rational side of the listener or reader. Soaring language, rich in imagery, can move individuals, an auditorium of listeners, vast media audiences, and even nations. Rational argument—the intelligent, calm method preferred in a court of law, however, is preferred in the college classroom. This will require adherence to the protocol of academic writing: a clear and strong thesis statement (now referred to as the *proposition*), valid and logical supporting data, and a powerful, unmistakable conclusion that will raise the reader's antennae.

The Most Complex Mode of Discourse

Persuasion and argument is the most complex, and therefore, the most difficult voice of discourse to read and write. It often includes the three other modes—description, narration, and exposition. So constituted, it can sound as believable as a factual essay. The added dimension is its appeal not only to the reader's sympathy, but also his vices, flaws, weaknesses, or desires. The "seven deadly sins"—lust, greed, envy, sloth, anger, gluttony, and vanity—while serving as frequent targets, when carefully masked in the points of the argument, can also serve as a writer's ally. A complex mode, indeed! Appeal to a reader's desire for equality or increased comfort, for example, can be tempting arguments.

Proposition, Issue, Solution

This fourth voice of discourse tells "what should or ought to happen." In full argumentative essays (as opposed to ads or other short pleas for readers' action), we must include the *proposition* (like the thesis statement) somewhere near the beginning. It will declare the *issue*—which means, simply, the topic. In an argumentative essay, the topic is generally a problem to be solved. The same paragraph patterns of exposition will be used in the internal paragraphs of P&A essays as well: comparison and contrast (C/C), cause and effect (C/E), definition and example (D/E), analysis (AN) and sequence (SEQ).

The last paragraph of a P&A essay often contains a *solution* to the problem. However, more often, no solution can be given. The writer may merely want to raise the issue, discuss the problem, and suggest to the reader that "something" be done about it. It is up to the reader to take up or just reject the cause.

This is what makes P&A so difficult, so sophisticated, and so very appealing to write. You can bring up something that you think is urgent. You can describe it fully. You can even provide a vivid example by telling a story about someone involved in the issue, or one like it. You can then explain, expose, and demonstrate why it is urgent, perhaps using published studies or actual statistics. You can just put it out there for the reader, the listener, or the huge audience in cyberspace, to contemplate. If you've done your job, they *will* seriously contemplate it. If they agree with you, and try to work out a solution, you will be a huge success!

Reading Persuasion and Argument

Earlier, we asked the question, is there a way to respond to P&A? And what can we learn from it? When you yourself have written a proposition–solution essay, you will recognize the process. You will have learned how it is done. You can identify the attention seeker, how s/he builds your confidence, appeals to your needs and your vices, and what it is s/he wants you to do. As an informed reader you will know that the task before you is to *judge*. You are the jury. Is the writer logical? You have to infer, to read between the lines, to think about the standard guideline for listeners and readers or persuasive and argumentative speeches, editorials, and essays. To add to your new knowledge of P&A, consider "The 30-Second Spot Quiz" on the following pages.

THE 30-SECOND SPOT QUIZ

Hugh Rank

"The pitch" is a slang term, long used in America, variously defined as "a set talk designed to persuade" (American Heritage Dictionary); "an often high-pressured sales talk; advertisement" (Webster's New Collegiate); "a line of talk, such as a salesman uses to persuade customers" (Webster's New World).

Now, "the pitch" is used here to describe a **basic pattern** of advertising, a five-part strategy described here in a **1-2-3-4-5 "fingertip formula"**—Hi, Trust Me, You Need, Hurry, Buy—easy to memorize, simple to apply, even to *non-rational* persuasion, yet accurate and elegant.

1   **What ATTENTION-GETTING techniques are used?**

Anything unusual? Unexpected? Noticeable? Interesting? Related to:

■ **senses:** motions, colors, lights, sounds, music, visuals (e.g., computer graphics, slow-motion)

■ **emotions:** any associations? (see list below):
sex, scenery, exciting action, fun, family, pets.

■ **thought:** news, lists, displays, claims, advice, questions, stories, demonstrations, contests.

(Popular TV **programs** function as attention-getters to **"deliver the audience."**)

Trust Me!

2 What CONFIDENCE-BUILDING techniques are used?

■ Do you recognize. know (from earlier repetition) the **brand name?** company? symbol? package?

■ Do you already know, like, and trust the **"presenters"**: the endorsers, actors, models?

■ Are these "presenters" **AUTHORITY FIGURES** (expert, wise, protective, caring)? Or, are they **FRIEND FIGURES** (someone you like, like to be, "on your side"; including "cute" cartoons)?

■ What key **words** are used? (Trust, sincere, etc.) **Nonverbals?** (smiles, voice tones, sincere look)

■ In **mail ads,** are computer-written "personalized" touches used? On the **telephone**: tapes? scripts?

You Need!

3 What DESIRE-STIMULATING techniques are used?

Consider (a) **"target audience"** as (b) **benefit-seeking**; and persuaders' **benefit-promising** strategies as focused on (c) **product claims**, or (d) **"added values,"** the intangibles associated with a product.

a. **Who is the "target audience"?** Are you? (If not, as part of an unintended audience, are you interested or hostile toward the ad?)

b. **What's the primary motive of that audience's benefit** *seeking*?

Use chart at right. Most ads are simple acquisition (lower left); Often, such motives co-exist, but one may be dominant. Ads which intensify a **problem,** (that is, a "bad" already hated or feared; the opposite, or the absence of, "goods") and then offer the product as a **solution,** are here called **"scare-and-sell"** ads (right side).

To keep a "good" (protection)"	To get rid of a "bad" (relief)
To get a "good" (acquisition)	To avoid a "bad" (prevention)

c. **What kinds of product claims are emphasised?** (use these 12 categories) what key words, images? Any measurable claims? Or are they subjective opinions, generalized praise words ("puffery")?

SUPERIORITY ("best")   STABILITY ("classic")
QUANTITY ("most")   RELIABILITY ("solid")
EFFICIENCY ("works")   SIMPLICITY ("easy")
BEAUTY ("lovely")   UTILITY ("PRACTICAL")
SCARCITY ("rare")   RAPIDITY ("fast")
NOVELTY ("new")   SAFETY ("safe")

d. **Are any "added values"** implied or suggested? Are there words or images which associate the product with some "good" already loved or desired by the intended audience? With such common human needs/wants/desires as in these 24 categories:

"basic" needs:
FOOD ("tasty")
ACTIVITY ("exciting")
SURROUNDINGS ("comfort")
SEX ("alluring")
HEALTH ("healthy")
SECURITY ("protect")
ECONOMY ("save")

"certitude" needs:
RELIGION ("right")
SCIENCE ("research")
BEST PEOPLE ("elite")
MOST PEOPLE ("popular")
AVERAGE PEOPLE ("typical")

"territory" needs:
NEIGHBORHOOD ("hometown")
NATION ("country")
NATURE ("earth")

love and belonging needs:
INTIMACY("lover")
FAMILY ("Mom" "kids")
GROUPS ("team")

"growth" needs:
ESTEEM ("respected")
PLAY ("fun")
GENEROSITY ("gift")
CURIOSITY ("discover")
COMPLETION ("success")

Hurry!

4 Are there URGENCY-STRESSING techniques used?

(Not all ads: but always check.)

■ If an urgency appeal: What words? (e.g., Hurry, Rush, Deadline, Sale Ends, Offer Expires, Now.)

■ If **no** urgency: Is this **"soft sell"** part of a repetitive, long-term ad campaign for standard item?

Buy!

5 What RESPONSE-SEEKING techniques are used?

(Persuaders always seek some kind of response)

■ Are there specific triggering words used? (Buy, Get, Do, Call, Act, Join, Smoke, Drink, Taste)

■ Is there a **specific response** sought? (Most ads: to buy something)

■ Is there a **specific response** sought? (Most ads: to buy something)

■ If **not**: is it **conditioning** ("public relations" or "image building") to make us **"feel good"** about the company, to get favorable public opinion on its side (against any government regulations, taxes)?

The Reading Experience: Questions for Study and Discussion

1. Have you ever purchased anything based on seeing its commercial? What was the product? What was the pitch? Was a free coupon offered? Was the item on sale for a limited time? Consider "The 30-Second Spot Quiz" sequence.

2. Do you consider yourself to be a logical person? Can you determine when a claim is manipulating you? Should political speeches and advertisements be read or listened to aesthetically or efferently? Why?

3. When an argument is not logical and rational, it is called a *fallacy*. For example: "If the most popular sports heroes wear Adidas Superstar, they must be the best sneakers. If you buy a pair, you will enhance your performance at your chosen sport." What is wrong with this argument? Can you name any commercials or ads that use famous spokespersons for their products? Which "step" in the quiz above addresses this fallacy?

4. When commercials for juicy burgers, shrimp dishes, or melting chocolate are shown on TV, how close are these items to the camera? How are the chosen phrases and the tone of the actors presented to enhance the product? Which of the four "desire stimulating" techniques above is used?

5. In an election year, how do candidates use techniques that match any of the steps in "The 30-Second Spot Quiz"?

The Writing Experience: Suggestions for Short Papers

1. List ten or more features of your personality that would be vulnerable to advertisements and commercials. (For example, "I am star-struck," "I love a bargain," "I want anything that will make my life easier.") How are these personality features, however slightly, connected to one of the "seven sins"?

2. Choose two public figures who are currently running for public office. Using their commercials, explain your impressions of their personalities, their integrity, and their effectiveness if elected in a 500-word paper.

3. Choose a film or music album that you have seen or heard recently. Write a one- to two-page review either criticizing features that you found lacking or features that you liked, explaining persuasively why others should listen to the album or see the film.

4. Look for a product's use of "senses, emotions, and thoughts" given for #1, the "Hi!" phase of the sequence in five ads in a recent magazine or newspaper. How does each ad attract a reader's attention? Write your analysis of these three facets of the ad. Include the ads with your assignments.

Recommended Films and eConnections

Words Writing Tips — Ads that Attract Customers. Learnwithgoogle. 19 Jul. 2011. YouTube video.

Adweek Art: Mad Men at the Movies. Adweek. 15 June 2011. YouTube video.

Art and Copy. Dir. Doug Pray. Perf. George Lois, Mary Wells, Dan Wieden, Lee Clow, Hal Riney. 2009. Documentary Film.

Mr. Mom. Dir. Stan Dragoti. Perf. Michael Keaton, Teri Garr. Fox. 1983. Film.

Quiz

_____ 1. "The 30-Second Spot Quiz" is:　　(a) an uncommon framework for a magazine advertisement; (b) a cartoon designed to make the reader laugh; (c) the "skeleton" underneath most ads and TV commercials; (d) an argument against television commercials.

_____ 2. The five-step sequence in itself is a pattern demonstrating: (a) analysis; (b) sequence; (c) definition and example; (d) both (a) and (b) are correct.

_____ 3. The "desire-stimulating ads" are geared to: (a) keep a "good"; (b) get rid of a "bad"; (c) get a "good"; (d) avoid a "bad"; (e) all the above.

_____ 4. An "urgency appeal" often includes: (a) the words "Offer Expires"; (b) the words "reliability and simplicity"; (c) the words "trust me!"; (d) the words "Buy" and "Get."

_____ 5. The somewhat coy smiling face that speaks the words "Trust me!" is a symbol of: (a) an authority figure; (b) a "friend" figure; (c) a familiar brand or package; (d) all the above.

WHY CAN'T THIS VEAL CALF WALK?

The Humane Farming Association

Q: Why can't this veal calf walk?

A: He has only two feet

Actually, _less_ than two feet. Twenty-two inches to be exact. His entire life is spent chained in a wooden crate measuring only 22 inches wide and 56 inches long. The crate is so small that the calf can't walk or even turn around.

_____

Most people think animal abuse is illegal. It isn't. In veal factories, it's business as usual. "Milk-fed" veal is produced by making a calf anemic.

The calf is *not* fed mother's milk. He's fed an antibiotic-laced formula that leads to diarrhea. He must lie in his own excrement—choking on the ammonia gases. He's chained with hundreds of other baby calves suffering the same fate.

Tainted Veal

According to the USDA, sulfamethazine (a known carcinogen), oxytetracycline, penicillin, neomycin, streptomycin, and gentamycin have all previously been found in veal.

Doesn't the USDA prevent tainted veal from being sold? Absolutely not. The USDA itself admits that most veal is never tested for toxic residue.

The industry claims that the drugs used in veal have been approved by the FDA. But don't buy it. The fact is: Illegal and unapproved drugs have been widely used in veal calves.

Veal factories maximize profits for agribusiness drug companies because they are a breeding ground for disease. To keep calves alive under such torturous conditions, they are given drugs which can be passed on to consumers.

It doesn't have to be this way. And with your help, it won't be. *Please join us.*

YES! I support HFA's National Veal Boycott.
Factory farms must be stopped from abusing animals, misusing drugs, and destroying the environment.
Enclosed is my tax-deductible contribution of:
☐ $20   ☐ $50   ☐ $100   ☐ $500   ☐ Other

_____
Name

_____
Address

_____
City/State/Zip

Free newsletter available upon request.
The Humane Farming Association (HFA)
1150 California Street—Suite C
San Francisco, CA 94109

The Reading Experience: Questions for Study and Discussion

1. The heading and photo for this ad are deliberately misleading. How? What is the intention of the advertisers? When and how did you figure out this puzzle?

2. The word "feet" is a *homonym* – a *homograph*, to be precise – which is a word that sounds, and in this case, is spelled, like another word with an entirely different meaning. A *homophone* is another type of homonym, a word that sounds like, but is spelled differently from another word; for example: *colonel* and *kernel*; *two, too,* and *to*. Together with a partner, create as many homonym word pairs as you can that are: (a) homographs and (b) homophones. Put these on the chalkboard.

3. Playing with words in order to fool the reader is not the only gimmick used in this ad. What other linguistic and visual chicanery is used in this ad? (Hint: look at the photo itself, as well as the coupon.)

4. What is the *issue* proposed in the ad? Is it a valid issue? What is the proposed *solution*? Is it a valid solution?

5. How does this ad affect you? Will it influence your future actions? How?

The Writing Experience: Suggestions for Short Papers

1. Using "The 30-Second Spot Quiz," follow the five-question sequence to identify the content of this advertisement. Write your findings in a short, critical essay.

2. Create an advertisement of your own for an existing issue or product. You may simply describe the layout, or actually craft an ad for a classroom demonstration. To use a graphic or photograph is your choice; however, your ad must include several composed paragraphs that discuss the issue, as the calf ad does above. The six or seven paragraphs shown may be used as your model. Standard English, correct spelling, and careful editing are necessities.

3. In a brief, one-page essay, discuss the importance of the photograph in the calf ad. How does it deepen the message? Would the ad be as successful without it?

4. Research other advertisements by the Humane Farming Association. Do they follow a pattern? How are they similar or different? What is the primary intention of that organization? Why, in your opinion, are they so successful? Prepare a report of your findings.

Recommended Films and eConnections

Farm Animal Abuse Video.[1]AnimalRightsFanClub. ebbtider. 5 June 2008. YouTube video.

Bill Bailey Comes Home! A Dog Rescue Story. AnimalAdvocates. 1 Oct. 2008. YouTube video.

Marley and Me. Dir. David Frankel. Perf. Owen Wilson, Jennifer Aniston, Eric Dane, Kathleen Turner, Alan Arkin. 20th Century Fox. 2008.

Gorillas in the Mist. Dir. Michael Apted. Perf. Sigourney Weaver, Bryan Brown. Universal Studios and Warner Brothers. 1988. Film.

Quiz

_____ 1. The intent of the Humane Farming Association advertisement is to: (a) describe the veal industry; (b) narrate the story of the veal industry; (c) persuade the reader to take some positive action against the factory farms; (d) explain objectively how veal cows are raised.

_____ 2. According to the ad, calves: (a) appear happy to spend their time in a crate; (b) are fed fattening food; (d) are fed too much solid food; (d) do not have enough room to turn around and stretch their legs.

_____ 3. The basic appeal of this advertisement is: (a) rationality; (b) emotionality; (c) sentimentality; (d) anthropomorphism.

_____ 4. Those who oppose animal protection according to the advertisement, portray the issue as a choice between humans and: (a) vegetarians; (b) veal cattle; (c) the Humane Farming Association; (d) animals.

---

1. Warning: This video may be disturbing to some viewers.

5. The answer within the advertisement to the question "Should this calf be allowed . . . .to walk?" is: (a) It really doesn't matter. (b) No. (c) Yes, of course. (d) The public is powerless to do anything about it.

I LIVE IN THE FUTURE & HERE'S HOW IT WORKS

Nick Bilton

There's a recent, often-quoted study, "Emails 'Hurt IQ More than Pot.'"

. . . Over and over at speeches and conferences, I hear the same kinds of fears and anxieties that new technologies and developments have generated for decades: Our brains weren't wired for all this fast-paced stuff. We're too distracted to do meaningful and thorough work. At the same time, our entertainment is also dangerous and damaging people tell me. Video games will destroy our children's brains and their relationships—if Twitter and Facebook don't do so first. We cannot effectively multitask or jump from e-mail to writing to video, and we never will be able to.

There may be some truth to some of this; we may well be fundamentally different when this is all over. But for the most part, I believe it's bunk. Just as well-meaning scientists as consumers feared that trains and comic books and television would rot our brains and spoil our minds, I believe many of these skeptics and worrywarts today are missing the bigger picture, the greater value that access to new and faster information is bringing us. For the most part, our brains will adapt in a constructive way to this new online world, just as we formed communities to help us sort information.

Why do I believe this? Because we've learned how to do so many things already, including learning how to read. . . . Today, when children learn their letters and form them into words and sentences and big, powerful ideas, their brains still have to re-form and readapt to make the information fall into place.

Stanislas Dehaene, chair of Experimental Cognitive Neurology at the Collège de France, has spent most of his career in neuroscience exploring how our brains learn to read and calculate numbers. He explains that human brains are better wired to communicate by speaking. In the first year of life, babies begin to pick up words and sounds simply from hearing them. Sure, they need some help identifying that a cup is a cup and Mommy is Mommy. But by two years old, most children are talking and applying labels to objects without any special lessons or drills.

This is not the case with reading. Most children, even if they share books with their parents and hear stories every single day, won't pick up reading on their own. Instead, they must learn to recognize letters one by one and put them together into sounds or words before recognizing whole sentences and thoughts. They must learn to decode symbols. . . .

* For examples of very young children's connection to technology, watch on YouTube the many videos of babies accurately dancing and singing to various performers (e.g., Lady Gaga and Elvis Presley) even while strapped into car seats.

Let's hypothetically travel back two thousand years and find a newborn baby. Imagine taking that baby and transporting him through our time machine forward to today. This child would be raised in our technology-rich society, growing up in a world of iPods, video games, the Internet, mobile phones, GPS, robotic Elmo toys, banner ads, and more. I asked several neuroscientists if this baby born two thousand years ago would likely grow up differently than would a child born today. The resounding answer was "no." A newborn's brain from two thousand years ago, I was told, would likely look and work exactly the same as a brain does today.*

But what if you took an adult—let's say a thirty-year-old man from two thousand years ago—and dropped him in the middle of Times Square. He might well experience a panic attack from all the crowds, cars, flashing lights, and stimulation. But, neuroscientists said, his brain would begin to adapt. He might never get to a point where he could talk and simultaneously send text messages, but numerous research studies show that our brains are capable of substantial adaptation in about two weeks and in some instances, seven days. Our two-thousand-year-old man would be just fine. His adaptation to society and the new stimuli would just take training, and not as much as you might think. . . .

What happens when we're online that keeps the brain so busy?

The online experience isn't simple or controlled; it's like the Wild West. The user interface alone is enough to send you running for the comfort of the printed page. Every last piece of real estate on the screen is vying for your attention. Your Web browser has back buttons, reload buttons, and a bright red stop button that screams, "Hey, look at me!" Other windows may be floating in the background of your computer screen. You probably have a desktop image of your cats or a cute baby.

Then there's the actual Web page, which includes eye-popping banner ads, search boxes, logos, and colored text showing you links to other Web pages, which then link to even more Web pages. In the course of a day, you might go to a few news websites, read a blog or two, look at the weather, search Google for a range of answers, and buy a book on Amazon or eBay. Before you know it, you may have visited well over a hundred Web pages in a day. That may not seem like a lot, but the amount of content you see can be mind-boggling. . . .

Beyond the links, the websites have plenty of words, too . . . the top two hundred news and information sites in the United States and the United Kingdom put forth an astounding grand total of 487,881 words and 66,248 links. And get this: Hitting those two hundred sites is the equivalent of flipping through Tolstoy's *War and Peace*, which is 480,000 words long. . . .

Our brains are stimulated while we're online by the physically interactive and unpredictable nature of using a computer: You're challenging your brain by holding a mouse, looking at a screen, and navigating through choices and buttons. It's a very hands-on experience that is completely different from the more passive and linear activity of reading a book or watching TV or a movie. When you're reading or watching a movie, your body and your hands are relatively still. And though you can certainly skip around, you're more likely to read or watch from the beginning to the middle to the end.

Although there is a beginning, middle, and end to most online content, those links also form thousands of branches of information that essentially allow you to devise your own narrative, creating a whole new form of storytelling. . . .

All of this is enough to make your head spin. It makes perfect sense that our brains are active as a scanner when we're online.

Online our brains are stimulated, calculating and exploring. They are working differently. This is consistent with another development researchers have found: Mastering another electronic challenge—video games—also engages the brain and may actually make us more adept at certain tasks.

But this doesn't mean our brains can't handle this new form of storytelling. It just means we are telling and consuming stories differently. . . .

As our brains adapt and continue to grow and change shape, the technology and storytelling will continue to do the same thing. Our brains have done this successfully for thousands of years as they have learned new forms of communications and storytelling.

The Reading Experience: Questions for Reading and Study

1. Nick Bilton, lead tech writer for the *New York Times* and largely responsible for the paper's switch from its full print edition to one online, argues with people who fear newer and newer technology. What are they afraid of? What is the *issue*?

2. What does Bilton think of the older generation's beliefs about technology? Does he agree with any part of it? Bilton's *proposition* is stated early in the essay; can you underline it?

3. If you *assay* this essay, you can find his argument's compelling conclusion right where it should be. Underline it; compare it to the proposition (thesis statement) you underlined earlier. How do they match? Do you see the *main idea*, in a nutshell?

4. Not alone in his beliefs, Bilton cites research done by French cognitive neurologist Stanislas Dehaene who spent much of his life studying how the human brain learns to read and calculate numbers, comparing it to using a mouse, studying the computer screen, responding to emails and talking to someone in the room, all at the same time. If you've done this, do you think you are lessening your ability to think, or improving it?

   Bilton asks us to travel back 2000 years and provide a baby from that time with the toys and machines of our modern technological society. He assures us that the child would grow up with the same capabilities as you or I. But Rome at that time (about 14 AD) was a thriving metropolis with sophisticated food and water supply systems, active religious cults, rich forms of literature, art, and sculpture—much of which is displayed today in the Metropolitan Museum of Art. It is not a stretch to imagine the first century's child's brain to be as fully developed—and capable of developing more complex thought processes—as any child's today. There seems to be no quarrel with that notion.

   But what of the adult? What would his or her problems be? Do you think, as Bilton does, that that person might never fully adapt? How does this example reinforce the author's *proposition*?

5. The author says this new form of storytelling (think of it as writing) and consuming (think of it as reading) is not destroying our brains at all, just functioning at the same level, but "differently." Do you agree with his *proposition*? Has he "solved" the problem explained at the beginning of his chapter?

The Writing Experience: Suggestions for Short Papers

1. Write from the point of view of Bilton's thirty-year-old man from 2000 years ago "dropped" in the middle of Times Square. Walk around in his shoes. What does he think of the lights, traffic, theaters, people, technology? Take Bilton's comments seriously, and incorporate them into your narrative.

2. Describe your own experiences when you're online, either on your computer or cell phone. Do you text (never in the car!!) and talk to others at the same time? Do you navigate more than one website or blog at a time? How often do you switch to a different Web page? Explain your process.

3. Compare and contrast reading print with digital text. Do you own an iPad, Nook, or other device? What are the similarities and differences between each process? Which do you prefer, and why?

4. Do you think your brain is being disrupted by media? To help you with this and other argumentative essay topics, download the free application from nickbilton.com and snap an image of the QR Code (two-dimensional barcode) at the beginning of each chapter to access additional original content.

5. Where do you think the digital world will take us next? What do you foresee in our technological future? How will newer tools continue to shape the way we communicate and perform? What do we need to do to take advantage of these opportunities? (Recommended reading: *The Diamond Age* by Neal Stephenson.)

Recommended Films and eConnections

Nick Bilton and the Future of News. IgniteNYC. 11 Sept. 2008. YouTube video.

Nick Bilton: Smart Content. poptech. 5 Mar. 2010. YouTube video.

The Back to the Future Trilogy. Dir. Robert Zemeckis. Perf. Michael J. Fox, Christopher Lloyd. Amblin Entertainment. 1985, 1989, 1990. Film.

Fit to Print. Dir. Adam Chadwick. Perf. Stephen Janis, Laura Frank. n.s. 2010. Film.

Quiz

_____ 1. Bilton's proposition is that: (a) our brains will adapt in a constructive way to the new online world just as they have done for thousands of years; (b) emails hurt IQ more than pot; (c) our brains will be fundamentally different as a result of video games, Twitter, and Facebook; (d) human brains are better wired to communicate by speaking.

_____ 2. Bilton cites Stanislas Dehaene in discussing: (a) how adults decode symbols; (b) how children naturally pick up words and sounds simply from hearing them; (c) how difficult it is for children to learn to speak; (d) how important it is for children to share books with their parents.

_____ 3. Bilton suggests that a baby born two thousand years ago: (a) has a brain inferior to babies born today; (b) had brains superior to babies born today; (c) had a brain that looked and worked exactly the same as a baby's brain today; (d) would not have had the ability to learn how to use an iPod or a robotic Elmo toy.

_____ 4. Bilton posits that an adult from the first century put in the middle of Times Square would: (a) panic; (b) begin to adapt; (c) eventually learn to talk and text at the same time; (d) all of the above.

_____ 5. Bilton argues that being online: (a) allows you to devise your own narrative by moving back and forth between the links, telling and consuming stories differently; (b) confuses your brain so you no longer can understand how to read; (c) destroys the art of storytelling; (d) none of the above.

HAND, EYE, BRAIN:
SOME "BASICS" IN THE WRITING PROCESS

Janet Emig

Much of the current talk about the basics of writing is not only confused but, even more ironic, frivolous. Capitalization, spelling, punctuation—these are touted as the basics in writing when they represent, of course, merely the conventions, the amenities for recording the outcome of the process. The process is what is basic in writing, the process and the organic structures that interact to produce it. What are these structures? And what are their contributions? Although we don't yet know, the hand, the eye, and the brain itself surely seem logical candidates as requisite structures (Emig, 1975, pp. 11–13). The purpose of this chapter is to speculate about the role or roles each may play in the writing process and to suggest hypotheses, with appropriate methodologies, to assess their contributions, as well as to determine the likely forms orchestration and interplay may take.

From "Hand Eye Brain: Some 'Basics' in the Writing Process" by Janet Emig, in *Research and Composing: Points of Departure,* Charles C. Cooper and Lee Odell (eds.). Copyright © 1978. Reprinted by permission of the National Council of Teachers of English (NCTE), Urbana, IL.

The Reading Experience: Questions for Reading and Study

1. Careful word choice is essential in framing an argument. Even before she states her proposition, note the language Emig chooses in her very first sentence: the words "confused," "ironic," and "frivolous" set the tone for her argument. How? Using a dictionary or Thesaurus, find synonyms for each of these words. If these were substituted in their place, how would the emphasis shift? How would changes either reinforce or weaken her opening statement? What "loaded" words can you find in the second sentence? How does this sentence further her point of view? Look for (actually, circle) other such words in the rest of this selection that strengthen her point, and her point of view.

2. How many times does Emig choose to use the word "process"? Is there a reason for this repetition? Note that in this short, but powerful paragraph, every single word counts.

3. Earlier in this textbook, Emig's proposition—her thesis statement—was quoted to demonstrate its clarity. A master of crafting language economically, choosing each word carefully, the proposition sets out precisely what Emig will focus upon. She tells us that we will look at three parts of the body—the hand, the eye, and the brain—for the purpose of analyzing the *roles* each may play in the *writing process.* What is a process? Without reading her full essay, what do you think she might say about each of these parts? Think about the way you use your hand, your eyes, and your brain when you write. How do these function? Why are they important?

4. Looking at parts of the body is not an argument; what is she arguing for?

5. Do you agree with her point of view? Do you think capitalization, spelling, and punctuation are really *basic* in writing well? Do these "amenities" deserve our most important focus? Should you be judged as a poor or proficient writer on your ability to capitalize, spell, and punctuate?

The Writing Experience: Suggestions for Short Papers

1. When reading P&A, a reader's role is *to judge*. Test Emig's hypothesis now. Together with a partner, watch one another write. Decide on a topic first. Then, as each of you writes in turn, the partner will observe what is happening. Follow these suggestions:

   - Look at the writer's hand. Is s/he right- or left-handed? What utensil is being used? Ask the writer about the preference of one tool over another—and include keying, or typing, as opposed to writing by hand. Does the writer use script, or print? Are any words crossed out, erased? How frequently does the writing stop?

   - Look at the writer's eyes: do they stay focused upon the paper, or do they wander upward, left, or right, when thinking? How are they important to the task? What would happen if vision were impaired? Would the writing process change?

   - Ask the writer what s/he is thinking about. How does s/he form ideas? How often does the writer stop to think? Is the writer fluent—does s/he keep going? Is s/he cheerful or anxious about the task?

   - Write your findings in a short essay, beginning with a proposition that seeks to "test" Emig's theory. Your conclusion, of course, must reflect your *judgment*.

2. How can we update the hand-eye-brain writing process described by Emig? What shall we look at as we use a computer, iPhone, or any other digital media? Design criteria for such an experiment and work with another student in a Writing Lab session. Compare the class experience with the lab experience. This suggestion may be replicated as homework if conditions are more feasible.

3. Use question #5 as the basis for a short essay, discussing the importance of capitalization, spelling, and punctuation in evaluating a college level essay. Use your own past experiences as a student to reinforce your argument.

4. What parts of the body are required for one of the following activities: reading, completing math problems, playing a musical instrument (choose one), knitting, pottery throwing, or painting. Choose one with which you are familiar. Sketch and construct your model before beginning observation. Then write a short paper that describes your chosen activity. (For additional help, see the online article, "Janet Emig: The Writer's Notebook," by Charles Bivona.)

Recommended Films and eConnections

Jerry Seinfeld on How to Write a Joke. The New York Times. 20 Dec. 2012. YouTube video.

The Writing Process. OnDemandInstruction. Aug. 2011. YouTube video.

Becoming Jane. Dir. Julian Jarrold. Anne Hathaway, James McEvoy, Julie Walters, James Cromwell, Maggie Smith. Miramax Films, 2007. Film. 3

Adaptation. Dir. Spike Jonze. Perf. Nicolas Cage, Meryl Streep, Chris Cooper, Cara Seymour, Tilda Swinton. Columbia Pictures, 2002. Film.

Quiz

_____ 1. The full essay to follow this excerpt will progress as follows: (a) the essay will discuss capitalization, spelling, and punctuation; (b) the essay will discuss confusion, irony, and frivolity; (c) the essay will discuss the hand, the eye, and the brain and how they contribute to the writing process; (d) the essay will discuss the current talk about the basics of writing.

2. The proposition/thesis of this argumentative essay is in: (a) the last two sentences; (b) the first two sentences; (c) the third sentence; (d) none of the above.

3. The paragraph opens by: (a) crediting the current studies of writing; (b) challenging the present level of importance put on capitalization, spelling, and punctuation; (c) reinforcing the status quo; (d) praising the current talk about writing.

4. Emig's paragraph indicates that the essay to follow will qualify for: (a) the aesthetic reading stance; (b) the efferent reading stance; (c) prolonged study by experts; (d) little effort in reading.

5. Most likely, Emig will conclude with the *solution* that: (a) the reader needs to do more research on composing; (b) writers need to begin with an outline and work through multiple drafts of their writings; (c) more research is needed; (d) focusing on the hand, the eye, and the brain is more basic to understanding the writing process than work on grammar.

CONTEMPLATING THE UNIVERSE: LINGUISTICALLY SPEAKING

Laura Kolnoski

"Awesome" is antiquated. "Whatever" is waning. "At the end of the day?" The end is near. If you're still using these so-yesterday terms, you're not up on the latest assault on the King's English. Today's trendy talkers are repeatedly using "sort of" in most annoying ways.

I'm sort of sick and tired of people increasingly inserting the phrase "sort of" into their conversation, which is particularly proliferating on television. The pundits speak of "sort of" policies, with various politicians being "sort of" concerned. Are they concerned or not? Commentators, interviewers, and their interviewees use it. Recently, I heard former presidential press secretary Robert Gibbs use it. It's astounding and disheartening how many supposedly intelligent speakers have allowed this pointless phrase to creep into their daily conversation.

During an otherwise enjoyable interview about love letters written to Lady Bird Johnson by her boyfriend Lyndon Baines Johnson in the 1930s, one of LBJ's granddaughters used it, calling them "sort of love letters." I submit they are, in fact, love letters, not "sort of" love letters, just as LBJ was president, not "sort of" president. More onerous than "kind of," "sort of" indicates the speaker can't make up their mind, or has serious commitment issues.

The verbal plague has crept upon the public lexicon slowly and insidiously. No doubt, a new annoying word or phrase will soon replace the overused "sort of," just as "groovy" has been replaced with the baffling "that's sick." I'm sticking with "groovy." Please do everything you can to eradicate this scourge upon the public discourse. It's sort of up to all of u to prevent language slaughter.

The Reading Experience: Questions for Reading and Discussion

1. The first paragraph and most of the second paragraph prepare the reader for the proposition, which declares the issue, at the end of paragraph two. Can you underline the proposition? Do you know which of the expository patterns has been chosen for this essay? Aha! If you said "cause and effect," you are right. However, there seems to be just a description of the "effect" — but no cause given. Can you supply one?

2. How does the author use the phrase "sort of" ironically? Does its use make the essay more or less persuasive? Is the tone serious, humorous, angry, melancholy? Explain.

3. Why does Kolnoski mention Robert Gibbs and "one of LBJ's granddaughters"? If you were writing an essay that criticized popular culture, how would you illustrate the issue? Does the author's citation of these public figures add to her credibility? Why or why not?

4. Does Kolnoski offer a solution to the problem? What does she expect of the reader?

5. Do you agree or disagree with the writer? Judging from your own experience, do you feel that there is a problem with people using the term "sort of" too often? Does the phrase bother you? Is Kolnoski's argument successful?

The Writing Experience: Suggestions for Short Essays

1. Compose an opening paragraph that sets out an issue about language usage in your school, community, or within your group of Facebook friends. Are there any expressions that are a bit too trendy and overly annoying? What do you suggest be done about it?

2. New slang terms enter the English language almost daily. They are largely a reflection of regional and generational culture. Create and then compare two lists of slang terms used today and a specific era in the past, perhaps the 1950s; or compare slang expressions used in your local area with slang used in a distant area of the United States. How do these reflect the generation or the region from which they spring? Are there any problems that occur when "East meets West"?

3. Are the following phrases logical? How did they begin? Are they still appropriate? Write a short essay that explains the origin and present usage of these expressions, concluding with a statement that expresses your feelings about their use.

   "You're the best thing since sliced bread."

   "Dead as a doornail."

   "It's a dog eat dog world."

   "Put that in your pipe and smoke it."

   "You're driving me nuts."

   "Avoid it like the plague."

   "She's a space cadet!"

   Add your own!

4. Choose a popular figure (singer, politician, talk show host) who uses non-standard English, or a way of speaking that characterizes him or her in the extreme. Write an analysis of that person's speech.

Recommended Films and eConnections

A Commentary on The Use of Slang. JWebgotSWAG. 12 Dec. 2010. YouTube video.

4 Magic Phrases You Can Use to Respond to Anything. Online Communication Skills Training. Videos with Dan O'Connor and Power Diversity. 27 June 2004. YouTube video.

My Fair Lady. Dir. George Cukor. Perf. Rex Harrison, Audrey Hepburn. Warner Brothers. 1964. Film.

Rocket Science. Dir. Jeffrey Blitz. Perf. Reese Thompson, Anna Kendrick. Picture House and HBO Films. 2007. Film.

Quiz

_____ 1. The author's *issue* is: (a) that too many people have allowed the phrase "sort of" to creep into their conversation; (b) famous people in public life set the standards for others to use improper language; (c) new annoying phrases come into the language too often; (d) LBJ's letters were forged.

_____ 2. Kolnoski wants her readers to: (a) check the facts about Robert Gibbs and Lyndon Johnson's granddaughter; (b) consider the validity of her argument and do everything they can to eradicate this scourge on public discourse; (c) read more enjoyable reviews about famous love letters; (d) stay alert when it comes to language.

_____ 3. The use of the words "sort of" in this article are called everything *except*: (a) a scourge; (b) antiquated; (c) language slaughter; (d) a verbal plague.

_____ 4. The article: (a) is more emotionally persuasive than logically argumentative; (b) is more logically argumentative than emotionally persuasive; (c) lacks a concrete solution; (d) both (a) and (c) are correct.

_____ 5. People who use slang or other deviations from standard English: (a) are not always aware that they are doing so; (b) do so deliberately, to sound "cool"; (c) are generally non-native speakers ; (d) none of the above.

SELF-RELIANCE
1847

Ralph Waldo Emerson

Trust thyself: every heart vibrates to that iron string. Accept the place the divine providence has found for you, the society of your contemporaries, the connection of events. Great men have always done so, and confided themselves childlike to the genius of their age, betraying their perception that the absolutely trustworthy was seated at their heart, working through their hands, predominating in all their being. . . .

Whoso would be a man, must be a nonconformist. He who should gather immortal palms must not be hindered by the name of goodness, but must explore it if it be goodness. Nothing is at last sacred but the integrity of your own mind. . . .

From "Self-Reliance" by Ralph Waldo Emerson, Essays: First Series, 1841.

The Reading Experience: Questions for Reading and Discussion

1. To whom is Emerson speaking? Pay close attention to the form of the verb. The first two words of his most famous quotation are a perfect example of the grammatical form "you understood." It recommends immediate audience involvement. The heart of his message is not just to engage your attention, but to almost startle you into obedience, and to make you want to obey, willingly. It is the perfect example of P&A. Emerson persuades us at once. Who would not want to trust themselves? This sets the level of positive response from the reader instantly.

2. Emerson believes that genius lies within each person's own heart and mind. But he does not shun others; on the contrary, he advises his reader to connect with others. Paraphrase the second sentence.

3. Why does Emerson advise us to be "childlike"? What do you think he means? A clue may be found in the words "betraying." If a man listens to himself while *in* the company of others, but does not let the others ("the society" of his "contemporaries") know or hear what he thinks at that moment, he is actually keeping silent, as a child does, when listening to the adults around him.[2] In a sense, he is "betraying" himself. How does this relate to you, "thyself"?

4. However, when he, like "great men," is silent, he is judging his contemporaries' words and actions, and the events that are taking place, and deciding how to act—how to "connect." He instead will show through deeds and actions (like the great men—"working through their hands") what he believes—what is "seated at [his] heart." His inner thoughts—the feelings of his heart—are "trustworthy." How do *you* respond to the events you are a part of? Do you act accordingly, without boasting? Without being pushy? Do you think quietly to yourself, and then do what you know to be right?

5. Explain what Emerson means when he says "Whoso would be a man, must be a non-conformist"? He most certainly does not intend harm to society. On the contrary, he seeks "goodness." So what does he mean by "the *name* of goodness"? Is everything that is called good, really good? Consider the title again, and those powerful two first words. Do you *trust thyself*?

The Writing Experience: Suggestions for Short Essays

1. In 1847, Emerson's audience was predominantly male. Women not only were routinely excluded from academic and professional life, but were certainly not encouraged to think for themselves, to trust themselves, to be "self-reliant." Such a woman would be considered unmarriageable, and even witchlike. Rewrite the opening paragraph as you would like to see it for women. This may be done from two points of view: one, advice for the passive, obedient 1847 woman, and the second, advice for today's woman.

2. Select a contemporary issue that you would like to address. Write a short essay that explains how your "heart vibrates to that iron string" inside yourself when you think of "the connection of events" in society to your role in it. The video below, "The Hunger Project: Women's Journey to Self Reliance" is an illustration of one such issue.

---

2. Emerson would have been familiar with the popular Victorian adage used since the fifteenth century to teach children obedience: "Children should be seen and not heard."

3. There are "nonconformists" in society from Emerson's era to our own who have "explore[d] . . . goodness" for the benefit of all mankind. Write an essay about these men and women, relating each to Emerson's essay, "Self-Reliance." Cite your sources appropriately.

4. Read "Nature," "The American Scholar," or another essay of your choice by Ralph Waldo Emerson. Select and quote from one important passage from your chosen essay and analyze it for its issue, its proposition, and its solution. Relate the theme to a modern-day issue that makes your heart "vibrate," arguing strongly for a solution.

Recommended Films and eConnections

Ralph Waldo Emerson — Trust Thyself. ajhande. 22 June 2008.

The Hunger Project: *Women's Journey to Self-Reliance.* thehungerproject. 12 Jan. 2010. YouTube video.

The American Dream. Dir. Jamil Walker Smith. Perf. Jamil Walker Smith, Malcolm Goodwin, Ming-Na, Louis Ferriera. Little Plow Films. 2012. Film.

Bowling for Columbine. Dir. Michael Moore. Perf. Matt Stone, Chris Rock, Charleton Heston, Marilyn Manson. United Artists, 2002. Film.

Quiz

_____ 1. Emerson's "iron string" is: (a) society; (b) one's self; (c) a life partner; (d) none of the above.

_____ 2. Emerson's proposition is that: (a) we need to conform to society's laws and moral codes; (b) we need to consider the tenets of faith and follow the Scriptures; (c) we need to seek goodness according to our own standards of goodness; (d) accept the place divine providence has found for you and remain obedient to its existing laws.

_____ 3. When Emerson states "whoso would be a man must be a nonconformist," he means: (a) to be a nonconformist, one must be a man, not a woman; (b) both men and women must not be nonconformists; (c) that one must not obey the law; (d) to become a full, responsible human being, one must be a nonconformist by obeying one's own search for goodness.

_____ 4. To read "Self-Reliance" in the most readerly manner, one should: (a) take the aesthetic stance, living through the experience of reading; (b) take the efferent stance, judging the proposition and conclusion for oneself; (c) predict, build, review, and interpret, looking at plot, characters, setting, and a narrator; (d) both (a) and (c) are correct.

_____ 5. Emerson is: (a) not persuasive; (b) questionable; (c) extremely conservative; (d) a successful writer of persuasion and argument.

COLLABORATION SENSATION: THE MOCK ELECTION— A PARTNER PROJECT IN THE POLITICAL PROCESS

- At least two class days may be needed for this project; one for planning the process, and the second for its performance.
- Divide the class into two political camps.
- Each camp will choose one student to run for political office (President, Governor, Mayor, etc.)
- Each candidate will write and deliver a campaign speech. S/he will collaborate with other student speechwriters to compose and edit the speech.
- Another contingent of students in the group will prepare and act in a political TV commercial for the candidate. It may be videotaped or presented live. Props may be utilized.
- A third contingent of students will create a full page ad against the opposition, using appropriate materials. "Smear tactics" are permissible.
- Students will present speeches, commercials, and ads to the entire class.
- An election will be held with all students voting for the the candidate of their choice.
- The instructor may or may not take part in the voting process.
- As an exercise in Journalism, an analytic paper of the event may follow.

THE WRITER'S HANDBOOK: TOOLS OF THE TRADE

For Extensive Writers

THE ESSAY-COMPOSING PROCESS

"Get Ready"

- *Step 1*

  Be calm. Work in a comfortable, quiet, well-lit, tranquil environment. Gather all your tools and materials. Have all your books/notebooks/notes within reach. Have snacks and water nearby. Focus.

"Get Set"

- *Step 2*

  Brainstorm. Write your ideas without stopping. Use either your computer or a large pad. Save all your materials. Try not to edit. Keep going.

- *Step 3*

  Cluster. Group similar ideas together. Draw a "map" if that helps you, with your main idea in the center. Your clusters will be your internal paragraphs.

"Go!"

- *Step 4*

  Prewrite. Begin to shape your essay. Begin with a technique that grabs your reader's attention. Your thesis statement will most probably be explained in the first paragraph, after the introduction. Keep an eye on your clustered ideas. Decide on the order. If it is a comparison/contrast paper or an analysis, which will be discussed first?

- *Step 5*

  If you are using quotations, add them now. Add your sources after you prewrite your first draft. Cite your sources in your text and on your Works Cited page.

- *Step 6*

  Proofread. Type a first draft.

- *Step 7*

  Conference. Talk over what you have written with your instructor, a tutor, or a good friend who can give you an honest opinion of what you have written.

- *Step 8*

  Revise, following suggestions if you feel they are valuable. Proofread again. Type your final draft. Make sure that you save a copy.

Composing an Introductory Paragraph for an Essay

Begin the paper with an introduction that contains the thesis of the paper, identifying your *topic* (what you will write about) and your *focus* (the direction the topic will take).

Creating Initial Interest

- To raise interest, you may want to introduce your thesis by means of a **question,** which the paper's internal paragraphs will then answer. (The final paragraph should state the full, conclusive answer to this question, to the best of your ability.)

- There are other ways to create interest when introducing your thesis. One way is to begin with a **quotation** related to your topic. Often, there are poems, songs, and stories that feature your topic. These can be quoted and then related to your topic. You may find a quotation by a scientist, a politician, or a celebrity, as well,—however, it must absolutely lead your thesis.

- Some writers open effectively with a specific **detail** which appeals to the reader's *visual* sense and helps him see a situation or a particular setting. For example, you may want to describe a person or a scene (to enrich your description, you may want to include one or more of your other senses besides sight). For example, describing one special photograph (perhaps of your great-grandfather) or one special family dinner that you attended would be a great idea, if you plan to speak about heritage.

- Although it is less common, the idea of opening with a **statistic**, if it is relevant, can also be effective. For example, you may want to begin by citing a source which provides hard data regarding your topic. Make sure you cite your source.

- For excitement, a **shocking statement** associated with your topic makes a great opener. A stimulating or terrifying point to make the reader take notice is one of the best ways to begin.

A funny or odd **anecdote** about your topic makes a great opening paragraph. Then link it solidly to your thesis statement.

The Thesis Statement

The thesis statement is the most important sentence in an essay. It tells the purpose of the essay; what the author is going to say. It tells the reader the focus of the essay.

Review Chapter 4, which explains how the thesis statement functions in exposition. Practice writing a few thesis statements. Begin very plainly. For example, "The purpose of this essay is to discuss my favorite Italian dishes, chicken Parmesan, ravioli, and pizza. I always have a hard time choosing number one." In the essay to come, one paragraph will be devoted to chicken Parmesan, the next to ravioli, and the next to pizza. The last paragraph may conclude which one is the favorite. Try your own topic. Fill in this blank:

"The purpose of the present essay is to explain _(the topic)_ because _(reason for writing)_." For a more sophisticated sentence, do not bluntly state "the purpose of this essay is. . . ." Just begin with a sentence about the topic. Then add your *focus*, the direction your topic will take. The thesis statement usually appears somewhere near the beginning of the essay, perhaps toward the end of the first paragraph or at the beginning of the second paragraph.

Composing an Essay's Internal Paragraphs

The internal paragraphs of an essay relate to the thesis statement, the "mother of all topic sentences" that announces the subject of the essay. Generally, the first sentence of each internal paragraph is its *topic sentence*. If the thesis statement is the mother, the topic sentences of each paragraph are its "children." Each internal paragraph contains a smaller, related idea related to the main subject, the thesis.

To help yourself write these paragraphs, ask yourself several questions, like: What is the subject doing? What are the qualities of the subject? Why or how is the subject related to this smaller idea? How will each internal paragraph achieve its purpose, to make the main topic clearer? Does each paragraph contain enough information for the reader?

Paragraph Patterns in an Essay

The most common patterns in writing internal paragraphs in an essay are *comparison and contrast*, *cause and effect*, *definition and example*, *sequence*, and *analysis*. Refer to Chapter 4 for a detailed explanation of each. Sometimes an essay will combine more than one, but all the patterns always focus on the chosen topic.

Transitions in an Essay

Once you have established the order you plan to use in your essay, you will need to connect your paragraphs smoothly to one another. Transitions are word bridges built by writers to carry readers over gaps between ideas. Without them, your essay will be choppy. Think of transitions as a link in a chain. Sometimes you can carry over an idea with a single word, but other times you need to use a phrase or even an entire sentence. Study professionally written essays to see how these are used. Watch for them, and learn to use them in your writing. The following is a list of frequently used transitions:

furthermore	what is more	first, second, next, etc.
in addition	on the other hand	without question
even so	in contrast	to this end

Composing an Essay's Conclusion

Your last paragraph should draw a conclusion or ask an important question of the reader. You may make a recommendation to the reader or a prediction of some kind about what may happen in regard to your chosen topic. A summary is appropriate as a conclusion, but use it wisely. An exact repetition of your opening can be dull. (Never repeat information from your internal paragraphs.) Think of your thesis statement as a query, and your conclusion as the response (Q → A). Often the techniques used for writing an attention-getting introduction may be appropriate as well for your conclusion.

Documenting Sources

Research must always be documented. Without citing your sources, you are in jeopardy of plagiarism, which in all academic institutions is a serious breach of protocol. It is not acceptable scholarship, and can and often does result in failure. Your instructor will explain his or her precise method for documenting sources, but some general guidelines are in order.

Most English instructors prefer the MLA (Modern Language Association) style. This is modified from year to year; therefore, the model for each type of citation does not need to be memorized. Each kind of publication has its own method. The most recent format may be found on the OWL (Online Writing Lab) website from Purdue University, or may be Googled under "MLA form." Follow this in the absence of specific instructions from your professor.

Sources used in your essay are listed on the last page, headed Works Cited. This list refers to the quotations used in your essay. The entries are listed in alphabetical order, according to the name of the author. Follow these easy steps for documenting a quotation from a print source.

- FIRST: If you know the author, write the author's name. Put the last name first, then a comma, then the first name. After that, put a period. For example:

  Smith, John.

- SECOND: Using italics, put the name of the book and then a period. Capitalize the most important words (usually four letters or more). For example:

  Smith, John. *Life is Wonderful.*

- THIRD: Put the city where the book was first published and then a colon [:]. If it is a major city, omit the state. For example:

  Smith, John. *Life is Wonderful.* New York:

- FOURTH: Put the name of the first major publisher followed by a comma. For example:

  Smith, John. *Life is Wonderful.* New York: Putnam,

- FIFTH: Put the year the book was first published and then a period. For example:

  Smith, John. *Life is Wonderful.* New York: Putnam, 2012.

- SIXTH: Last, if it is a printed book, put the word Print with a capital P, followed by a period. For example:

  Smith, John. *Life is Wonderful.* New York: Putnam, 2012. Print.

Note: The following is available on most computers: Scroll to **References.** Click on **Manage Sources** or **Bibliography**. If you have prepared a list of your sources, your computer can format these *for* you.

Composing a Summary

A summary can be one paragraph or several, but essentially it is a small fraction of the length of the essay as a whole. A summary is a distillation of the major ideas in the essay. Often a student needs to practice summary writing by completing several revisions, taking out unnecessary words until only the bare bones of the essay remain.

Do:

- Begin with a broad, general statement about the topic as stated in the essay's thesis statement. Provide the name of the author and the text.
- Add key words that support the topic, or explain the thesis statement. These often appear in the first sentence of every internal paragraph.
- Put these in sentences using your own words.

Don't:

- Do not include minor details.
- Do not evaluate the essay in any way. (Never use the word "I.")
- Do not use an entire sentence as it appears in the original essay.
- Do not use more than a single word for a quotation. (Avoiding quotes entirely is best.)

Grammar Tips

Fragments

One of the most frequent errors college students make when writing papers is the *sentence fragment*. Like a piece of broken glass, it is incomplete, just a part of a sentence. It is just a broken piece of a sentence. Perhaps glass can't be fixed, but sentences can!

Every sentence must have both a subject and a verb. If one is missing, it is only a fragment. "Ate dinner and went to bed" is a fragment. The subject is missing. Who ate dinner? Add the name of the person or a pronoun and the sentence is whole. "A ship without a rudder" is a fragment. The verb is missing. What is the action? Add what such a ship does and the sentence is whole. "Never again." This is missing both the subject and the verb. Never again, for whom? I? She? He? Never again, what? Consider these repaired fragments:

Tiffany ate dinner and went to bed.
A ship without a rudder flails in the open sea.
I will never again overeat.

Active and Passive Voice

The very words *active* and *passive* sound positive and negative. In writing sentences, the concept is the same. Using the *active voice* is always recommended; the *passive voice* makes your writing sound almost dead. Consider these sentences. Which sounds more vibrant?

The hikers explored the cave.
The cave was explored by the hikers.

In the first case, we can envision people moving. In the second, there is absolutely no movement. The cave, immobile, is there, with just a memory of people having been there.

Subject–Verb Agreement

In grammar, as in life, there is nothing better than to cheerfully agree. People who habitually disagree, frankly, are disagreeable. So it is with subjects and verbs.

If the subject is singular, its verb must be singular.

> A *pilot*, along with his crew, *plays* a critically important role in our nation's security and safety.

If the subject is plural, its verb must be plural.

> *Students* attending Open College Night *need* to register at the front door of the gym.

Subject and Object Pronouns

A *pronoun* takes the place of a noun. It may either be a *subject pronoun* (aka subjective *case*) or an *object pronoun* (aka objective *case*). This means that the subject pronoun takes the place of the sentence's subject. Subject pronouns—I, he, she, we, and they (as well as who)—begin a sentence.

> *I* love to dance. *He* loves to dance. *She* loves to dance. *We* love to dance. *They* love to dance. *Who* loves to dance?

Object pronouns—me, him, her, us, and them (as well as whom)—move toward the end of the sentence, after the verb has done its job.

> He loves to dance with *me*. She loves to dance with *him*. He loves to dance with *her*. They love to dance with *us*. We love to dance with *them*. Who loves to dance with *whom*?

Misplaced and Dangling Modifiers

If you have ever misplaced your cell phone, you know how disorienting that can be. No one wants to be left dangling, or hanging, either! That's pretty disorienting as well. The same is true of words in a sentence. *Modifiers*—words that describe or explain—must be placed near the words they modify; otherwise, the meaning is lost, or just dangling in midair. When that happens, the meaning is scrambled, often sounding positively silly.

> Eating dinner with my big family, the dishes piled up in the sink. (What was eating dinner? The dishes?)

> Crawling on the wall, I saw a spider. (Who crawled up the wall? Was it the speaker?)

Use common sense and place those modifiers where they belong!

Capitalization and Punctuation

Capitalize names, geographic locations, institutions, countries, cities and states, acronyms, holidays, days, months, languages, types of music, nationalities and religions, titles of people and publications, and the first word in every sentence.

> Susan, Grandma, Harlem, the North Pole, the Middle East, the South, Harvard, Ocean County College, Peninsula High School, England, the United States of America, Chicago, CBS, AIDS, NASA, the White House, Windsor Castle, the Louvre, Yankees, the Girl Scouts, the Stone Age, the Renaissance, Columbus Day, Cinco de Mayo, Tuesday, February, Italian, German, Pop, Rock, Grand Opera, Catholicism, Judaism, Shinto, Dr., Mrs., Sergeant First Class (SFC), *The Great Gatsby*, the Constitution.

End every sentence with a period, question mark, or exclamation point. Commas have multiple uses, but their most important functions are to separate main clauses, words in a series (see the list directly above), words of direct address, and three digits in large numbers.

> I forgot my umbrella, but it didn't rain.

> Modes of transportation in the early part of the twentieth century included the railroad, the steamship, the trolley car, the blimp, and the very first automobiles.

> Friends, Romans, countrymen, lend me your ears.

> Last year, Wal-Mart earned $469,200,000,000 and gave $1,000,000,000 to charity.

Semi-colons separate two independent clauses. Each could be a sentence, if it wanted to.

> Maria will be home early; otherwise, she will call you.

Colons announce. Think of the two dots as the sound that comes out of a little trumpet.

> Pay attention to the following: all latecomers will be asked to wait until the end of the first scene, no cameras will be allowed, and cell phones must be turned off.

Parentheses set off material (like this), but brackets set off corrections [not all corrections]. For the record, brackets go inside parentheses (when needed [as in this example]).

Use a *hyphen* to connect two words that are not compounds, like all-American, but use a *dash*, which is twice as long and often surrounded by space — as it is used here — when you require a short statement that is an important part of the sentence (as opposed to parentheses, which set off statements that are not important).

Spelling

Spelling requires that you become a prolific reader. The more English-language publications you read, the easier it will be for you to recognize correct spelling. English is the world's largest "second language." Students from foreign lands have little trouble with learning to speak English, but writing it engenders numerous problems, as it does for native English speakers who spend limited time reading, and today, are reliant on abbreviated text-talk.[1] Some tried and true rules are in order.

The oldest adage for spelling confusing *i* and *e* words, "I before E, except after C, or when sounding like A, as in neighbor or weigh," is an attempt to solve only one spelling problem.

Homonyms present another tough hurdle. Words that sound the same, but have different meanings, can take two forms: homo*graphs* and homo*phones*. While there may be difficulty for a listener in understanding what the talk really is about, there is no *spelling* problem with homographs, since spelling is the same for a swimming pool, a game of billiards, a shared car ride to school, or a lottery-type fund that pays money from the combined giver's contributions to the winner. But in words like the famously confused "*their, there,* and *they're,*" or "*too, two,* and *to,*" spelling is definitely an issue.

It can't be stressed any more strongly: to write well, read, read, read! If you have trouble, use your computer's spell-check or a dictionary.

---

1. A surprising study by Dr. Clare Wood of the University of Conventry, however, posits that the opposite may be true. Textism usage was found to have a positive effect on students' ability to spell correctly. Clare Wood et al. *British Journal of Psychology*, Aug. 2011. Vol. 102, Issue 3, pp. 431–442.

THE READER'S HANDBOOK: TOOLS OF THE TRADE

For Efferent Readers

Finding the Main Idea

All sentences are not equal. Some are more important than others. When reading exposition, the most important sentence is somewhere at the beginning of the essay or textbook chapter. This sentence is the *thesis statement*. It tells the reader what the essay will be about in broad terms. Most of the time, it connects to the title of the essay or the textbook chapter.

The next most important sentence is the *conclusion*, which tells what the essay was about. These two sentences put together provide you with the *main idea* of the essay in a nutshell.

The topic sentences that generally head each internal paragraph in an essay—or the subtitles in a full textbook chapter—provide less important ideas, but these illustrate the main idea. These sentences provide *support* for the main idea.

Items that are not sentences at all, like sub-headings, graphs, charts, and illustrations, are visual aids to learning. These also support the main idea, but are less important than the internal topic sentences.

To find the main idea easily and quickly, a reader must look at the essay in the following order.

- FIRST, read the essay until you find the thesis statement. Underline or copy it.[1]
- SECOND, read the paragraph until you discover the conclusion. Underline or copy it.
- THIRD, put these two sentences (thesis + conclusion) together. You will have the main idea in a nutshell.
- FOURTH, underline the first sentence in each internal paragraph. Nine times out of ten it will provide a topic sentence that gives an important supporting detail.

---

1. All instructions involving writing in the book assume that the reader owns the book.

These four steps will give you an *outline* of the essay or textbook chapter. After performing these steps, when you read the essay from start to finish, you will feel secure in zipping through it, because you will now know what you are reading for. Now is the time to enjoy the graphics.[2]

Annotating and Highlighting

To begin, above all, do not highlight too much, or you will never know what to study. Using the method above, *highlight* with (preferably) a yellow marker just the thesis statement and the conclusion. Write "TS" or "C" in the margin, or use a symbol (asterisk, star, check) to attract your attention to these sentences when studying. *Underline* in a different color (or in pencil) the first sentence in each internal paragraph (most of the time, topic sentences). *Annotate* these topic sentences in the margin, designating them as specific support sentences. In addition, write a shortened note you will understand later in the margin next to these sentences.

Circle important terms like names, dates, or statistics. Put these key words in the margin, fully or in abbreviated form. If it is a word new to you, write its definition in the margin.

Write questions in the margin next to passages or sentences you do not understand.

Write a very short summary at the bottom of a page or in the margin at the end of a section.

If you wish, transfer the marginal notes to good, old-fashioned note cards. Put one important term on the back. Quiz yourself, using these as flash cards.

SQ3R[3]

The SQ3R formula for reading and study purports to present a strategy to college students that will help them move efficiently through a large amount of textbook material and help them to retain its information. In recent years, the now-generic technique has been expanded by several researchers, but this is its original formula:

- Survey
- Question
- Read
- Recite
- Review

A land survey is an inspection of geographical boundaries, and the relationship of specific points of the terrain to those boundaries. In reading, to *survey* means to perform a fast overview to determine how specific subtopics relate to the main idea. The best way to begin is to "assay" the material as explained above in the "Main Idea" section and in Chapter 4 of this book; but in a survey, you will need to do this very quickly, by skimming the sentences. The skimming rate is generally considered to be between 800–900 words per minute. Next, skim individual sections of the article or chapter to see its subheadings and graphics. Look for questions at the end of a textbook chapter before reading through the chapter later, to help yourself know what the author finds important. This should take less than five minutes.

The second step, *question*, requires your personal interest: what do you want to know, and what do you need to know about what you have just skimmed? What do you already know about the

---

2. Carmen Collins' "How to Assay an Essay" is the source of this method. See Chapter 4.
3. Francis Pleasant Robinson is the author of two books: *Effective Study* (1946) and *Trucking: A Truck Driver's Training Handbook* (1981). The SQ3R formula derives, of course, from the former.

subject? Ask the 5 Ws and an H as they apply to the reading. This should only take about a minute or two.

The next step, *read,* is the act of reading through the material from beginning to end at an average reading rate — 250 words per minute for easy material, 300 words per minute for college texts. These rates result in approximately 70% comprehension. If you are studying for an important exam, however, striving for 100% comprehension, the rate will be slower. (If you are quickly reading a magazine, newspaper, or internet article for your own pleasure, the rate may be as high as 500 words per minute.) How fast you read depends on your purpose. When you read a college text, try to find the answers to the *questions* you posed earlier.

To *recite,* close the book and say aloud everything you remember, answering your own questions. If you are in an environment where speaking is not possible, quickly jot down in a notebook as much as you remember.

To *review,* open your book and check to see if you left anything out of your recitation. Indicate with a check or an "x" the material that you missed. Go over this material again.[4]

Vocabulary Building

There are three major methods of building vocabulary, all of which can be recorded in a Vocabulary Word File. For journal-keepers, this can be stored in the last section of your notebook for safekeeping and referral. As a new word is discovered, it should be entered in this word file.

The best way to learn a new term is through *context.* Words are isolated items that can mean many things, but the way they are used in a sentence or paragraph indicates its *semantic* meaning — the meaning as it relates to the article being read. Consider the various contexts for the word "good": "Good morning!" "Good heavens!" "For your own good. . ." "A good dinner" "Good luck!" "He was good and sick." Note how the context, the way the word is used in a sentence, changes its meaning.

The next best method is *analysis* through *word parts,* taking the word apart before putting it back together again (*synthesis*).

Every word has a *root.* Roots may derive from other languages, such as Germanic, Latin, or Greek. The root of the word *cardiogram* is the Greek word *cardia,* meaning "heart." You can see the root with various spellings, as in the word *coronary,* from the Latin *cor-.* Related languages use it too: in French, the word is *coeur*; in Spanish, *corazón.* So, every word had a root — *core, a heart* — at its center.

Prefixes can be added to the beginning of the word; *suffixes* at its end, creating more complex meanings, but meanings that link to its root. Some common prefixes include *pre-, a-, anti-, micro-, para-, astro-, bio-, un-, multi.* Some common suffixes include *-ive, -ment, -able, -ate/ite, -ian, -arian, -ish, -ology, -tion.* Even the word part *-burger* is a suffix, although it has come to mean a meat patty. Actually, it is any chopped substance, molded into a patty. Think about it!

The third, but least effective way to build your vocabulary is to look up the unknown word in a dictionary. The reason it usually is not effective is because there are approximately 600,000 words in an unabridged dictionary. It is impossible to memorize and remember the meaning of each. However, when you do look it up, write down the meaning in your Vocabulary Word file. Try using it in a sentence. Then, try to use it in speaking, as part of your new active vocabulary.

---

4. For another perspective on the SQ3R method, watch the YouTube video *SQ3R. MrGWilson1.* 5 June 2010.

Skimming and Scanning

Skimming is rapidly getting the gist of the material. Leave out sections that contain specific examples, or sections that repeat. Look for clue words that say "in other words," "for example," "in addition," "furthermore," "also," "too," "to repeat," or "once again." Keep going when you see these words. Zip through the material. Look at the questions or the summary, which will speedily give you what the author thinks is most important.

Scanning is a technique used to pinpoint a specific word or number, as in looking up someone's phone number. Scanning requires moving your eyes rapidly down a column or a page to locate a printed item. It is actually not reading; it is *finding*.

Literal, Inferential, and Applied Questions to Ask When Reading

There are basically three types of questions that can be asked and answered in every reading selection: literal questions, inferential questions, and application questions. Knowing the difference can *make* the difference when writing an essay or taking tests.

Literal questions ask for answers which are given right in the sentences by what the author says. The information is *stated*. For example, in the sentence "Columbus discovered America in 1492," literal questions would include "Who discovered America?" or "In what year did Columbus discover America?" Extensive writing/efferent reading are verbal forms that provide factual information. "True and False" and "Multiple Choice" test questions are literal.

Inferential questions require that you think and search; these questions ask for rational answers which are not specifically stated in the sentences, but given through information that relates to the question. The answers to these questions are not as easy to find, but will yield almost the same answers from everyone. The information is *implied*. Inferential questions about our sentence above could include "Were maps accurate in 1492? Why not?" or even "Knowing the hazards Columbus faced on his voyage to the New World, was Columbus happy when he saw land?" For students who have studied the course material carefully, test answers will be obvious. Logic and good judgment are essential in a student's ability to respond correctly, with confidence.

Application questions put you "on your own." These are outside the text, asking for answers which are not stated in or implied by the reading itself. The information must be derived from your knowledge of the situation closest to the printed description, which is known from *your own life*. Therefore, you are applying to a brand new situation a "pattern" or "code" you have learned previously. (Unfortunately, sometimes these yield stereotypical answers, like male and female behaviors or characteristics.) Neither stated nor implied, the information is not there at all; you need to provide it. Using the example above, application questions might ask "Where would you be if Columbus had not discovered America?" or "Do you think Columbus actually is responsible for discovering America?" or even "Was America really 'discovered,' or was it there all along?" In a test situation, when the question calls for your opinion (as in "What if . . .?" questions), you can state it, but you will always be asked to explain and to provide support for your opinion.

How Reading Connects to the Cycle of Learning: What? So What? Now What?[5]

Efferent reading by definition is reading to take away literal information from the text for the purposes of practical use either immediately or at a future time.[6] However, after asking the question "What?" and finding out the literal answers (this is what the lesson was about), a learner's next question is more likely to be, "So what?" That level of learning signals interpretation, a search for meaning. Why do I need to know it? What can it do to help my life? How do I feel about it? But the very highest level of learning is achieved when the learner begins to use the information in her own way—to make it into something new and better, reapplying it to relevant, but entirely different situations. "I'm going to design..." "I'm going to build..." "I'm going to write..." "Now, I'm going to do..." something that no one has ever thought of before.

Final Thoughts Considering Extensive Writing, Efferent Reading, Reflexive Writing, Aesthetic Reading, and the Human Experience

In a broad sense, if we consider the "Now what?" phase of learning, the efferent stance might well turn into an aesthetic response, where readers and learners extract knowledge and make it personal. At such a point, they would indeed be moving into a reflexive mode; that is, experiencing reading and writing for themselves, for life.

---

5. Questions originally posed by educator Terry Borton in *Reach, Touch, and Teach*. Cambridge: McGraw-Hill, 1970, pp. 88–91.
6. Louise Rosenblatt's famous example—quickly reading the label of a poisonous liquid accidentally swallowed by a child in order to find out its antidote.

About the Author

Sandra G. Brown, a graduate of Douglass College, received her Ed.D. from Rutgers University, where she studied with Janet Emig and Louise Rosenblatt. She is the co-author of several editions of *Reading as Experience* with William J. McGreevy as well as articles for NCTE and MLA, and has presented over three dozen papers for various educational organizations. As a contributing member of TYCA-NE, she has served on the Regional Executive Committee as a former editor of its newsletter *The Nor'easter.* She has taught reading, writing, literature, and humanities courses to high school, college, and graduate students as well as underprepared adults and professionals in the workplace. Sandra G. Brown is presently a full professor at Ocean County College, Toms River, New Jersey, where she has taught since 1986.